Real Estate for Professional Practitioners
A Wiley Series

DAVID CLURMAN, Editor

RETIREMENT HOUSING

A STEP-BY-STEP APPROACH

JAMES L. LAUGHLIN
S. KELLEY MOSELEY

WILEY

JOHN WILEY & SONS
NEW YORK · CHICHESTER · BRISBANE · TORONTO · SINGAPORE

Library of Congress Cataloging in Publication Data:
Laughlin, James L.
    Retirement housing : a step-by-step approach / James L.
Laughlin, S. Kelley Moseley.
        p.   cm.—(Real estate for professional practitioners)
    Bibliography: p.
    ISBN 0-471-63476-X
    1. Retirement communities—Finance. 2. Aged—Dwellings—Finance.
3. Real estate investment. 4. Real estate development.
I. Moseley, S. Kelley. II. Title. III. Series.
HD1390.5.L38 1989
362.1′6′0681—dc19

Printed in the United States of America

10 9 8 7 6 5 4 3 2 1

SERIES PREFACE

Since the end of World War II, tremendous changes have taken place in the business and residential real estate fields throughout the world. This has been evidenced not only by architectural changes, exemplified by the modern shopping center, but also in the many innovative financing responses that have enabled development of new structures and complexes, such as multiuse buildings. It can be expected that real estate development will speed in new directions at an ever increasing pace to match the oncoming needs of our time. With this perspective, the Real Estate for Professional Practitioners series has been developed in response to professional needs.

As real estate professional activities have become divided into specialties, because of intensive demand for expertise at all stages, so has there developed an increasing need for extensive training and continual education for persons directly involved or dealing in business ventures requiring detailed knowledge of realty procedures.

Perhaps no field of business endeavor is more in need of a series of professional books than real estate. Working in the practical world of business and residential construction and space utilization, or at advanced levels of college training covering these areas, one is constantly aware that too little of existing creative thinking has been transcribed into viable books. Many of the books that have been written do not thoroughly enough encompass both the practical and theoretical aspects of complex subjects. Too often the drive for immediate answers has led to the overlooking of fundamental purposes and technical know-how that might lead to much more favorable results for the persons seeking knowledge.

This series will be made up of books thoroughly and expertly expounding existing procedures in the many fields of real estate, but searching as well for innovative solutions to current and future problems. These books are intended to offer a compendium of each author's wide experience and knowledge to aid the seasoned professional.

The series is addressed to professionals in all walks of realty endeavor. These include business investors and developers, urban affairs specialists, attorneys, accountants, and the many others whose work involves real estate creativity and investment. Just as importantly, the series will present to advanced students in many realty fields the opportunity to review professional thinking that will help to stimulate their own thoughts on modern trends in housing and business construction.

We believe these goals can be achieved by the outstanding group of authors who will create the books in the series.

DAVID CLURMAN

PREFACE

This book is about planning and developing living environments for seniors. It is designed to enlighten a variety of professionals on development issues specific to the seniors housing industry. Such professionals include developers and sponsors, consultants, lenders who finance these properties, seniors housing property managers, and students interested in alternative living arrangements for seniors. The material is based on the authors' experience and suggestions from others who have been involved in developing seniors projects ranging from nursing homes to leisure lifestyle seniors communities.

Like senior consumers, the seniors housing industry is diverse and not well defined. As a result, the industry suffers from conflicting approaches, definitions, and concepts. This situation is understandable, since contemporary seniors housing programs are less than 10 years old. Even veterans in the industry often disagree on the appropriate terms to use in describing certain types of seniors housing. It is hoped that this book can provide a point of reference, by offering uniform terms supported by a detailed description of services. The introduction devotes considerable space to defining and describing the concept of retirement housing and the types of housing likely to be encountered.

Seniors housing is not a single product or type of development. In fact, it spans a wide variety of housing products and services, including nursing homes, personal care facilities, congregate living environments, lifecare facilities, apartments, and the seniors' own home. Further, the various segments are not distinct. The types of housing offered often overlap, and differences in their services tend to blur. Obviously, this blending of concepts promotes the confusion surrounding seniors housing.

Recognizing these issues, the authors prepared a book that attempts to clarify the key issues, concepts, and techniques in developing retirement housing. Much attention is paid to the development process: planning tasks and understanding the unique character of the senior consumer. The reader will notice that two elements of development—financing and architectural design—are not discussed in great detail. The authors, publishers, and other experts believe that financing of real estate and investment are adequately covered in several existing texts. Moreover, specific programs directed toward financing seniors housing are changing rapidly and would make any material in this book quickly outdated. Architectural design is not presented as a separate concept or chapter because the design of seniors housing is a function of elderly needs, abilities, and lifestyle. These issues are adequately addressed throughout the book, and their relationship to design is indicated. A number of excellent texts are available on design.

It is the expressed desire of the authors that this book will fill a gap in the literature concerning the development of retirement facilities.

The issues addressed throughout each chapter have been organized to give the reader a better understanding of the intricacies involved with the retirement industry.

JAMES L. LAUGHLIN
S. KELLEY MOSELEY

Eugene, Oregon
Houston, Texas
December 1988

ACKNOWLEDGMENTS

The coauthors of this book are indebted to those individuals who played key roles in its preparation. We express our appreciation to the four contributing authors without whose individual efforts, energy, and dedication we could not have written this book: Charles Carter (Chapter 7); Ricci Casserly (Chapter 3); Keith Kirschbraun (Chapter 5) and Dianne Love (Chapters 4 and 7). Readers will benefit greatly from the experience and background each author brought to vital areas in the development process of retirement communities addressed in this book.

Further, we recognize Maureen Laughlin who worked tirelessly proofreading and editing the manuscript, as well as preparing all illustrations. In addition, we appreciate the help provided by Donna Ospina, Cyndi McDowell, and Linda McCarty, as well as all the developers, consultants, lenders, architects, care providers, and seniors who have taught us the lessons related in this book.

J.L.L.
S.K.M.

ABOUT THE AUTHORS

JAMES L. LAUGHLIN is the founder and president of Community Association Services, Inc., headquartered in Eugene, Oregon. CAS provides the experience for the developer and/or sponsor from planning to completion of retirement communities, including project feasibility, marketing and sales strategy, site review, concept design analysis, formation of legal structure (operational prospectus), assistance with securing finances, and establishment of management services to meet initial and ongoing needs of the community. Clients have represented a cross-section of developers, sponsors, lenders, health providers, and real estate professionals throughout the country. To date, Community Association Services, Inc., has been responsible for the planning (project analysis, financing, and marketing), formation, and operational management of 180 retirement communities. Mr. Laughlin's education includes an undergraduate degree in business administration and graduate degree programs in financial management, real estate management, land planning, and urban development. His background encompasses 16 years' experience with residential and retirement properties—"for sale" projects as well as rental and entrance fee developments. He has written numerous articles for magazines and newspapers and is the author of *Business Condominiums,* published in 1985 by the National Association of Home Builders (NAHB). He is also a founder and past president of Community Association Institute. Mr. Laughlin is a member of NAHB and serves on the Senior Housing Committee, the Commercial, Industrial, and Institutional Professional Advisory Committee, and the Multi-Housing Committee. He has a Certified Property Manager® designation from the Institute of Real Estate Management as well as a Professional Community Association Manager® from Community Association Institute.

S. KELLEY MOSELEY, MBA, Doctor, Public Health, Chief Executive Officer, Affiliated Medical Companies, Inc., holds a bachelor's and a master's degree in business administration. His doctoral study in health services dealt with assessing the characteristics of effective organization. A licensed nursing home administrator, Dr. Moseley began his work with health care facilities in 1966 and has provided management and planning consultant services to over 150 health care, real estate, and developer clients. He has served as hospital administrator for large and small facilities and currently gives management assistance to hospitals, retirement communities, and nursing care and rehabilitation facilities. As a faculty member and Director of Graduate Programs in Health Services Administration, University of Houston, Dr. Moseley taught courses in management, planning, and long-term care. He has also prepared and published more than 50 articles and presentations, and recently he has completed a book on retirement housing. As a licensed nursing home administrator, Dr. Moseley has been active nationally, regionally, and locally in the development, planning, and management of alternative lifestyles for elderly adults. Currently, Dr. Moseley serves as Chief Executive Officer of Affiliated Medical Companies, Inc. This multifaceted health care company has a network of over 45 member and managed health facilities, encompassing long-term care, home health, and related health service programs. Professional memberships have included the following: Management Committee, Select Council on Senior Housing, National Association of Home Builders; Delegate Council, National Institute of Senior Housing, National Council on Aging; Board Member, National Association of Senior Living Industries; Advisory Board Member, National Hospice Organization, American Hospital Association, American College of Health Care Executives, American Association of Health Care Consultants.

CHARLES A. CARTER, BS, LNHA, Executive Director of Affiliated Senior Living Systems, Inc., has been involved in the planning, development, and management of senior housing alternatives for over 15 years. As an author and lecturer on senior housing management, he assisted in the development of a national association certification program for senior housing managers. Licensed as a nursing home administrator in Texas and Illinois, he has been involved in the operation of more than 40 retirement communities and nursing homes. He has also served on both state and national committees associated with the long-term care industry.

RICCI IVERS CASSERLY, BA, MS, is a consulting services specialist of Affiliated Healthcare Consultants, Inc., a subsidiary of Affiliated Medical Companies, Inc. This company provides a variety of consulting services, including market feasibility analyses for retirement housing projects. Ms. Casserly has 12 years of experience in the health care field. Four of these have included the planning and development of retirement housing projects. She is a member of the American Hospital Association and retains an active involvement in community-based concerns of the elderly.

KEITH D. KIRSCHBRAUN is a partner in the law firm of Wood, Lucksinger & Epstein. His practice includes representation of clients in the structuring and formation of health care joint ventures. Since joining the firm in 1980, Mr. Kirschbraun has been involved in structuring of health care venture opportunities, including those involving nonprofit entities. He has also assisted in the restructuring of nonprofit entities in order to facilitate participation in such opportunities with for-profit entities. Mr. Kirschbraun received both his BBA in finance and JD from the University of Texas at Austin.

DIANNE B. LOVE, PhD, is Assistant Professor of Accounting and Administration of Health Services at the University of Houston, Clear Lake. She is the author of numerous articles in the health care as well as the accounting field. In addition, she has served as a consultant to the health care industry. Dr. Love has over 15 years of experience in the accounting and finance field, the last five of which have been concentrated in the health care and retirement industry. She is a member of the Healthcare Financial Management Association in addition to memberships in numerous accounting organizations.

CONTENTS

CHAPTER 1

INTRODUCTION

JAMES L. LAUGHLIN

All generalities are false. For every example or rule of thumb that is discussed here, there are one or more exceptions. For example, sound reasons can be given for and against placing a kitchen in each apartment of a supervised living environment. Not including a kitchen removes an element that encourages independence among elderly residents. But many developers believe that any size or type of kitchen will always be underutilized by the residents in a supervised living community and would unnecessarily increase the costs of building the unit.

This is just one illustration of the many issues for which an easy solution cannot be offered. Readers must decide how to meet the needs of the residents of a particular community.

The following decision makers should find this book useful:

Developers, converters, and sponsors of retirement properties. Developers will be proprietary (for profit) or nonprofit. Converters will wish to redirect existing properties or facilities to an age-segregated community. Sponsors may be nursing homes, hospitals, fraternal or religious organizations and their affiliates.

Professionals who support and assist the developers, converters, and sponsors during the many stages of development, design, construction, operations, marketing, and sales.

Financial community members—lenders, savings and loan institutions, commercial banks, mortgage brokers, and syndicators

1

who finance the development, building, and conversion of retirement communities.

The decisions of these professionals are often based upon insufficient or inaccurate data, with results ranging from unfortunate to catastrophic. This book attempts to bring together the essential data concerning retirement communities, to enable all three groups to make informed decisions. The differences and similarities between approaches, steps, and procedures necessary to create, operate, sell, or lease various forms of residential retirement communities will be compared and contrasted.

Anyone who wishes to venture into this business must do so with the understanding that it is a long-term commitment and an ongoing business, and not simply the sale or leasing of a multifamily shelter. It is *consumer sensitive*. The consumer in the retirement community industry is different from the nursing home industry consumer or the single- or multifamily housing industry consumer.

DEFINITIONS

The methodology discussed throughout this book in general is applicable to retirement developments regardless of where they are located or the level of services and support the developer or sponsor wishes to implement. Key concepts are defined below.

Levels of Lifestyle.   Throughout the book there are references to levels one through five of lifestyle.

Level one equates to the fully independent elderly, those who can perform all tasks of daily living without any assistance, including managing the home, preparing meals, shopping, and arranging transportation. These older adults have the capability of living anywhere they wish, within financial limitations only. Any form or type of shelter can provide an option to them. The level is also referred to as first-generation retirees. Fully independent persons may purchase services such as home repairs or housekeeping, but do so for convenience rather than out of necessity.

The point at which a fully independent person needs the additional services of a semi-independent living environment is not clear. Each individual makes that decision based on his or her personal life situation and motivation. As a result, persons capable of independent living may choose or demand supportive living for convenience or relieve the burden of home management and maintenance.

Level two housing and lifestyle is for the semi-independent resident who needs some support with home management and social services but does not need personal care or medical care. Support is most often needed in the areas of transportation, housekeeping, meal preparation, maintenance, social, and educational needs. Individuals in this level are often between the ages of 75 and 84 and are labeled as second-generation retirees. The retirement population in this category needs assistance but is still independent and wants to be able to age in place as long as possible. An adult congregate living facility usually contains the services required by the elderly who require this level of support.

Level three includes the moderately dependent resident who requires supervised or assisted living. This person can be any age but is usually in the 80-plus age group and needs regular daily living assistance but does not have to be placed in a nursing home. Frail but not ill, this individual needs assistance with activities of daily living such as bathing, dressing, medication, toiletry, and mobility. Examples of housing include personal care homes, also known as domiciliary care, assisted living, catered living, or board and care communities.

Level four designates a dependent resident who requires intermediate care in a nursing home. A level four nursing home patient requires more intensive care than level three, but less intensive care than level five. Individual care is given to residents who need medication administered and restorative services to prevent further deterioration in independence.

Level five residents require skilled nursing care, including around the clock supervision and medical assistance. Traditionally, skilled facilities administer care to residents who have been recently discharged from hospitals and need rehabilitation services.

Additional Levels of Support Services.   Prior to selecting one of the earlier listed levels of lifestyle, housing, and service, the developer must consider the services provided by the community at large. What types of outreach programs are offered by organizations and associations for the elderly? For example, a community in the west has such a comprehensive networking system established that it would be very difficult to make a large impact with a level two product since many of the level two services are provided currently to the home. Services such as adult day care, respite care, meals on wheels, visiting nurse programs, home health care, and elder-port (transportation for citizens over the age of 60) allow older adults to age in their current homes. With this kind of support system adults can maintain their frail parent or parents in the parents' own home or in the adult child's home for a much longer period of time because of the assistance provided by community agencies and organizations. One should research such programs to determine how they would impact any level of community planned by the developer or sponsor for a given market area.

Adult Congregate Living Facility (ACLF).   The market segment of an ACLF community is generally second-generation retirees, 75 to 84 years of age. More singles than couples make up the residents within an ACLF. Generally there is no on-site health care provided; however, there may be a nurse on duty and a variety of wellness services such as pharmaceutical education, a mobile health unit, and other programs. These communities provide shelter plus support services for the semi-independent elderly who have their own furnishings. The units usually have carpeting, kitchen appliances, and drapes. Units also normally have an emergency call system. Seldom do these types of communities require entrance fees. Usually the fees (including rent) are collected on a month-to-month service basis. Rarely is a lease required. The parties simply have a rental agreement.

In addition to shelter, services provided are housekeeping, meals (one to three a day), maintenance, laundry, transportation, security, communications, and social and educational programs. There is health linkage even though there are no nursing beds within most communities. Unfortunately, no one definition for any term will apply to every case. For example, Florida includes personal services such as bathing, grooming, and dressing, as part of an ACLF definition.

Age-integrated Community.   This type of community permits any age resident, from infants through 100-plus years of age.

Age-segregated Community.   Residents of an age-segregated community are restricted to a specified age group, such as 45 and older, or 62 and older. The communities that will be discussed throughout the book are age segregated rather than age integrated.

Personal Care Facilities.   This housing is developed to meet the needs of the level three resident who requires supervised living. The operator must be licensed in most states. Usually, the resident will live in a personal care facility (supervised living or assisted living) for only one to three years. The residents range in age from 80 to 85 or older. Personal care facilities can be found in a continuing care retirement community (CCRC), which provides supervised living for some residents as well as a freestanding personal care community for those who require level three support.

The individual in a personal care facility can no longer live alone. About half the living areas have no kitchen facilities, and those residents have all meals in a central dining facility. Room service is provided for residents who are unable to attend the central dining room.

Condominium. A condominium owner has separate ownership of an air-space unit, together with common (undivided) ownership of the land and improvements in the project. Any level or type of product can be developed as a condominium from fully independent (level one) communities through nursing home facilities (level five).

Continuing Care Retirement Community (CCRC). This community provides full care and services, meeting level one needs through level five needs. Designed to be a multilevel community or campus plus shelter, it entails independent living units, assisted living units or board and care facilities, and intermediate and skilled nursing facilities. Entrance age varies, from 75 years to 80 years.

More often than not residents will have to pay an entrance fee (also called an endowment or an accommodation fee) plus a monthly fee. Some communities have refundable fees, many do not. Some utilize an amortized endowment approach. Fee approach will be addressed in Chapter 4, "Financial Feasibility." Currently 23 states have regulations concerning continuing care retirement communities. Topics include disclosure requirements to prospective residents, contents of the contract, the handling of deposit money, and any requirements regarding audits. A certificate of need may be required for assignment of nursing beds, and each development with nursing beds is required to be licensed. The two most important motivators for residents who move into a CCRC seem to be security and lifestyle.

Life Care. Life care is differentiated slightly from continuing care by the market. Life care assumes a one-time payment for all future housing and health care needs. Continuing care assumes those costs to the residents will change over time. The concept of life care or continuing care is not new in the United States. Fraternal and religious organizations have provided this service since before the American Revolution.

Sheltered Bed Nursing Facility. This takes place when a state licenses a continuing care or life care community, granting it the right to have nursing beds. The beds must be occupied by private pay patients after a specified date. No Medicare or Medicaid patients may utilize the beds after the cutoff date, if ever. During the early fill-up years the developer may be allowed to have the beds utilized by Medicare and Medicaid patients to help alleviate some of the negative cash flow. After the period of time stipulated by the state, only private pay patients and, in many instances, only patients who are residents of a given community may occupy the beds.

Nonsheltered Bed Nursing Facility. This type of nursing facility is not restricted or limited by the state as to patients' income or insurance. A nonrestricted or nonlimited use license is issued—the ideal approach if the state licensing agency will grant it to the developer.

Senior Adult Community. Preretirees and first-generation retirees between 55 and 74 years constitute the senior adult community. Such communities draw from large intrastate areas and often from out of state. The principal services are recreational and social amenities. Pricing approach may be fee simple or rental. A retirement community is often called a campus, center, or club.

OVERVIEW

Retirement development is a blend of the housing industry, service industry, and health care industry. The mixture is determined by how much the developer, sponsor, or converter wishes to enhance a piece of real estate. The market can be summed up in a word—*diverse*. It is like no other type of development because it possesses the broadest range of services, approaches, and strategies that a developer will ever experience. Creating a retirement community environment (lifestyle) is a joint venture effort in combining shelter with service.

If a developer is fortunate enough to have the required background and expertise and is able to bring together all components necessary to create a successful project, the venture can be realized independently.

However, most developers don't have all the necessary prior experience for creating a business; providing hotel, health care, social, housing management, leisure, recreation, and transportation services; and structuring a minigovernment if the development is planned to be sold as a condominium or cooperative. The retirement community concept, regardless of the form the community may take, is far more complex than general residential development.

CONCEPT

How do we define the concept of retirement housing? *The developer's product in retirement housing is the concept.* The product is not housing. The product is not real estate. The product is the concept. The concept is comprised of three major components—shelter, service, and amenities—and several elements make up each of the three components.

Shelter   The elements that pertain to the shelter component include location, housing, value, convenience, physical and psychological security, functional design, acceptability, and accessibility to community. The shelter must be located in a feasible site. (See Chapter 3, "Product Analysis and Assessment.")

The design should attempt to be as barrier free and accident proof as possible. Too many designers seem to forget who will be living in the community. Poorly thought-out design will undermine the ability of older residents to function as they would like. As an example, ramps are often constructed at such a steep angle that residents are unable to negotiate them safely.

The convenience element includes external support services located in the surrounding neighborhood as well as interior amenities of the community. Such services impart physical and psychological security from loneliness by providing support from peers and staff.

Services.   The second major component of the concept is services. Basic services include: meals (one to three meals per day); utilities (electric, gas, water, telephone); housekeeping (weekly, twice a month, once a month, or as requested); maintenance and repair of individual units, equipment, and appliances; laundering of linen and towels and of personal items; transportation; maintenance and repair of building exteriors and common areas.

Optional services may include resident service programs (financial counseling, social services, mental health programs, consumer education); safety and security programs (telephone answering service, emergency medical assistance, security guard for buildings and grounds); personal care (bathing, dressing, toiletry, walking, medicating); home delivery of meals; beauty and barbershop appointments.

Other resident service programs may include religious or spiritual counseling, legal advice, continuing education, and assistance with medical claims.

Personal enrichment programs may include travel, recreation, social activities, and educational and employment opportunities. Wellness programs encompass exercise programs, pharmaceutical counseling and education, health education, speech therapy, physical therapy, appointments with doctors and dentists, visitation of mobile health unit, clinics staffed with nurses, swimming, and hydrotherapy.

Additional programs could include volunteer opportunities, location of vacation exchanges, and establishment of resident councils or committees, to name but a few. While all of these services are not provided in all communities, the listing indicates the range of services that can be made available.

Amenities.   The final component encompasses the amenities that may be planned for a retirement community: multipurpose rooms, auditorium, central dining room, lobby/reception area, convenience store, gift shop, guest lodging, library, chapel, beauty shop, barber shop, walking paths, and areas for flower and vegetable gardens.

Other amenities may include master cable and antenna system, meeting rooms, arts and crafts rooms, lounges, coffee shops, private dining rooms, exercise rooms, greenhouse, fireplace, game rooms, dark rooms, club rooms, wellness center, dispensary (clinic), health center (nursing beds), swimming pool, whirlpool, saunas, tennis courts, putting greens, picnic areas, lawn bowling, covered parking, administrative office(s), staff dining room, staff locker room, central supply storage, trash removal systems, delivery areas, loading docks, maintenance shops and storage, housekeeping office and storage, facility storage (furniture, furnishings, equipment supplies), marketing and public relations office, health center office, board meeting room, automatic teller machine, postal facilities, mail boxes.

These components and their elements make up the concept of a retirement lifestyle, and the concept is the product. It is extremely difficult, however, for anyone who is venturing into the retirement community business to be able to select items from within these lists of amenities, services, and shelter without defining *retirement*. If one is unclear about what retirement means, it can make defining the product that much more difficult.

Defining Retirement. Any developer who ventures into the retirement field must define clearly what retirement means and then create a product that meets the existing needs of the elderly in the community. *Funk & Wagnall's Dictionary* (J. G. Ferguson Publishing Co.: Chicago, 1960) defines one who is retired as having "withdrawn from active service, business, office or public life." When one retires, one does not necessarily withdraw from lifestyle, financial responsibilities, value system, or sex. One simply stops working. Too many sponsors or developers tie down a site and then attempt to force a product on the site without understanding the retirement market.

The difficulty of defining retirement can be illustrated by asking the reader to think of retirement housing as congregate housing, which would be comprised of many services (e.g., meals, transportation, housekeeping) but would not include nursing care. Most people would not be thinking of the retirement market but more likely would be imagining frail elderly women who are in fact in postretirement—over the age of 75, probably nearing the age of 80. That postretirement market's expectations, needs, and demands are completely different from those of the retirement market. The congregate market for the frail elderly woman is a service-intensive market.

One segment of the retirement market may require more mandatory levels of service than another segment. For example, level one comprises older adults who are self-sufficient and able to perform all activities of daily living. They are not seeking or expecting to have transportation, central meal service, and housekeeping provided for them. However, level two residents would be desirous of a congregate living lifestyle that has transportation, preparation of meals, and housekeeping available. Those services would be considered mandatory for the level two residents, but would be considered discretionary services for the level one residents.

It is also important to understand that each market level or segment of a market has some portion of services, amenities, and shelter requirements that overlaps other levels of services and care. Not all elderly of a certain age would be considered level two, and not all level two elderly would want the same services. Retirement would be much easier to understand and define if it could be stated that all residents in any level will always be in need of certain services, but remember, all generalities are false.

As another example of how difficult it is to define the retirement market, consider the difference between ambulatory and mobile and how those two terms may be interpreted. One can be ambulatory (able to walk) or mobile with the aid of a walker or cane. Those confined to a wheelchair can be mobile, although not ambulatory. A marketing director must understand the distinction. Some individuals who are mobile through the use of walkers and wheelchairs consider themselves ambulatory. At least for the first few years, a developer may decide not to permit wheelchairs and walkers in a community. Problems may arise because of the misunderstanding of the terms ambulatory and mobile.

Developers who plan to undertake the development of a retirement community and have not clearly defined the product, concept, lifestyle, or community to be served are their own worst enemies. Inaccurate and insufficient data in the preplanning stages of retirement communities can cause developers and sponsors to draw the wrong conclusions.

UNDERSTANDING THE RETIREMENT MARKET

Among the key factors that need to be understood before one ventures into developing retirement housing is demographics, which will be addressed in detail in Chapter 3.

How important is demographics to a developer? The story is told of a city dweller who decided to move to the country and was kept awake three nights in a row by the noise the frogs were making. Being an enterprising person, he decided to solve two issues: eliminate the problem of the noise by selling frogs to the restaurants in the city, and develop a new business. He drove into town and persuaded several restaurants that they should buy their frog legs from him and that he could produce as many frog legs as they would need. After signing up a number of restaurants he went back to the country to fill the orders. Alas, he found very few frogs and realized there were a lot more croaks than there were frogs. The moral of this story is: Be sure there is a market. Be sure that the market cares about, wants, and needs the product a developer plans to develop.

Exhibits A through Q illustrate the elderly demographics through 2030. One need only look at the exhibits briefly to realize that there is a growing senior market throughout this country. Taken alone, the numbers can be misleading. Surveys and studies have demonstrated that regardless of the product and services, approximately 19 percent

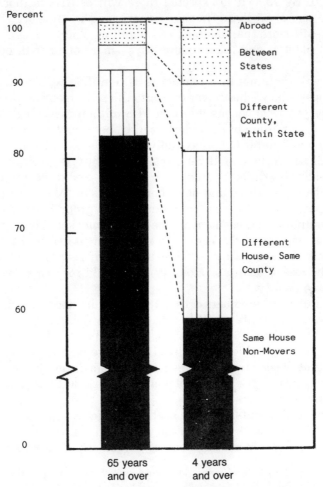

SOURCE: Based on data from US Bureau of the Census.

Exhibit A. Mobility and migration status of the population 65 years and over and 4 years and over.

of the elderly will relocate and 81 percent will age in their current location and find other alternatives to a retirement community. (See Exhibit A.) Of the 19 percent who will ultimately relocate after reaching age 65, approximately 5 percent will move to a different state, and the remaining 14 percent will move intrastate. Of the 4 to 5 percent who move out of state, 40 to 50 percent (4 to 5 in 10) will return eventually.[1]

Exhibit B demonstrates the trends and projections between 1950 and 2030. By 1990 it is expected there will be 31.8 million persons over the age of 65 living in this country, and in 40 short years that number will more than double to 64.3 million elderly. These numbers can be looked at and taken many ways—more often than not, incorrectly.

Why will there not be a market of 31.8 million persons in 1990 for a developer who wishes to venture into the retirement market? Using the projected 1990 census figure of 31.8 million individuals over the age of 65, 18 million of the elderly will be between the ages of 65 and 74. (Refer to Exhibit C.) Many individuals who are turning age 65 in 1990 will be World War II veterans. Their lifestyle and value system are considerably different from their parents', and therefore, they will not want to live where and how their parents do. Most will not want to be a part of a retirement community. This group is what is known as a demand-driven segment of the elderly market. They are not in need of a retirement facility. They may want to live in a retirement community because of the services and amenities promised but don't suffer the loss of health or mobility that would require a level two or level three facility.

Certainly some members of that 18 million are need driven, but only a very small percentage. Of the 31.8 million individuals who by the year 1990 will turn 65, 10.3 million individuals will constitute the second-generation elderly (Exhibit D). A large percentage of these individuals need level two accommodations and facilities. It is anticipated that at any given time between 4 and 6 million elderly need an assisted living environment.[2]

Exhibit E illustrates the size of the third-generation or old-old population (85 and older), which in the year 1990 will number 3.5 million Americans. The old-old segment of the elderly population has the

[1]Dennis M. Horn, "Developing and Financing Retirement Center Housing," *Real Estate Finance* Vol. 2, No. 2 (1985): 28.

[2]Marie McGuire Thompson, "Enriching Environments of Older People." In *Congregate Housing for Older People*, edited by R. D. Chelles, J. F. Seogle, and B. Seogle (Lexington, MA: Lexington Books, 1982), 4.

Millions of Persons

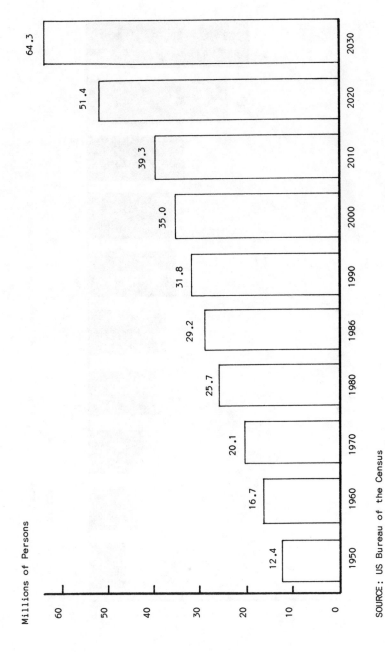

SOURCE: US Bureau of the Census

Exhibit B. Population age 65 and over, trends and projections, 1950–2030

14

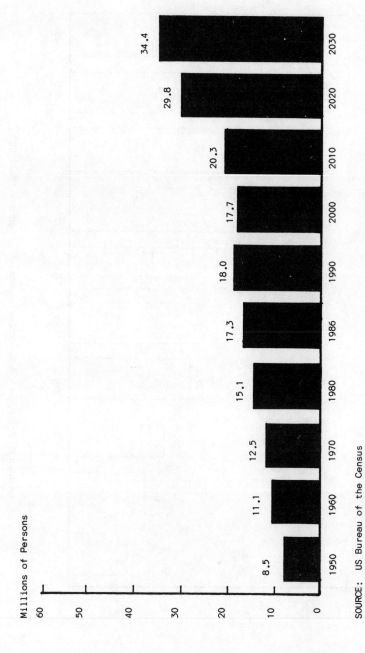

Millions of Persons

60	
50	
40	
30	
20	
10	
0	

8.5   1950
11.1   1960
12.5   1970
15.1   1980
17.3   1986
18.0   1990
17.7   2000
20.3   2010
29.8   2020
34.4   2030

SOURCE: US Bureau of the Census

Exhibit C. Young old population (65–74), trends and projections, 1950–2030

Millions of Persons

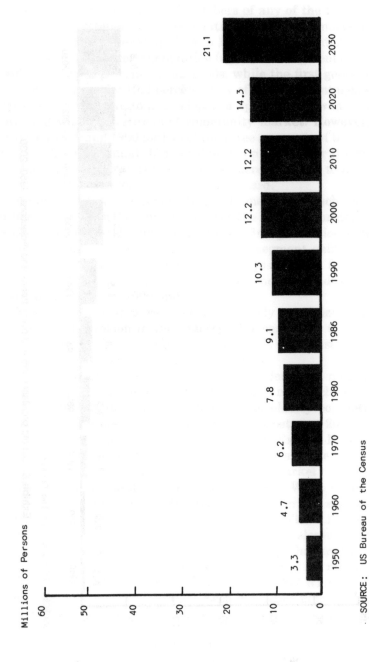

SOURCE: US Bureau of the Census

Exhibit D. Middle old population (75–84), trends and projections, 1950–2030

15

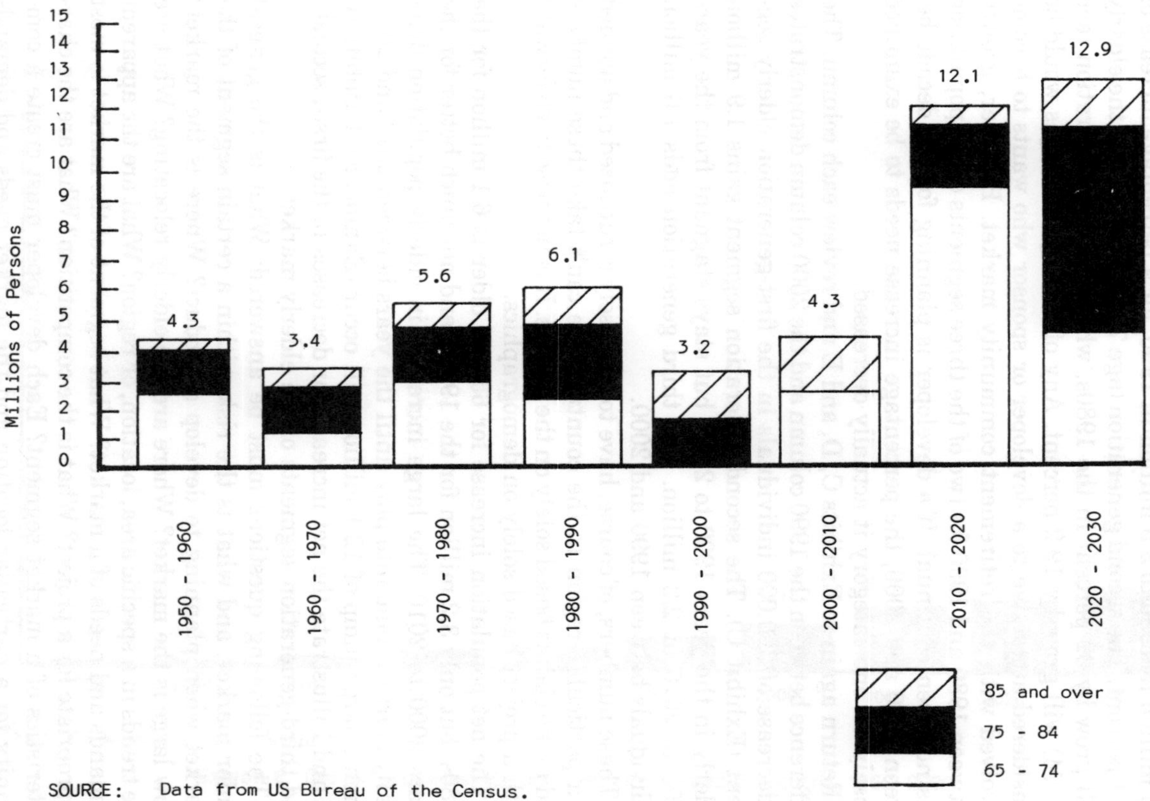

Millions of Persons

4.3 · 1950 – 1960
3.4 · 1960 – 1970
5.6 · 1970 – 1980
6.1 · 1980 – 1990
3.2 · 1990 – 2000
4.3 · 2000 – 2010
12.1 · 2010 – 2020
12.9 · 2020 – 2030

85 and over
75 – 84
65 – 74

SOURCE: Data from the US Bureau of the Census.

Exhibit F. Net increases of older population, 1950–2030

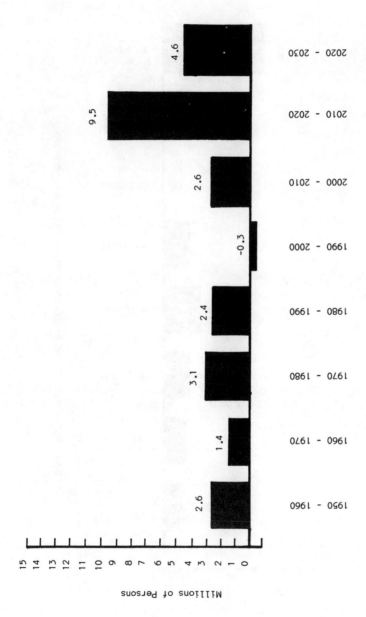

SOURCE: US Bureau of the Census

Exhibit G. Net increases of young old population (65–74), first generation

19

20

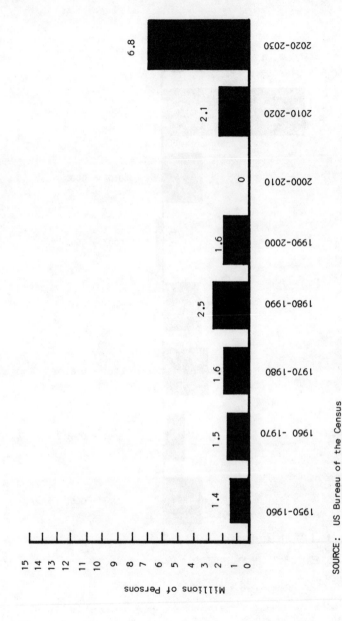

SOURCE: US Bureau of the Census

Exhibit H. Net increases of middle old population (75–84), second generation

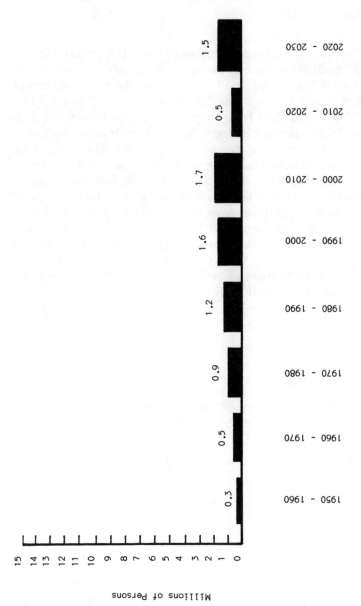

SOURCE: US Bureau of the Census

Exhibit I. Net increases of old old population (85 and over), third generation

21

work for a given retirement community. Success in St. Louis doesn't mean success in San Diego.

Economic Profile. It has been estimated by the U.S. Bureau of Census that of the 28 million people over the age of 65 in 1986, approximately 75 percent owned their home and the remainder were renters, except for a small percentage who lived with relatives. (See Exhibit J.) Of those elderly who own their home, approximately 80 percent have no mortgage on their current residence. It is also estimated that more than 14 million homeowners are over the age of 65. The equity they have in their current home ranges between $45,000 and $50,000, which collectively equals approximately $500 billion. The Bureau of Census estimates that persons over the age of 55 have an annual income of $350 billion. As a group, those over the age of 65 have more discretionary funds to spend per person ($5700 per year) than any other age group in the United States. All other age groups have an average of $3400 of discretionary funds to spend per person. In 1900, one in 60 citizens in the United States was over the age of 65. In the year 2000, it is projected that 1 in 5 will be over the age of 65.

	1980 Household Heads 65+		1986 Household Heads 65+	
	Number	Percent	Number	Percent
Owner Households	11,919,413	75%	13,950,000	75%
Renter Households	4,968,244	25%	4,650,000	25%
Total Occupied Households	16,887,657	100%	18,600,000	100%

SOURCE: Data from US Bureau of the Census. Copyright 1988 by American Association of Retired Persons. Reprinted with permission. Profile of Older Americans, 1988.

Exhibit J. United States owner and renter households headed by older persons

Disability by Age Group. Anyone who wishes to venture into the retirement housing market must understand the older American, which is not an easy task. The customer's needs, demands, concerns, problems, and fears as well as health needs must be seen through the eyes of the elderly.

The physical limitations that elderly customers may have prior to entering the community must be considered. Approximately 86 percent of all elderly Americans (65 and older) will have some type of chronic illness.[3] Such disabilities range from arthritis to hypertension.

Each disability can impair mobility, taste, vision, and hearing to some extent. Older individuals often experience difficulty in discriminating normal conversational sounds from competing background noise generated by building mechanical systems, traffic, echoes, music, and so on. High frequencies are harder to perceive, which affects the older person's ability to respond to warning signals. The developer may include a number of large interior plantings that can assist in diverting traffic noises, or tight windowsills to alleviate external noises. The physical design of the dwelling units, the overall community and its relationship to the surrounding environment, must all be planned in response to the realities of aging.

Aging Process. Aging is a general term that can be defined as a process of continual changes involving physical, psychological, social, and chronological aspects.[4]

Although everyone ages, they do not do so at the same rate. Some individuals show signs of aging before they are chronologically old. Others who are chronologically old may show few signs of aging.[5]

Older individuals for the most part have a positive view toward their health. In 1982, 65 percent of non-institutionalized elderly described their health as excellent or good when compared to individuals their own age.[6]

The presence of chronic disease can cause varying degrees of limitations in activities. The majority of Americans 65 and over do not

---

[3]E. Rosetta Parker, "Housing for the Elderly," *Institute of Real Estate Management of the National Association of Realtors* (Chicago, IL: 1984), 53.

[4]Jon Hendricks and C. Davis Hendricks, *Aging in Mass Society: Myths and Realities* (Cambridge: Winthrop, 1977), 23.

[5]Cary S. Kart, *The Realities of Aging: An Introduction to Gerontology* (Newton, MA: Allyn & Bacon, 1985), 75.

[6]U.S. Special Committee on Aging and the American Association of Retired Persons, *Aging Americans: Trends and Projections* (1985–1986), 84.

have health problems that limit ability to perform daily activities. About 20 percent have some degree of limitation caused by chronic illness. Limitations increase 13 percent for ages 65 to 74; 25 percent for ages 75 to 84; and nearly 50 percent for ages 85 and over.[7] For those disabled individuals living outside institutions, friends, spouses, and relatives represented about 80 percent of care givers.[8]

As illustrated in Exhibit K, less than 1.5 percent of individuals between the ages of 65 and 75 are living in nursing homes or personal care homes. Less than 7 percent of 75- to 84-year-olds are in nursing homes or personal care homes. The largest segment (23 percent) of nursing home or personal care home residents are persons 85 and older. Of that percentage, approximately four out of five residents are female.

The elderly have fewer mental impairments than other age groups. Their major mental health problem is cognitive impairment, or loss or deterioration of mental powers, which is one of the primary reasons for institutionalization. The National Institute of Mental Health found that 14 percent of persons over age 65 have mild cognitive impairment; 6 percent of men and 3 percent of women in this age group demonstrated severe impairment.[9]

Aging and Sexuality.   Negative attitudes toward sex and aging are very apparent in our society. Sexual dysfunction is not an eventuality of the aging process. The few physical changes in the female and male genital systems do not preclude older persons from having an active and satisfying sex life.

Overall, older individuals are less active sexually, but for social rather than physical reasons. Many older persons succumb to the stereotypes attached to sex and aging. They feel ashamed to engage in sexual activity or have a fear of failure.[10]

Psychological Changes.   Some psychological changes that occur with aging are normal, but others are not. Stereotypes associated with thinking, memory, and personality that fit some elderly usually occur with poor health, mental illness, or social impairments. The fear that most people seem to have with respect to aging is a loss of mental ability—learning, memory, intelligence, creativity, and personality.

[7]Ibid., 86.
[8]Ibid., 96.
[9]Ibid., 91.
[10]Cary S. Kart, *Realities of Aging*, 75.

	Percent of Population in Nursing and Personal Care Homes
Under Age 65	0.1
Age 65 - 74	1.4
Age 75 - 84	6.4
Age 85+	22.6
Total Over Age 65	4.7

SOURCE: US Bureau of the Census

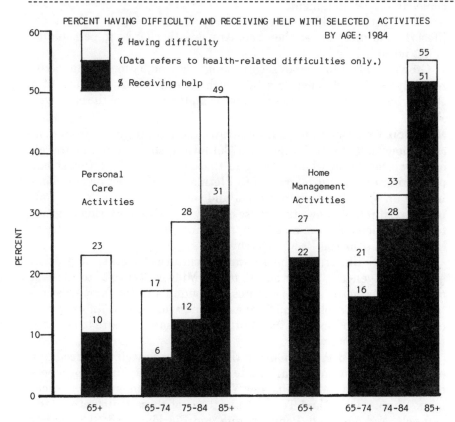

SOURCE: Data from US Department of Health & Human Services. Copyright 1988 by
American Association of Retired Persons. Reprinted with permission.
Profile of Older Americans, 1988.

Exhibit K. Percentage of population utilizing nursing and personal care homes

Most people, however, do not lose intelligence as they age. A decline may be the result of an untreated health problem such as heart disease or high blood pressure. The key to maintaining intelligence is to retain interest in what is happening in the world. The ability to learn does not decrease with age. In fact, one aspect of intelligence, verbal ability, tends to increase through the 50s and 60s. The only difference between learning ability in the young and old is that the process may take an older person slightly longer. In fact, today's older adults often go back to college, intent on developing new careers. With increasing age also comes improved judgment.

Personality is stable over time; however, some people change their lifestyle and interests as they age. Any drastic change in personality is not normal.

Growing old encompasses social changes and adjustments that occur not only in an older person's life, such as retirement or death of a spouse, but also in the world's perception and treatment of the elderly.[11]

Migration Trends.   Exhibit L illustrates the out-migration from non-contiguous states into Florida and California, showing where the elderly relocate from when moving to these states. The Northeast has predominately an out-migration to Florida; the Midwest has predominately an out-migration to Florida and secondary migrations to California. Exhibit M shows that those elderly who live in Florida migrate to the Northeast for the most part, and those in California relocate to the Southwest or the Pacific Northwest.

Exhibit N illustrates the relocation patterns of other migration streams. In general, senior adults in the Midwest relocate to Arizona or to one of several southern states. Individuals in the Northeast relocate to North Carolina and Tennessee. Individuals in California who do not relocate to Texas or the South seem to have a desire to relocate to the Pacific Northwest.

Exhibits O and P demonstrate the numbers as well as percentage of elderly population for each state. States with the largest numbers of elderly include California, New York, Florida, Pennsylvania, Michigan, Illinois, Ohio, and Texas. Only three of these states are in the sun belt, and only two, Pennsylvania and Florida, have 13.3 percent of their total population comprised of persons 65 years old or older. Other states with 13.3 percent or more elderly population include Massachusetts, Missouri, Iowa, Arkansas, Kansas, Nebraska, and South Dakota.

[11]Elaine M. Brody, *Mental and Physical Health, Practices of Older People* (New York: Springer, 1985), 232–236.

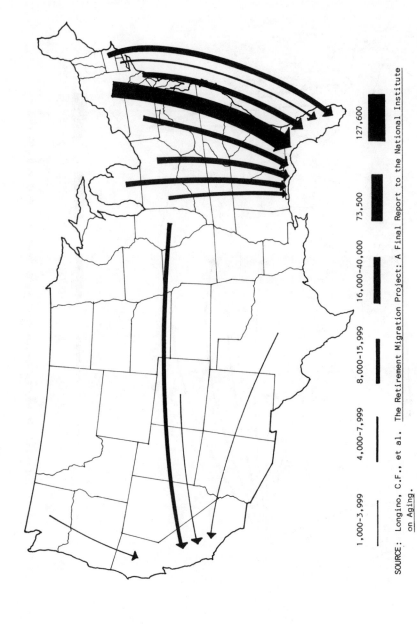

1,000-3,999   4,000-7,999   8,000-15,999   16,000-40,000   73,500   127,600

SOURCE: Longino, C.F., et al. <u>The Retirement Migration Project: A Final Report to the National Institute on Aging.</u>

Exhibit L. Salient streams from noncontiguous states into Florida and California

27

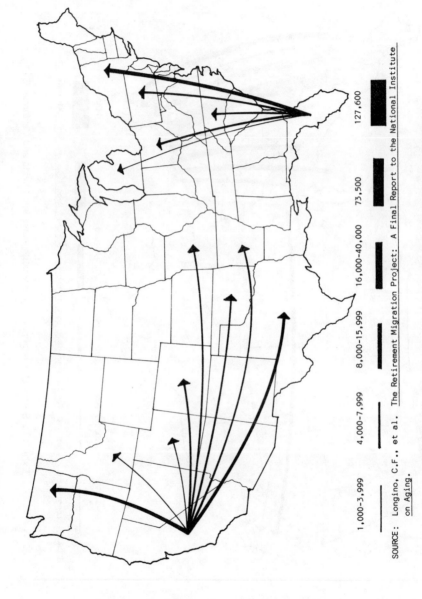

1,000-3,999   4,000-7,999   8,000-15,999   16,000-40,000   73,500   127,600

SOURCE: Longino, C.F., et al. The Retirement Migration Project: A Final Report to the National Institute on Aging.

Exhibit M. Salient streams to noncontiguous states from Florida and California

28

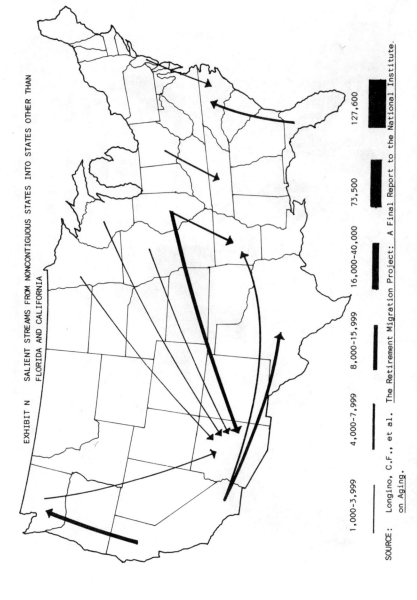

EXHIBIT N   SALIENT STREAMS FROM NONCONTIGUOUS STATES INTO STATES OTHER THAN FLORIDA AND CALIFORNIA

1,000-3,999   4,000-7,999   8,000-15,999   16,000-40,000   73,500   127,600

SOURCE: Longino, C.F., et al. The Retirement Migration Project: A Final Report to the National Institute. on Aging.

Exhibit N. Salient streams from noncontiguous states into states other than Florida and California

29

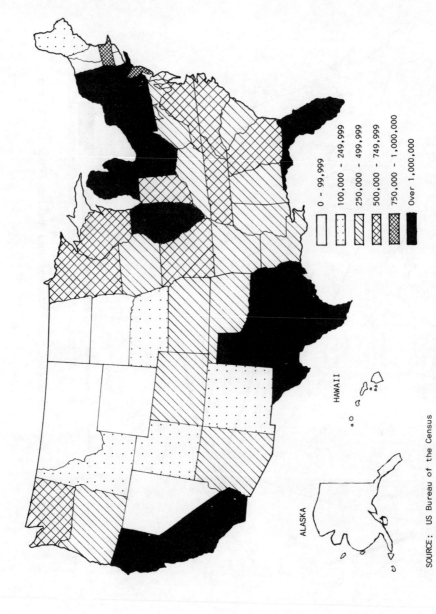

ALASKA

HAWAII

	0 - 99,999
	100,000 - 249,999
	250,000 - 499,999
	500,000 - 749,999
	750,000 - 1,000,000
	Over 1,000,000

Exhibit O. Population 65 and over by state, 1985

SOURCE: US Bureau of the Census

30

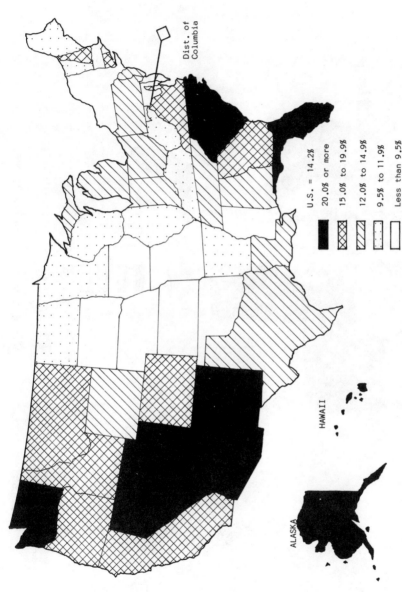

U.S. = 14.2%

■ 20.0% or more

▨ 15.0% to 19.9%

▧ 12.0% to 14.9%

⬚ 9.5% to 11.9%

☐ Less than 9.5%

Dist. of Columbia

HAWAII

ALASKA

SOURCE: Data from US Bureau of the Census. Copyright 1988 by American Association of Retired Persons. Reprinted with permission. Profile of Older Americans, 1988.

Exhibit P(A). Percentage change in population 65 and over, 1980 to 1986

31

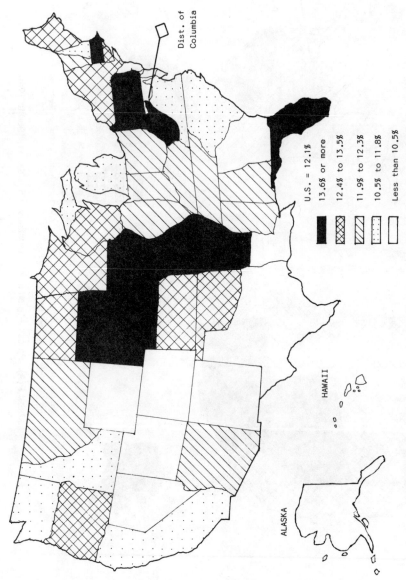

SOURCE: Data from US Bureau of the Census. Copyright 1988 by American Association of Retired Persons. Reprinted with permission. _Profile of Older Americans, 1988._

Exhibit P(B). Persons 65 and over as percentage of total population, 1986

U.S. = 12.1%

■ 13.6% or more
⧉ 12.4% to 13.5%
⧄ 11.9% to 12.3%
⋰ 10.5% to 11.8%
☐ Less than 10.5%

Dist. of Columbia

HAWAII

ALASKA

32

Developers and sponsors should remember that they do not have to plan to relocate their business to join the retirement housing industry. Even though the numbers may look impressive in Florida and California, they only represent a small percentage of the total population. The majority of senior adults will not relocate, and many who do will relocate less than 20 to 25 miles from their current home. The market really exists in every state.

Lifestyle Preferences. Older consumers often look for a total supportive community offering shelter, community involvement, and a hedge against inflation, along with a myriad of other elements discussed previously. Older people, of course, differ in their lifestyles. Some find restricted or age-segregated communities isolating and depressing, others choose a lifestyle that exactly suits them, and some try a particular lifestyle but reject it after relocating to a retirement community.[12]

The retirement community offers as many and varied housing types as any cross-section of the general population. The senior adult is interested in condominiums, rental apartments, mobile homes, high rises, single-family homes, multifamily housing, and townhomes. It would be a mistake to state that one type of housing or any single amenity would always or never be acceptable to a given number of older adults.

To have a successful senior community one must understand the consumer and the aging process. An effective market targeting process and the right offering can be developed with the help of an experienced team. Even with a first-rate product and a superior management organization a developer still may have no better than an even chance of success.

Reasons Why Elderly Relocate. Surveys have been conducted by many national organizations including the American Association of Retired Persons (AARP) to determine why individuals decide to relocate and, conversely, why they decide to stay in place. Ironically, most older Americans are better housed than ever before and are generally satisfied with their housing situation. The AARP survey confirms previous studies indicating that housing satisfaction is greater if one ages in place, even though the housing tends to be older, in greater need of

---

[12]Michael Sumichrast, Ronald Shafer, and Marika Sumichrast, *Where Will you Live Tomorrow?* (Homewood, IL: Dow Jones-Irwin, 1981), 257–260.

repair, and more expensive to maintain relative to income. This phenomenon may occur because one's home is a reflection of self and therefore, one hesitates to denigrate it. It has also been suggested that the aging process is accompanied by a reduction in aspirations and/or the older aged cohorts are socialized to have lower expectations. In the AARP survey, 97 percent of the respondents mentioned things they liked about their current homes, whereas only 47 percent mentioned things they disliked. The positive attributes named most often were location and comfort, and the primary negative attributes were stairs and maintenance.[13]

Most older people are very satisfied with their housing. The top three concerns expressed by the survey respondents were failing health, upkeep of their homes, and loss of their independence. These findings support the notion that older people have difficulty balancing household maintenance versus health maintenance needs when personal or financial resources are strained.[14]

Demographic trends in conjunction with health care advances will result in more vulnerably frail individuals living for longer periods of time, thus strengthening the link between housing and long-term care.[15] The following list shows the reasons some older adults relocate and others do not.

Reasons for Relocation

1. *Upkeep of Home Is Too Expensive.* Many homes are energy inefficient. The average older adult home is approximately 40 years old. Even if home maintenance assistance is available, it may be too expensive. The home probably does not have central air conditioning, if air conditioned at all. Frequently, the kitchen and baths are outdated. There may be more steps to negotiate than older adults care to deal with. However, only 19 to 20 percent of the elderly will relocate; the remainder are satisfied with the physical condition of the house, the amount of space, and the overall neighborhood in which they are currently located.

2. *Current Home Is Too Large.* Many seniors age 65 or over, particularly those over 75, purchased their home early in life and raised two or more children. Now they have little need for an 1800-square-

---

[13]Leah Dobkin, "AARP Releases Nationwide Survey of Older Consumers," *Aging Network News* Vol. 4, No. 2 (1987): 6–7.

[14]Ibid., 7.

[15]Ibid.

foot home which must be clean and heated. Homeowners must also deal with increased utility costs and rising property taxes.

3. *Capital Is Tied Up in Home.* Many elderly relocate to buy a smaller home, so that they can use their excess equity from their current home to offset monthly living expenses. Often after the sale of the home has been completed, there is sufficient money left to reduce monthly living costs, even after the purchase of a smaller home. This is particularly true if the older consumer decides to rent and invests all the equity. The passive income generated from the capital investment of the sale proceeds can be utilized for monthly expenses.

4. *Climate Is Disliked.* This is a concern of more and more older consumers who have fought the harsh cold of winter and the humid heat of summer for 60 or 70 years and have run out of patience. They therefore wish to find a milder living environment.

5. *Neighborhood Is Unstable.* A good number of the elderly find themselves in transitional neighborhoods or run-down metropolitan areas. Residents of these neighborhoods feel unsafe and insecure, particularly some older adults.

6. *Opportunities Are Few.* This translates into few or no services, physical activities, or cultural events within a reasonable distance. Health facilities and special services may be lacking, too expensive, or poorly managed.

7. *Children and Friends Are Moving from Immediate Neighborhood.* Senior adults may find they are becoming isolated, with few or no neighbors in some locations, and the familiar is becoming rapidly unfamiliar.

Reasons Against Relocation

1. Current home meets the needs of the residents.
2. Relocation is too difficult.
3. Long-term establishment of friends and neighborhoods causes the elderly to feel safe and secure; a support network exists to meet their needs.
4. The expense of maintaining current home is not a strain on the cash flow or morale of the homeowner.
5. Children and friends live nearby.
6. Climate is pleasant, with tolerable weather conditions; all support services are available.

7. Neighborhood is stable, so the resident feels safe and secure in current location.
8. Individual is mobile or ambulatory.
9. Present community meets needs for health care, transportation, cultural activities, churches, and shopping.

Dependent versus Independent Capabilities. First time developers in retirement housing often overlook or underestimate the need to design into the community services and programs that meet the residents' changing needs. If a developer plans only independent living residences, flexibility in design to meet the realities of the aging process may be unnecessary.

It is important to allow residents to remain a part of the community as they age and become more frail. Often developers set aside reserves to maintain aging buildings but do design flexible and functioning programs that allow residents to maintain their independent units and remain in their community.

Factors that determine the level and length of time residents can age in place include the activeness or inactiveness of the population and the architect's design features for frail or handicapped residents. Before planning and designing a community, the developer and team members need to decide which of the following groups they want to serve:

Third generation resident (old-old)	or	First generation resident (young-old)
Frail or handicapped resident	or	Able resident
Disoriented resident	or	Alert resident
Inactive resident	or	Active resident

A developer who assumes that the community will encompass all the elements listed in the right column is looking at an independent, or level one, community. If the items in the left column are being considered, then a nursing home is the likely choice. However, a person looking at some balance between the two columns needs to plan for a ACLF or CCRC development.

From a practical viewpoint the majority of the older adults who relocate want to make only one such move rather than repeated ones as their needs change with age. One major task of an ACLF or CCRC developer or sponsor is to plan a retirement community that can age effectively with each of the residents.

Facts and Fictions Concerning Aging. Numerous polls and surveys have indicated that the vast majority of Americans between the ages of 18 and 64 have many misconceptions about the elderly. Developers who are planning retirement communities should note that the members of their staff are generally in the same 18-to-64 age bracket; therefore, many team members may have misperceptions and stereotypes about the elderly ingrained in their value system.

An established stereotype is often extremely difficult to change or eliminate. One poll was conducted among people under age 65 to learn what they thought about individuals over age 65. Only 35 percent of the group felt that the elderly were very good at getting by and living independently; 29 percent believed that the elderly were bright or alert; 19 percent thought that the elderly were open-minded and could learn new ideas. The majority of nonelderly felt that in general an elderly individual was sick or frail, disabled, lonely, and depressed.[16]

The U.S. Department of Labor classifies an individual as an older worker after the age of 45, which reinforces the stereotypes.[17] Older people are not all the same, often are not dependent on others, and resemble other segments of our population in most ways.

The typical elderly individual is a woman. Longevity alone ensures that women will dominate the ranks of senior adults. In 1900 there were only 98 women to every 100 men over 65 years of age. By 1970 there were 138 women over 65 to every 100 men. By the year 2000 it has been projected there will be 154 women over 65 for every 100 men.[18]

Today, a 65-year-old man or woman can expect to live 16 years longer. At age 75, the longevity for men and women combined is another 10 years.[19] The U.S. Bureau of the Census breakdown by gender at age 65 is as follows: a male will live an additional 14 years, a female will live 18.4 years; at age 75 a male will live an additional 8.6 years, a female will live 11.5 years.[20]

Surveys of older workers have determined that they have less absenteeism, fewer on-the-job accidents, and less tardiness than other segments of the working population. The elderly—capable, willing, and

[16]National Council on the Aging, Inc., *Facts and Myths About Aging* (Washington, DC, 1981), 8–9.

[17]Ibid., 13.

[18]Elizabeth W. Markson, "Placement and Location: The Elderly in Congregate Care." In *Congregate Housing for Older People,* edited by R. D. Chelles, J. F. Seogle, and B. Seogle (Lexington, MA: Lexington Books, 1982), 57.

[19]National Council on Aging, *Facts and Myths,* 4.

[20]U.S. Bureau of the Census, *Demographic and Socioeconomic Aspects in the United States: Age Years of Life Remaining* (Washington, DC: 1978).

anxious to learn—acquire a great deal of additional information after retirement. Being fiercely independent, the elderly will not be forced into purchasing, renting, or relocating against their best interest. Elderly consumers will listen to advisors and adult children, but will make their own decisions.

Older Americans, then, are as dissimilar as younger Americans. They are neither all poor nor all rich, and they do not all suffer from senility. They do not all live alone, and many who do wish they didn't. Loneliness is a major concern of the elderly, who can and do function in society, assuming there isn't a serious mental or physical disability. Older citizens, in fact, form a most positive, active, and economically prosperous population segment in the United States today. They are not, and do not want to be, a burden on society or their adult children.[21]

Ethnic Tradition. Ethnic tradition is extremely important in some parts of the country. Adult children may care for their parents for a much longer time, rather than having the parents move into a retirement community or nursing home. If this tradition affects a large portion of the target population, it can have a devastating effect on the absorption of units in the projected market area.

In essence, ethnic tradition may in some locales make a retirement product unfeasible. For example, in one Eastern metropolis, a developer building a CCRC west of the city has little or no chance of success. East of the city, there are two or three very successful CCRCs because that community segment is more transient and does not have the same ethnic traditions.

DETERMINING THE COMPOSITION OF A RETIREMENT COMMUNITY

Essential Components. Five components have to be evaluated in determining the population segment a retirement community will serve: (1) levels of care and service capabilities, (2) functional ability of the residents, (3) age, (4) income levels, and (5) payment approach.

1. *Levels of Care and Service Capabilities.* These include needs of independent residents, semi-independent residents, moderately dependent residents, and dependent residents.

2. *Functional Abilities of the Residents.* Functional abilities are generally classified as first generation (fully functional), second gen-

[21]National Council on Aging, *Facts and Myths,* 10.

eration (frail to moderately impaired), third generation (seriously impaired to bedridden).

3. *Age.* This factor can be considered in the following way: Preretirees, 50 to 64 years of age; young-old, 65 to 74; middle-old, 75 to 84, and old-old, 85 and older. Not everyone falls into a category discussed in this section. Some individuals under 50 years of age are very dependent for mental or physical reasons, and other persons over the age of 90 are very independent. These components are merely guidelines.

4. *Income Levels.* Percent distribution by income for 1986 is illustrated on Exhibit Q. The median income of older persons in 1986 was $11,544 for males and $6,425 for females. Although higher than in 1985 the figures did not represent increases in real income for females after adjusting for inflation rate of 2% but do represent a gain of 4% in real income for males.

Families headed by persons over 65 reported a median income in 1986 of $19,932 ($20,716 for whites and $12,477 for blacks). About one of every seven families with an elderly head had less than $10,000 income.[22]

The retirement communities addressed in this text cannot cover the spectrum of income levels. Unfortunately no one in the private sector has discovered a way to build and service the support systems necessary for level two residents, as an example, and reach all income levels. It is unrealistic to assume that the private sector can provide housing and services easily for the elderly whose incomes fall much below $18,000.

In 1986 some 38 percent of families headed by 65-year-olds and older had an annual income of $25,000 and over; 10.3 percent had an annual income of $50,000 or more.[23] The communities and levels described in this volume are suitable for the elderly whose income levels are in the top 45-to-50 percent range.

Until programs economically supported or underwritten by the federal government are developed, it is impracticable for the private sector developer or sponsor to subsidize low or very low income elderly projects. Some fraternal and religious organizations provide limited support services and housing to lower income elderly through donation of land and facilities, the use of volunteers, and charitable contributions. At least at this writing, it is not very likely that the private sector can undertake such ventures.

[22]American Association of Retired Persons and Administration on Aging, U.S. Department of Health and Human Services, *A Profile of Older Americans* (Washington, DC: 1987), 9.

[23]Ibid., 9.

FAMILIES WITH HEAD 65+

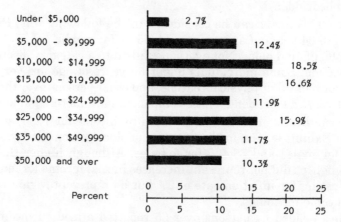

Under $5,000   2.7%

$5,000 - $9,999   12.4%

$10,000 - $14,999   18.5%

$15,000 - $19,999   16.6%

$20,000 - $24,999   11.9%

$25,000 - $34,999   15.9%

$35,000 - $49,999   11.7%

$50,000 and over   10.3%

              0   5   10   15   20   25
    Percent   ├────┼────┼────┼────┼────┤
              0   5   10   15   20   25

UNRELATED INDIVIDUAL 65+

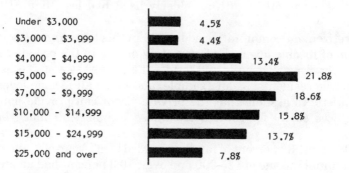

Under $3,000   4.5%

$3,000 - $3,999   4.4%

$4,000 - $4,999   13.4%

$5,000 - $6,999   21.8%

$7,000 - $9,999   18.6%

$10,000 - $14,999   15.8%

$15,000 - $24,999   13.7%

$25,000 and over   7.8%

$19,932 median for families with heads 65+
$7,731 median for unrelated individuals 65+

NOTE: Income categories in each half of chart vary in size and
        differ from those in other half.

SOURCE: Data from US Bureau of the Census. Copyright 1988 by American
          Association of Retired Persons. Reprinted with permission.
          Profile of Older Americans, 1988.

Exhibit Q. Percent distribution by income, 1986

For persons who have developed a multilevel age-integrated community and have worked with the yuppies and empty-nesters market, the next segment of the market to consider can be called the *muppies.* The acronym stands for mature upscale postprofessionals. This is the target market that will be economically feasible for most developers and sponsors.

5. *Payment Approach.* This refers to the various payment plans that have been devised and implemented in retirement communities. The major approaches are endowment, rental, menu, and ownership.

Endowment. This approach, also known as an entrance fee or accommodation fee, generally takes one of four forms.

The first type is 100 percent owned asset. All assets of the individual are signed over, usually to a fraternal or religious organization, to pay for housing, health care, and support services for the remainder of a person's life. This approach was in vogue 15 to 20 years ago. It has become more and more difficult to convince the senior adult as well as his or her adult children that the plan makes economic sense. A monthly rental fee is usually not charged.

The second plan is 100 percent endowment or entrance fee. In this approach, a large sum of money is paid to cover the cost of the unit, leaving sufficient funds for operational and health care costs for the remainder of the resident's life. It is nonrefundable and there may be additional monthly rental charges as well.

The third plan, partial endowment, is also known as the amortized approach. As an example, a cash amount of $100,000 is paid by the retiree to the developer and is amortized over 50 months in equal amounts of $2000 per month. After residing in the unit for 50 months, the retiree is not entitled to any refund upon moving from the community. If, however, the resident decides to move after month 10 he or she is refunded $2000 per month for 40 months ($80,000). If the resident should die prior to the end of the amortization period, then the facility or developer usually retains the balance. The facility has the use of all the money, of course, and most often keeps any interest earned on the initial amount. Additional rent is normally charged.

The fourth plan is a refundable endowment or entrance fee. A portion of the entrance fee, typically 50 to 90 percent is refunded when the resident vacates the premises, assuming that the unit can be remarketed. The facility keeps any interest earned from the principal. Usually in case of death the refundable portion of the entrance fee or endowment is returned to the individual's estate. An additional rental amount is usually charged.

Rental.   The second major approach is a rental arrangement. It is the least complicated for the resident and is often a straight month-to-month rental agreement. All services are usually included in the monthly rent. This is a *bundled* approach, meaning that housekeeping, transportation, and one to three meals a day are included in the monthly fee. An *unbundled* rental approach covers only rent for the apartment or unit; all of the services are charged on a pay-as-you-go basis, commonly referred to as an *a la carte plan.*

Menu.   The menu approach combines the payment plans in a retirement community. Each resident can then select either a refundable plan, partially refundable plan, totally refundable entrance or endowment plan, or a straight monthly rental approach.

There are more and more CCRCs that do not require an endowment fee approach but operate solely on a rental approach, charging either a bundled or unbundled monthly fee, based on the level of care and services. The majority of level two and level three communities are on a rental basis with a good number having bundled services. This approach is chosen because it is easier to fix the costs of operation, whereas under the unbundled approach a developer is never sure, for example, how many residents will opt for lunch on a given day, making planning for staffing, raw food, supplies, and utilization of space very difficult.

Ownership.   The final approach is ownership. It is applicable for condominiums, cooperatives, or homeowners' associations that require the resident to buy the unit and pay a monthly assessment to cover the maintenance of the exterior and the support services. The approach is gaining interest and becoming a viable marketing approach. At one time many developers thought that the elderly did not wish to own real estate. In fact, the elderly want to own real estate as much as younger people.

Insurance Programs.   For years private insurance underwriters hesitated to provide long-term health care and joint benefits to older people. That picture, however, is changing. The number of elderly Americans over age 85 has been growing rapidly, and is projected to increase from 2.6 million in 1980 to 13.3 million by the year 2040. The need for long-term care increases with age as chronic disabilities and functional dependency develop.

Insurance underwriters are developing many varied programs for level three through level six residents and patients. It should be noted that Medicare does not pay for all nursing home care, but only for skilled nursing home occupancy that begins within 30 days of discharge from a hospital stay of 3 or more consecutive days. Approximately 20 underwriters today have developed various forms of long-term health care packages to alleviate some of the expenses for resident patients who live in a community with nursing beds or custodial care units.

Advantages and Disadvantages of Varying Payment Approaches. Practices and approaches utilized in retirement communities vary along the continuum of options. As increasing sophistication in the marketplace exerts greater control over entrance fee investment, terms of leases, or maintenance fees, varying advantages and disadvantages may develop in any fee structure and payment approach.

Nonrefundable Entrance Fees. Advantages of nonrefundable entrance fees are reduced indebtedness, reduced resident turnover, subsidized operating costs, reduced construction financing, smaller entrance fees compared to refundable entrance fees, health service reserves established from front-end payments, and reduced monthly fees.

Disadvantages of nonrefundable entrance fees are the following: A resident has no flexibility in relocating; a resident who is unhappy with management must relocate; a sizable front-end fee payment is generally required; the market size of qualified residents is smaller than other options; it is difficult for an inexperienced for-profit developer to achieve the credibility necessary to develop this approach.

Refundable Entrance Fees. Advantages include these factors: Part or all of the fee is returned to the resident, with minimal financial loss relocation is much easier, health care reserves can be established in front-end fee, and adult children prefer this approach versus the nonrefundable fee. Unbundled health care is often the norm, making this payment approach easier to finance, since it is unrelated to the health of the resident.

Disadvantages of the refundable entrance fee are these: Rents may increase more rapidly; there is need to be more flexible; the entrance fee is generally 50 percent higher than the nonrefundable entrance fee, making marketing more difficult; marketing is toward higher income brackets; and except for entrance fee increases, very little income is derived from turnovers.

Rental Approach. Advantages are as follows: A larger qualified market is available because there are no entrance fees or front-end fees, residents have no initial financial risk, residents are free to relocate, the senior's estate is preserved, and for-profit developers can more easily enter the retirement market through this vehicle.

The rental approach has these disadvantages: Residents can move easily, causing increased turnover rates; minimal health care is provided, reducing the length of time a resident can age in place; lack of entrance fee makes rental increases likely; and the monthly rental payment is higher than the monthly payment for a facility that charges an entrance fee.

Ownership. Ownership provides these advantages. The resident is protected against increased rents and loss of units. A resident needing to relocate can rent or sell the unit. Rising costs are generally controlled more closely when the debt service (if any) is each owner's responsibility. Unit owners can choose the services and amenities covered by their operating fees and exercise some control over management compared to the other options. Interest and tax expenses are deductible. Residents realize appreciation on their investment, and equity in the unit will pass to the estate. A broader market is established when congregate lifestyle is offered on an ownership approach. Rentals usually attract the over-75 market, but ownership attracts the 65-year-olds as well.

Disadvantages include the following: Property may be difficult to resell, depending on financial climate; condominium or cooperative documentation, platting, and mapping add additional expense and require a top-end site; potential buyers usually must sell their current home; ultimately, the developer loses control of the board of directors to the residents. However, several projects have placed the service program under a separate entity controlled by the developer, even though the residence owners control the condominium units and common elements.

Enhancement of Real Estate. Retirement housing development epitomizes the term *enhancement of real estate*. Each additional level of services or amenities and programs introduced to a given piece of property should increase the total value of the real estate product. For example, a garden apartment rents for an average of 50 cents per square foot on a monthly basis in most locations of the country. Thus, the typical one-bedroom apartment of 800 square feet with a separate bath, living room, dining room, and kitchen rents for $400 a month. Included in the rental fee are parking space, utilities (excluding phone), and a nicely landscaped location. By enhancing this location with level two support services, the square footage value increases to between $1.25 and $2.00. If it is assumed that $1.50 per square foot is an average rent per month, the unit that rented for $400 as shelter will command $1200 a unit as a ACLF unit.

The third step in enhancing the same garden apartment is a conversion into a level three support system (supervised living). The additional services provided include personal care for the individual resident(s) within the unit, including dressing, medication, and bathing. The rent for the same 800-square-foot unit will now range between $1.75 and $3.00 per square foot per month. At an average monthly rate of $2.25, rental for the enhanced apartment would equal $1800 a month.

Continuing care retirement communities and life care developments are the fourth and final step in enhancing the subject real estate. By far the most complicated and involved stage, it commits the developer to introducing a nursing facility as well as all the services and shelter outlined in the previous three steps. Encompassed in the lifestyle of the CCRC are levels one through five, including intermediate and/or skilled nursing beds.

In many instances that garden apartment will now not only command a higher monthly fee but also an entrance fee or endowment. Unlimited stays in the nursing facility may be included in the entrance fee, may be charged as an extra, or may be limited to a specific number of days (usually 10–60). In the latter case nursing facility days exceeding the limit are charged on a daily rate in addition to the unit rent and support services. The range for this unit can now reach $4.50 to $7.00 per square foot per month. Life care communities or CCRCs in affluent locations can command as high as $12 per square foot when the entrance fee is combined with the monthly rental amount and amortized over the life of the unit. The real estate does not change. The utilization of that real estate has changed.

MISPERCEPTIONS CONCERNING RETIREMENT DEVELOPMENT

There are many misperceptions concerning senior housing and support services.

Easy and Quick Development Phase.   There is nothing easy or quick about developing retirement housing if the developer and team members are to be successful. The development stage comprises four phases described in detail in Chapter 2. Development ranges from identifying the market to product definition.

Equity Injection Requirements. Conservatively speaking, it is not unusual initially to invest between $300,000 and $1 million to determine the viability of the market and to define its needs. When considering preconstruction expenses such as professional fees, insurance, interest, down payment for land, premarketing costs, documentation cost, and taxes, it is easy to see how a developer of a 200-unit ACLF project can and will spend $300,000. Data, information, and research to determine the viability of the market for a CCRC or life care community requires investing between $750,000 and one million. Consider this expenditure to be insurance money—it is better to spend $300,000 to save $10 million in the case of an ACLF, or $1 million to save $50 million in the case of a CCRC, than to discover that there is no market need or demand for the finished product.

Reduced Standard of Living on Retirement. Many elderly have the financial means to continue their lifestyle after retirement. Their value system does not change, they simply stop working and are planning to sustain if not improve their lifestyle and standard of living.

Quick Turnover of Units and Coverage of Debt Service. Although quick turnover of units may have occurred 15 years ago when life care and CCRC communities were just taking hold in this country, it is no longer happening. There is still too little data or historical perspective to be able to understand this phenomenon. Some of the earlier CCRCs have first-generation residents who have lived in their independent units for 15 to 20 years. Developers have found, in fact, the actuarials in many instances have been incorrect. Improved health care, support services, companionship, and security have extended the physical and mental well-being of residents, creating a much longer residency in the communities.

Presale or Preleasing Not Important. Presale or preleasing is a two-edged sword. To obtain funding, preleasing or preselling is usually necessary; however, most older consumers are not going to sign binding contracts, until they can see the finished product. The elderly, to the same degree as other consumers, are tire kickers.

The lender, on the other hand, needs assurance that the product, including the planned unit mix, pricing, location, and amenities, is correct for the market. The lending community believes that presales indicate reliable interest and acceptance by intended residents. The problem with this assumption is that in a rental project, often only 10 percent of the preleased units are actually occupied by those lessees. In a CCRC, one needs to presell about 50 percent more units than will be available to be assured of 100 percent occupancy. If the plan is to sell 300 units, then the marketing department needs to presell 450 units. However, the developer may not have enough units if more than 66 percent of the 450 presold units do come to fruition. Also, in some states it may not be legal to oversell a project.

Supply Outstripped by Demand.   Demand is often overstated. In some locations, demand may be minimal or nonexistent. The level one segment of the retirement market is clearly demand driven. Level two is a hybrid of the need and demand market. Need-driven consumers fall in levels three, four, and five. What an individual would like to have available versus what will motivate that individual to make a move often differ considerably. If a new 100-bed nursing facility came on line every week between now and the year 2000 the market still would have the demand and need for 500,000 additional beds. However, a given locale may have an oversupply of beds. Demographics that illustrate need must be analyzed closely before beginning a new project.

Unregulated Business.   All 50 states require nursing homes to be licensed. Many states also require a certificate of need application process to be undertaken prior to having a license issued. If the developer is planning to create a life care retirement community or a CCRC, 23 states currently have some form of regulation covering these developments: Arizona, Arkansas, California, Connecticut, Colorado, Florida, Illinois, Indiana, Kansas, Louisiana, Maryland, Michigan, Minnesota, Missouri, New Jersey, New Mexico, New York, North Carolina, Oregon, Pennsylvania, Texas, Virginia, and Wisconsin.

In addition, Florida regulates ACLFs, and New Jersey requires a developer who plans to market 10 or more retirement units at any level to file certain information. New York currently prohibits CCRCs or life care projects, but at this writing is considering permitting CCRCs with up to 1000 beds, on a limited basis. In addition, zoning codes often do not fit or meet the needs of retirement housing.

Special use permits are required to make most sites viable. These special uses will impact density, set-back, and parking, among other things. Regulations should not be considered as prohibiting entrance into the retirement market. Regulations help keep the serious developer involved in the business and assist in forcing out persons who are less serious about the industry. In states that regulate CCRCs, various departments and bureaus have the responsibility to enforce regulations, including the Department of Insurance, Social Services (in the case of California), and the Department of Public Health (Illinois and Indiana). In Maryland the Office of Aging and in Michigan the Corporation and Securities Bureau oversee retirement housing regulations.

It is likely that by the year 2000, three fourths or more of the states will have some regulations protecting the consumer who ventures into an entrance fee community. Perhaps as many as one fourth of the states will also have some regulations affecting residents who move into level two and level three communities.

Penetration Rate versus Capture Rate. Penetration rate can often be misleading. Developers entering into this market often will hear that they should not exceed a penetration rate of 5 percent. It depends on the needs and demands of the individual market.

Do not take a generalized rate and force it into a particular market. For example, if a developer plans to build a 300-unit CCRC and there already exist 1000 completed units, there would be 1300 potential units in that market. Assume there are approximately 8000 qualified households meeting the age and income requirements for entering a CCRC. (Generally people must own their home and have sufficient equity in it coupled with adequate monthly income to qualify for a CCRC.) The penetration rate, including the additional 300 units, would be 16.25 percent. Looking at just the 1000 units the penetration rate would be 12.5 percent. In some communities in this country either rate can be viable to go forward with a project because the demand may exist to support those penetration levels.

In the St. Petersburg market, for example, the penetration rate exceeds 5 percent. On the other hand, there are markets in the oil-dependent areas of the United States that currently may have a penetration rate of less than 1 percent; yet it would be a poor decision in today's economy to place a CCRC of any size in these areas.

Do not accept rules of thumb, rates, percentages, and directions without analyzing how the rules of thumb can be applied to any given product. Taking the penetration rate one more step, it is important to have a handle on the number of real consumers versus the ones who are just daydreaming. The *capture rate* helps determine this factor. It places cash requirements on the presale or preleasing to consumers. There are no formal standards for establishing the capture rate.

Assume that the penetration rate in a market area is 5 percent. What portion of that rate can be captured? How many persons will, in fact, close on their entrance fee, sign a lease, or put down the required deposit for purchasing a unit? A cash deposit is a method of validating the penetration rate. A developer who asks for a $250 refundable, or even nonrefundable, deposit would capture many individuals. They may, however, find it quite easy to forfeit that amount. A nonrefundable deposit for $10,000 would attract only serious individuals. The percentage of capture will be reduced as the cash deposit amount and restrictions on refunding are increased.

Fill Versus Full.   An additional concern of developers is when to permit occupancy. An initial response would be, as soon as the project is completed. However, if residents are permitted to move in too early, they will utilize only a few of the units and a very small percentage of the common area. Prospective residents touring the facility may react negatively to the depressing sight of only 7 individuals having their dinner or lunch in a central dining room designed for 350. It is wise to hold off until at least 15 or 20 percent of the units have been leased or sold, so that there will be enough residents to make a positive impression on prospective purchasers.

Size.   One of the earlier misconceptions articulated by sponsors or developers who want to enter the retirement housing market is that there must be a minimum number of units, often 200 or more if planning a rental product, and 200 to 300 if planning an entrance fee or a life care project. In addition if services are bundled, the number of units stated here is considered a minimum size for a successful project. Along the same line of reasoning, a developer who plans to develop an unbundled service approach, meaning services are paid for as consumed, may be able to reduce size to as few as 150 units for a rental project.

There are, however, several exceptions to these standards, particularly because this market is relatively new and the state of the art is changing constantly. Some highly successful projects have been as small as 16 units, nursing facilities as small as 20 units have done well, and projects have prospered as full service condominiums, with 80 sold units and an additional 40 rental units that share common areas with the owners. However, special characteristics, such as the combined sales and rental approach, usually need to be present in order to undertake the small size project.

Health insurance packages are being developed that cover long-term health care, major medical care, catastrophic illness, Alzheimer's disease (not covered under Medicare), and home health care. The elderly who purchase such a plan can relocate anywhere in the United States, because the insurance benefits are not tied to a specific location or facility. Smaller projects can target this market approach because nursing beds are not required.

Some smaller projects have been phased; some have shared services with hospitals or nursing homes. In addition, several smaller projects have been on a land lease with terms very favorable to the developer because the facility serves the needs of the lessor hospital or nursing home by being located on contiguous land.

Flexibility in design, by including kitchens in some units and being able to add kitchens relatively easily in other units, has also helped. Units can be designed for conversion ease, to permit expanding a unit to two bedrooms or splitting a unit to create two one-bedroom units. In other cases, a joint venture with a nonprofit organization in a landlord-tenant relationship may be advantageous to both parties.

Small size projects often need to contract for more services than larger projects would. Meal services that are catered instead of using in-house staff, save the capital required to build kitchens. Taxi, limousine, or bus companies can provide transportation. Housekeeping, laundry, maintenance, and janitorial services all can be contracted for, as can on-site health care.

Cost-effective measures to make smaller size projects affordable can be instituted, such as having some meals open to the public at prices that help offset the cost of providing the meal. Renting out the public areas for Saturday night dances, lectures, use by other elderly groups, day-care centers, and meetings of various organizations can generate income. Covered parking spaces can provide additional income as can the phone system, through extra charges for message and answering services.

A hidden work force can be tapped by utilizing the residents as host or hostess for the dining room, chef's helpers, purchasing agent, menu planner, social director, security force, maintenance staff, drivers, landscapers, and gardeners. When the residents work with and for a developer, both the residents' cost and the developer's expense can be reduced.

Do not place limitations on the provision of services for smaller size projects without understanding every available option.

Backdoor Policy. What will the lender or developer do with a project that fails as a retirement community? One of the major problems for a lender is how to utilize the public area if the project does not work as a retirement development and must be turned into an age-integrated community.

There is very little use for nursing home space if that portion of the community is not successful. This very real problem is often overlooked or understated prior to beginning a project. Some have used the central community areas for health centers, others have converted some public areas into additional apartments and rented out the total project as an age-integrated community. Alternative uses for extensive common areas must be considered to reduce the risk inherent in this product.

Elderly Ownership. There is a misconception that a person past a certain age is no longer interested in owning real estate, but prefers renting or entering a CCRC under a resident contract agreement.

It is estimated by *Florida Trend Magazine* that more than one third of the state of Florida is owned by individuals over the age of 50. The notion that an elderly person wishes to change lifestyle and no longer be responsible for owning real estate has not been demonstrated in any surveys.

Ownership is synonymous with independence and self-sufficiency. The third-generation retiree may not be interested in owning but younger generations of retirees certainly are, and they find many advantages to ownership.

Elderly residents want management to work for them, and owning gives them that kind of control. Ownership protects against increased rents and loss of the unit if the resident becomes physically ill or less ambulatory. Many elderly people believe that there is a fixed cost associated with owning, even though the cost of services escalates for either a rental or ownership approach. A big reason both the elderly and their children like ownership is that equity is retained.

There is little or no depletion of any part of the estate when one purchases a unit, assuming that the unit value remains constant or appreciates. If the unit appreciates, it is an additional advantage to ownership versus renting or an entrance fee approach. If further proof is needed that ownership is a viable option, consider that every unit located in the Leisure Worlds throughout the country is either sold as a cooperative or a condominium. A condominium in California has a nursing home that is administered by the condominium association, and all of the independent units are sold fee simple. It has been a very well-received concept.

ELEMENTS OF A SUCCESSFUL RETIREMENT COMMUNITY

The developer's responsibilities are to be the project manager, the major decision maker, and the coordinator for other members of the team. The developer must be well informed about all aspects of development, including such components as location, access, design criteria, product, parking, unit mix, marketing approach, cost, pricing, document development, internal unit improvements, construction and permanent financing, common services and amenities, management plan, phasing, timing, insurance, budgets, construction operations and reserves, construction coordination, and public and community relations. This list is not exhaustive, but it illustrates the breadth of knowledge and experience required to successfully develop and lease or sell units in a retirement community.

A developer must also enjoy the elderly and have sincere concerns about their well-being. Going into the retirement market just for the money usually will not work for the elderly or the developer. The developer who has the financial wherewithal to deal with retirement development but lacks background will need advisers with experience on senior issues.

The developer must also be prepared to commit resources of time, money, and reputation. A strategic plan must be mapped out with competent staff. Both the staff and developer must have credibility with the elderly population.

The job of construction coordinator illustrates the need for an experienced developer and competent staff. This is a prime responsibility of the developer of any retirement community. Only a portion of most retirement communities, however, need the multifamily stick-and-brick expertise that forms the background for many developers. In such situations, the developer needs a contractor who understands commercial and mid- to high-rise construction. A good number of square feet make up the kitchen and common areas. A construction coordinator must understand to some extent kitchen design, engineering, architecture, landscape architecture, and interior design. Some marketing background with experience in residential and commercial design is necessary to fill the multilevel professional requirements needed for retirement community development.

The end product must give elderly consumers the feeling that their relocation is an upward, or at least a lateral, move. An institutional look is undesirable. All this has to be done within a budget and, for most developers, with a profit at the end of the process.

The remaining chapters should provide the information necessary to increase the success factor, enabling each developer to make a profit and each sponsor to be compensated for risks and efforts.

CHAPTER 2

THE PLANNING PROCESS

S. KELLEY MOSELEY and JAMES L. LAUGHLIN

INTRODUCTION

Success in retirement housing depends on careful and thorough planning, a difficult and time-consuming process. This is particularly true in today's environment of uncertain access to capital, competition, governmental involvement, unknown market demand, inexperienced developers, and little historical precedent.

Real estate developers and health care institutions are both embarking on new territory in developing retirement housing. Critical questions such as the following need answers and are the focus of the planning process:

What is retirement housing?
Is this product consistent with my mission and goals?
What are the risks and opportunities?
What are my internal strengths and weaknesses relative to developing the project?
What type of support is needed to strengthen my team?
Is there a need or demand for the product(s)?
What buildings, programs, and spaces are required?
What government regulations impact the products?
What staff and equipment are needed?
How much does it cost to build?
How much does it cost to operate?

Does the project produce a profit?

How is it marketed?

How is it managed?

How is it financed?

The first step in planning retirement housing is a strategic or positioning step, designed to take the manager, developer, or owner through a series of questions that analyze alternatives. The analysis should result in selecting one or more alternatives to positively direct the organization's future.

Once a direction is identified, then detailed analysis, design, and product development can occur. Subsequent planning steps include product analysis and assessment, product design and program planning, financial feasibility, development and construction, marketing and promotion, and management and operations. Table 2-1 graphically describes these seven major phases of the planning process.[1,2] These phases will form the framework for subsequent chapters in this book.

The information in Table 2-1 also depicts the correct order of the planning steps. Positioning and strategic thinking should precede product assessment, and likewise, product assessment precedes design. Although the table implies that the steps are sequential, it is possible to fast track the process and complete several steps concurrently. The following pages describe these major phases and their contributions to the planning process.

PHASE 1. STRATEGIC THINKING—POSITIONING AND ORGANIZING

Need for Strategic Thinking. A dynamic business environment demands strategic thinking. It is clear that situations are constantly changing. However, during the past five years, these changes, particularly in the elderly shelter industry, have seemed to come more quickly, producing increasing uncertainty. Any organization considering a new line of business such as elderly housing must conduct strategic thinking within the organization as the first step in planning.

Strategic thinking is a process, or set of activities, that helps to

[1]Owen B. Hardy and L. P. Lammers, *Hospitals: The Planning and Design Process* (Rockville, MD: Aspen Systems, 1977), 32, 37.

[2]Louis E. Gelwicks and R. J. Newcomer, *Planning Housing Environments for the Elderly* (Washington, DC: The National Council on Aging, 1974), 67–74.

manage changing situations. It involves, as its outcome, actions that position the organization to take advantage of change. In its most basic form, strategic thinking comprises the traditional decision-making process. It encompasses activities that actually precede planning a specific project.[3]

In order to survive and prosper, an organization must constantly evaluate its position and make corrections in structure, approach, and services. As a result, strategic thinking is an ongoing activity, not merely a report prepared every three to five years.

Purpose of Strategic Thinking. The strategic assessment assists the organization in identifying opportunities, risks, and options in order to remain responsive to its current and future clients. The assessment should address the existing state of the organization, the attitudes of key administrative staff and clients, as well as critical issues facing the organization. The outcome should provide recommendations for new or modified services, role, and mission, and it should prioritize those recommendations.[4]

The primary objectives of the strategic assessment are to:

1. Ensure the continued viability of the organization
2. Identify major environmental forces expected to impact the organization
3. Assess future direction, function, and focus
4. Develop within the organization the skills to continue the assessment and planning process
5. Determine the resources needed to achieve the identified goals.

Table 2-1 identifies the series of steps in Phase 1 of the planning process. This phase identifies options and aids in deciding whether to develop one or more elderly oriented products. The following steps of Phase 1, should be completed before embarking on any project or program:

1. Motivation to develop a project
2. Identification of mission, role, and goals

---

[3]J. Rakich, B. Langert, and K. Darr, *Managing Health Service Organizations* (Philadelphia, PA: W. B. Saunders, 1985), 228–234.

[4]Jon Jaeger, "The Concept of Corporate Planning," *Health Care Management Review* Vol. 7, No. 3 (Summer 1982): 43.

TABLE 2-1. Phases of the Planning Process

1. Strategic Thinking—Positioning and Organizing

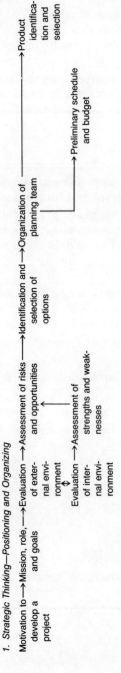

Motivation to develop a project → Mission, role, and goals → Evaluation of external environment ⇄ Evaluation of internal environment → Assessment of risks and opportunities ← Assessment of strengths and weaknesses → Identification and selection of options → Organization of planning team → Preliminary schedule and budget → Product identification and selection

2. Product Analysis and Assessment

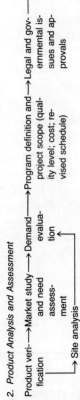

Product verification → Market study and need assessment → Site analysis → Demand evaluation → Program definition and project scope (quality level; cost; revised schedule) → Legal and governmental issues and approvals → Project description definition and restrictions

3. Product Design and Program Planning

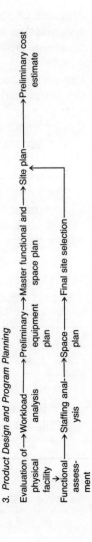

Evaluation of physical facility ⇄ Functional assessment → Workload analysis → Staffing analysis → Preliminary equipment plan → Space plan → Master functional and space plan → Final site selection → Site plan → Preliminary cost estimate

4. Financial Feasibility

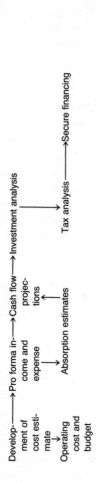

Develop-ment of cost esti-mate → Pro forma income and expense → Cash flow projections → Investment analysis → Tax analysis → Secure financing

Operating cost and budget

Absorption estimates

5. Development and Construction

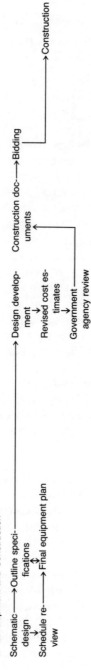

Schematic design → Outline specifications → Design development

Schedule review → Final equipment plan

Revised cost estimates

Government agency review → Construction documents → Bidding → Construction

6. Marketing and Promotion

Marketing objectives → Marketing plan → Marketing budget → Marketing schedule → Implementation → Evaluation

7. Management and Operations

Predevelopment → Preopening → Initial → Ongoing

Sources: Owen B. Hardy and L. P. Lammers, *Hospitals: The Planning and Design Process* (Rockville, MD: Aspen Systems, 1977), 32, 37; Louis E. Gelwicks and R. J. Newcomer, *Planning Housing for the Elderly* (Washington, DC: The National Council on Aging, 1974), 67–74.

3. Evaluation of external environment
4. Evaluation of internal environment
5. Assessment of strengths, weaknesses, risks, and opportunities
6. Identification of options
7. Organization of planning team
8. Product identification and selection
9. Preliminary schedule and budget

Motivation to Develop a Project.   Before any project can begin, someone of authority in an organization must be motivated to change. Although this step may seem obvious, it is nevertheless important. Many organizations maintain the same operating structure and approach for years. If they are profitable, or at least if the setbacks are not too painful, management may have little motivation to change. In other cases, perhaps, subordinates in an organization desire to develop a new product or program. If the top management cannot be persuaded to change, then it is unlikely that a new activity will be undertaken or even assessed for its merit.

Motivation can result from a variety of factors and forces including loss of market, increased competition, legal and tax issues, changing demand, and loss of revenue. Obviously, these are negative forces, and the motivation is to reduce the pain. Planning based on this motivation can produce results, but it is reactive and may be too little or too late.

Alternatively, planning based on recognition of changing market forces, understanding and research, is proactive, and responsive. Such an approach characterizes market leaders. At times such planners seem out of step or inconsistent with their peers. However, such anticipation of market forces is critical.

Mission, Role, and Goals.   Assuming that the organization is motivated to at least assess possible opportunities, the next step is to develop a clear understanding of the current situation and mission. There should be a review of the existing mission statement, describing the purpose of the organization and the limits on its activity. If a statement does not exist, one should be developed.

The mission statement will define what the organization does, where it carries out its activities, who its clients are, and how the mission is to be accomplished. For example, a hospital mission statement may read, "To provide quality medical and surgical services to the residents of Smith County at a reasonable cost, regardless of ability to pay."

Conversely, a real estate developer's mission statement may specify,

"To develop office buildings in Phoenix and maximize profits," or "To develop multifamily housing in St. Louis for moderate and upper income families."

Examining the preceding statements produces evidence of potential conflicts for development of elderly housing. First, elderly housing is not a goal of any of the organizations. Second, the identified geographic boundaries may prohibit opportunities outside those areas. Third, none of the statements offers clear authority to begin development of elderly housing.

If an organization were to proceed in developing elderly housing, without addressing the mission statement, then it is possible that the board of directors and/or shareholders might be very disappointed. Therefore, it is recommended that a mission statement be developed and approved by the board of directors to provide the authority and support for new product development.

Following completion of the mission statement, it is useful to examine the existing strategies, goals, policies, and objectives within the organization. In other words, how is the mission being accomplished? Are these strategies consistent with the mission? Are they supportive of an innovative philosophy and approach? If conflicts are observed, it will be necessary to undertake administrative changes to put the organization in a posture that is supportive of change and innovation. Such administrative actions may include altering board membership and revising the organization structure. [5,6]

Evaluation of External Environment. This step involves examination of forces outside the organization that will influence its operation and performance. It is a scanning tool to identify both the positive and negative factors that may produce risks and opportunities. The following are examples of forces that impact both health care institutions and the real estate industry:

Economic trends	Legal and tax issues
Demographic trends	Government regulation
Competitors and their products	Employment
Capital market activity	Population migration
Real estate prices and trends	Health and disease trends
Reimbursement for health care	

[5]Philip Reeves, David Bergwall, and Niau Ladside, *Introduction to Health Planning* (Arlington, VA: Information Resources Press, 1984), 2–6.

[6]B. A. Fournet, *Strategic Business Planning in Health Services Management* (Rockville, MD: Aspen Systems, 1982), 5.

These trends should be examined over at least the next five years. Some issues and trends are national; others are representative of the organization's local community.

The environmental assessment is not a market or need study for a specific product. Instead, it is an attempt to scan the political, economic, social, and demographic horizon in order to avoid pitfalls and anticipate opportunities. Data collected in this process include these items:[7]

Economic Trends

Bank deposits
Retail sales
New industry formation
Interest rate trends

Capital Market Activity

Financing vehicle changes
Investor requirements
Mortgage rate trends
Sources of capital

Demographic Trends

Population growth by age
   and sex
Income per capita and
   household
Migration
Birth rate
Poverty levels

Real Estate Trends

Home sales
Office vacancy rates
Apartment vacancy rates
Housing values
Land values

*Health, Social, and
Disease Trends*

Death rates
Diseases and illnesses
Problems of society
Social needs and activities
Elderly needs and problems

Health Care Trends

Hospital occupancy rates
Payment/reimbursement
   climate
Nursing home occupancy
   rates
Alternative delivery system
   trends

Evaluation of Internal Environment. This step provides a picture of the organization's current activities, strengths, and weaknesses. It includes a complete review of current programs, products, activities, resources, and finances. In many cases, this process also includes interviews with key staff, as well as a survey of community or client attitudes and opinions regarding the organization.

[7]Reeves, *Health Planning,* 179–183.

The following data are needed to complete this evaluation:

Income and expense statements (five years)

Balance sheets (five years)

Trends in programs and products (trends will vary by organization— health care institutions are concerned with utilization of beds and services; real estate developers must consider product sales, completions, and vacancy rates of existing properties)

Available staff and their qualifications

Consumer, client, or community leader attitudes and opinions regarding the organization

Key staff attitudes regarding strengths and weaknesses

Assessment of strengths and weaknesses of the organization should be started by the staff. However, it is difficult for an employee or owner to be objective regarding weaknesses, as well as to be accurate in documenting success. It will probably be necessary to request outside consultation to complete this task.

The evaluation assesses whether the organization is properly structured or positioned to undertake a new product or project, such as retirement housing. It further identifies weaknesses in staffing, finances, and organization that must be overcome in order to develop new programs or projects.[8]

Strengths, Weaknesses, Risks, and Opportunities. At this point, it is possible to develop a statement of strengths, weaknesses, risks, and opportunities facing the organization, based on information from the internal and external evaluations. The key point is to state these issues as clearly as possible in order to develop a strategy or approach that will avoid or overcome negative factors, build on organization strengths, strengthen the organization, and identify profitable opportunities.[9]

The listing or narrative statement should address these issues:

Strengths and Weaknesses	Risks	Opportunities
Financial position	Economic trends	Demographic
Competitive position	Competition	Location
Staff qualifications	Demographics	Competition
Location	Real estate market	Product
Programs or products	Capital market	Approach
Physical facilities		

[8]Reeves, *Health Planning*, 238–243.
[9]Rakich, *Managing Health Service Organizations*, 229–231.

Identification and Selection of Options. Based on all previous evaluations, it is possible to identify one or more options or products that warrant more serious assessment and perhaps development. A variety of options may have been identified, including nursing homes, hospitals, rehabilitation facilities, hospice care, home health services, rental congregate housing, outpatient clinics, Alzheimer's care, and others. The difficult task is to select one or more for further analysis. It is possible that outside professional expertise may be required, because most organizations do not have skilled internal staff who understand this process.

The identification of options for further consideration depends on whether the program or product is consistent with certain selection criteria developed during this positioning and organizing phase. The criteria arise from the internal and external evaluation discussed earlier and are determined from answers to the following questions:

1. Is the program or product consistent with the mission and role of the organization?
2. Does the product have support within the organization?
3. Is competition limited or significant?
4. Is the organization in a good market position to undertake this activity?
5. Can the program be implemented rapidly or slowly?
6. Is existing staff adequate, or must it be enhanced?
7. Does the product require large equity dollars up front?
8. Does there appear to be a general market for the product?
9. Are other successful operators in existence, and/or have unsuccessful products been identified?

When these aspects have been addressed, a decision will be made whether to conduct further analysis on the identified product or program. It should be noted that an approved product or program can still be rejected at other phases of the planning process; for example, if quantitative need is not demonstrated, the project is not financially feasible, capital is not available, or an adequate site cannot be found. At this point, however, the planning team can be organized and the products identified for further analysis.

Organization of Planning Team. The organization and selection of planning team members is critical to the success of any project. Of foremost importance is that the team receive its direction and support from the highest authority, that is, the board of directors or owners.

If the organization is directed by a large board structure, it is recommended that a planning committee be established and given the responsibility for project oversight. A planning director is usually hired by the committee to carry out day-to-day activities and to provide staff support.

In organizations that do not have large boards, the owner should delegate or employ a planning director. It is suggested that a single individual be given the responsibility of coordinating the planning tasks. Previous assessment of organization strengths and weaknesses will have determined whether such a qualified individual is available in-house.

It is unlikely that a single individual has the skills to conduct all of the planning tasks required. In fact, it is perhaps wiser to have the planning director supervise and coordinate the various players and participants. The skills needed include demographic analyses, architectural design, marketing, and management. As a result, during the development of a project, a variety of players may be required at different times. The role and function of each player are based on the requirements of the development process.

Although individual team members may not all be required for every project skill, the following tasks are generally necessary. Small-sized projects cannot often afford to include all persons listed on these pages, yet the developer should ensure that the tasks or activities are being completed by some member of the planning team or an outside consultant.

These skills are required on most planning teams:

Fund raising	Financial management (feasibility consulting)
Development	
Market research	Financing (investment banking)
Legal advice	Marketing
Functional planning	Association consulting
Architecture and design	Management and operations
Real estate	Insurance expertise
Construction management	Government liaison

The roles and responsibilities of the development team members are presented next.[10,11,12]

[10]American Association of Homes for the Aging, *Planning Housing and Services for the Elderly* (Washington, DC, 1977), 7, 8.

[11]C. W. Griffin, *Development Building: The Team Approach* (Washington, DC: The American Institute of Architects, 1972), 11–13.

[12]Hardy, *Hospitals*, 16–22.

Fund Raising. It is clear that no development project will proceed very far without financial support and authority. Someone must pay the consulting and development fees and decide to assume the risk of development. Only the owner or responsible financial partner can serve this role. All others in the process are consultants and agents, who do not usually bear the full risk of their recommendations. The owner is responsible for assembling the development team and selecting the qualified professionals needed.

Development. In many cases, the developer and owner will be the same person. However, in other cases, such as a complex health care project, a skilled developer will be required who may not be the owner. Coordination of the planning tasks is the developer's primary role. This includes supervision of market studies, economic feasibility, site selection, design, preparation of financing packages, and supervision of construction, fill-up, marketing, and sale or ongoing management.

One of the principal responsibilities of the developer is coordinating members of the team by means of compromise decisions, to obtain the goal of creating an optimum environment and lifestyle for the residents. As an example, a marketing director's primary responsibility is to lease or sell apartments and to package the lifestyle as attractively as possible to prospective residents. The attorney member of the team, however, may be concerned about providing protection for the developer or organization from claims by unhappy residents. Often the marketing director and the attorney may review a brochure and provide conflicting recommendations. The developer must arrive at a compromise that allows the marketing staff to reach maximum sales, within the guidelines of protection required by the developer's counsel.[13]

An additional responsibility of the developer is to be sure that all team members have reviewed and understand each of their individual roles as well as the roles of other members of the team. There should be specific meetings for certain members of the development team, and general meetings for all members of the development team to reinforce and coordinate responsibilities, timing, and other job requirements.[14] The specific meetings involve only certain members of the team and address specific issues. The developer is also responsible for creating a single vision of the goals and objectives of the product. Though this coordination is extremely important, it is often overlooked.

---

[13]F. Scott Jackson and James L. Laughlin, *Business Condominiums* (National Association of Homebuilders and Community Association Institute, Washington, DC, 1985), 9.

[14]Ibid., 10.

Market Research. The market researcher is responsible for assessing the need and demand for the product or program. This individual should be skilled in demographic analyses and experienced in conducting studies of the particular product. Tasks and activities of market research include market area definition, population projections, competitor analysis, and need assessment. In most cases, this specialist will be an outside consultant with extensive experience in assessing need and demand for retirement housing and elderly care services.

Legal Advice. The legal issues of elderly care extend beyond the normal development issues of land acquisition, zoning, or financing. In many cases, legal guidance will be required to deal with state, local, and federal regulatory agencies, such as state health departments or Medicare. In many instances, a certificate of need must be obtained from the proper authorities. Further, construction of leases, condominium agreements, or life-care contracts will require legal input at an early stage.

The attorney is also responsible for establishing the development entity or entities and for providing the appropriate tax planning together with the financial consultants. The attorney may also handle acquisition of the site and negotiation of the contracts, as well as negotiations with existing or potential lenders. Many times, the attorney is asked to deal with any tenant issues if the developer plans to convert an existing building to a retirement community. A myriad of tenant issues could arise, such as evictions or relocation.

It is not unusual to have the attorney involved in dealing with the zoning and site plan approvals as well as the politics of special use permits, which are often required for a retirement community or project. If the project is to be sold as a cooperative or condominium, legal input is required to ensure the project's compliance with state law. Further, the attorney should prepare disclosure documents and create rental agreements, leases, purchase agreements, or resident contracts. In many cases, an attorney may also act to educate the purchasers or residents of a given community at closing or settlement, if applicable.

Functional Planning. Functional planning is the process of describing the relationship of departments or activities within a building. It consists of identifying what goes on in a facility, how traffic and circulation occur, and how a facility is staffed and operated. Occasionally, management and operations consultants can provide this input if they are experienced in planning and developing elderly facilities. It is generally preferable to have this task completed by specialists. The most successful approach would be to use a combination of experienced managers and architects with extensive functional planning background in retirement housing.

Architecture and Design.   The role of the architect is to design, specify, and document the physical characteristics of the desired facility. The architect should have experience in elderly projects and have available on staff or access to specialists, particularly in kitchen or restaurant design, landscape design, and interior design. Experience in designing a specific type of project or product is critical to its success. The architect should also be aware of the physical and psychological needs of the elderly.

Real Estate.   The developer or a consultant should have direct knowledge of land availability, prices, and real estate trends in the community. This individual should also be skilled in negotiation and real estate transactions.

Secondarily, a real estate appraisal specialist is required during the planning process. This individual will develop the required documentation for lenders and investors under approved guidelines. The individual should be qualified as a Member, Appraisal Institute (M.A.I.) and possess experience in conducting appraisals of the defined product. The M.A.I. should also be familiar with the local real estate market.

Construction Management.   The construction manager provides important contributions from the beginning to the end of the development process. The primary role of the construction manager is to provide realistic estimates of project cost and to vigorously control project costs during construction. The role of the construction manager combines traditional activities of the general contractor and architect. The benefit in using an independent construction manager is that costs are controlled without loss of quality. However, it is perhaps more costly in terms of fees to have someone other than the architect perform this task.

Financial Management (Feasibility Consulting).   The financial feasibility consultant will conduct the analysis of income, expense, cash flow, and investment. This individual receives construction cost estimates from the architect and construction manager, and operating cost and revenue estimates from the management consultants or team members. Independently, the financial analyst assesses the economic feasibility of the project. In some cases, the project will require modification or perhaps even be abandoned if financial feasibility results are not consistent with owner needs and objectives.

Financing (Investment Banking). The investment specialist's role is to structure the financing for the project. The task is to define a financing approach that meets the needs of the owner-developer, but is also satisfactory to the investment community. The investment specialist will generally join the team after the financial feasibility evaluation has been completed. However, the financing consultant can provide input during financial analysis and project definition, because some financing sources require specialized projects, design, or regulatory approvals.

Marketing. Although the actual marketing tasks will probably not begin until financing is secured, the marketing specialist can provide insight into consumer acceptance of project design and amenities. Marketing professionals can also assist in conducting consumer opinion polls, developing marketing budgets and plans for financial projections, and developing an image-building campaign in the community.

Association Consulting. In a condominium project, this individual assists the developer in forming a workable association that will meet the needs of resident owners.

The association consultant is one of the few members of the development team who will be involved with the community on a long-term basis. Condominium consultants must act as an advocate of the association's interest, as well as being concerned with the developer's desires. The consultant should review legal documents to affirm that the association is created from an operational perspective, assisting the developer's attorney in creating practical and functional documents that permit residents the flexibility to age in place. Documents for a condominium can be perfectly legal and still place undue restraints on the association's operation.[15]

Management and Operations. Individuals who are knowledgeable about how a project or facility is operated and staffed are critical to both the design process and feasibility analysis. These specialists can provide cost-saving advice in functional planning, design, budget preparation, and financial analysis. The role of the management specialist is to review all architectural plans to ensure they are consistent with effective operations as well as meet the needs of residents.

[15]Ibid., 12.

Insurance Expertise. The insurance agent's interaction is primarily with the manager, attorney, and the developer. Frequently, insurance agents are unaware of the differences and unique requirements of a retirement community. Care should be taken in selecting an insurance carrier and an agent who is knowledgeable about retirement housing.[16]

Government Liaison. Because the city and county must approve the construction of projects in accordance with zoning, building, and subdivision codes, a continual liaison must be created between the development team and the municipality charged with overseeing the construction.[17]

Other Necessary Skills. In addition to personnel for the positions that have been outlined, other individual professionals may need to be considered depending on the form the retirement community takes. These include title insurer, escrow agent, tax specialist, medical specialists, security consultants, telecommunications consultants, and others.

Product Identification and Selection. A final step in the strategic positioning phase is the identification of specific products for further analysis. These products, which may include congregate housing, assisted living, nursing care, or for-sale housing should be specifically described. The planning team can perform a very useful role in creating this description.

Careful product identification is critical to the subsequent phases and tasks to avoid errors in market analysis and design, as well as many other components.

Selecting the Form of Retirement Product. The developer-owner has three basic options to determine the approach or model for developing a retirement community: rental, entrance fee, and ownership. There are several variations of each approach, such as a combination of the three basic approaches. There are advantages and disadvantages to any approach for both the developer-owner as well as the residents. Certain approaches are more favorable depending on the part of the country where the project is to be developed.[18]

A resident can be treated one of four different ways, each with

---

[16]Ibid., 13.

[17]Ibid., 13.

[18]Wilson H. Worley, "Retirement Housing: Should We Be in the Business," *Retirement Housing Report* Vol. 1, No. 10 (June 1987): 2–4.

varying degrees of rights, liabilities, and restrictions, as shown in Table 2-2.

The resident can be an owner, tenant, licensee, or patient, depending on the contractual arrangements established between the developer and resident. Each of these arrangements permits or restricts certain rights and responsibilities of the resident. Conversely, each approach permits or restricts the developer's rights and responsibilities in implementing covenants, conditions, restrictions, and rules that might apply to a certain project.

Owners of real estate, including owners of condominiums and cooperatives, have certain statutory rights in every state. Tenants on the other hand fall under a tenant–landlord relationship through use of a month-to-month rental agreement or a lease.

Certain stipulations are set forth in both instances to be followed by the developer-owner in dealing with a tenant or owner of an individual unit. That is not the case for a resident who moves into a continuing care retirement community (CCRC) and executes a resident contract. Such a contract can be equated to a personal service contract in that as long as the resident meets the contractual obligations, he or she may occupy and use the space addressed in the agreement. The agreement is a revocable license. It is not a lease or a monthly rental agreement, nor is it an easement. The agreement does not transfer or grant to the resident any interest in real property owned by the developer or sponsor.

Under the rental approach or ownership approach, real estate laws protect the resident-tenant to some degree, and the resident-owner to a greater degree.

The nursing home resident is a patient who signs an admission form,

TABLE 2-2. Ownership Forms

	Ownership	Rental	CCRC	Nursing Home
Resident status	Owner	Tenant	Licensee	Patient
Contract form	Deed	Lease	Resident agreement	Admittance form
Contract type	Real estate	Real estate	Service contract	Service contract
Resident relationship	Buyer-seller	Landlord-tenant	Right to use	Purchaser of goods and services

72

and occupancy is on a day-to-day basis. The patient transferred to a nursing home that is part of a CCRC may lose the right to continue occupying his or her apartment unit according to the resident agreement with the sponsor or developer. Various forms of retirement housing are shown in Table 2-3.

Preliminary Schedule and Budget. A final important step in the strategic positioning phase is construction of a preliminary project schedule and budget to guide all planning and feasibility steps and consultants. Although the schedule may change, the planning team will have established both timing and financial benchmarks to monitor the initial assessment and design phases.

This budget consists of planning and feasibility costs only and is not intended as a development budget. Predevelopment costs and schedules are identified to determine the amount of funds and time required for the project and enable the developer-owner to decide if the project should proceed. Included in this budget are costs such as option money for the site, feasibility consultants, preliminary architectural design and cost estimating, development of lender package, and corporate overhead.

In order to prepare the planning budget, it is necessary to understand the previously discussed steps of the planning process. Each step has costs associated with its completion. Further, a lender generally requires completion of these steps prior to the award of financing. As a result, funds expended in this planning process are at risk if the project does not move forward. From $300,000 to $1,000,000 may be needed to secure necessary financing for a project.

Summary. Strategic positioning involves assessing strengths, weaknesses, risks, and opportunities facing the organization, as well as determining if retirement housing is the business you want to be in. The primary purpose of this phase is to scan the environment both internally and externally to seek development opportunities and assess your capabilities. Strategic thinking is a key first step in deciding whether to pursue development of elderly products and services. This process also defines the specific products that will receive further analysis in the planning process. Finally, strategic positioning consists of organizing the planning team and preparing to move forward with the project. Careful selection of team members and creation of realistic schedules and budgets help ensure a well-organized project.

TABLE 2-3. Retirement Housing Options

Level	Development Segment	Market Segment	Age	Development Size	Size of Unit (square feet)	Market Area	Key Services	Pricing Approach
1	Senior adult community (independent)	Preretirees, young/-old couples, some singles	50–74	100 + units	1-, 2-, 3-bedroom, (700–2000)	Intrastate, many times out of state	Recreational and social amenities, preferred climate	Fee simple
2	Congregate living facility (semi-independent)	Old, old/old, more singles than couples	75 +	150–200 units	Studio (350–600) 1 bedroom (600–850) 1 bedroom with den (700–950) Two bedroom (900–1400)	Metro and submarkets	Meals, health linkage, social, transportation, security, housekeeping, recreation, laundry	Rental, fee simple
3	Board and care (moderately dependent, personal care)	Old/old, singles	80	25–30 + units	Studio (300–400)	Submarkets	24-hour supervision, personal care, three meals, transportation, housekeeping, recreational, social security	Rental
1–5	CCRC and life care (multi-level complex)	Old, old/old, couples, singles	75 +	200 + units, 40–60 nursing beds, 25 assisted-living units	Studio (400) 1 bedroom (600) 2 or more bedrooms (900)	Metro	Full congregate services and health services including nursing facility	Entrance fee or rental

PHASE 2. PRODUCT ANALYSIS AND ASSESSMENT

The purpose of product analysis and assessment is to conduct a thorough evaluation of each product. Traditionally, this phase has been described as market analysis or need-and-demand assessment. However, for purposes of this review, product analysis and assessment will be defined as need assessment, demand evaluation, legal and governmental review, and program definition.

The outcome of this phase is generally a market feasibility study defining the characteristics of the community, competition, need for the product or project, and a description of the potential product. The results will indicate whether the community has a sufficient population and market to justify the project and whether existing resources are adequate (evaluation of the competition). The assessment should also provide an estimate of the number of units or beds needed by the community; the size of the project; the proper mix of beds and units; and the amenities or services that would meet community desires and regulation requirements.[19]

The following pages address each step in the assessment phase, as diagrammed in Table 2-1. The steps of Phase 2 will be discussed in greater detail in Chapter 3. They are:

Product verification

Market study and need assessment

Site analysis

Demand evaluation

Program definition and project scope

Legal and governmental issues and approvals

Project description and restrictions

Product Verification. This step verifies that the products identified in Phase 1 are accurate and agreed upon by the planning team. It also forms the basis for guidance to both the market research consultant and legal adviser. Basically, the planning team states that the project will be, for example, retirement housing, or a nursing home, or a hospital.[20]

---

[19]American Association of Homes for the Aging, *Planning Housing*, 10–12.
[20]Ibid., 12.

Market Study and Need Assessment. Need analysis for senior retirement housing involves many variables, including not only the number of elderly in the market area, but also their lifestyle, housing condition, income level, and the existing competition. In this regard, the assessment of demand or need for the project depends on both quantitative and qualitative factors. In order for the consultant to make an accurate assessment of the market for the product, the elements listed under the following task areas must be researched.

Proposed Project Scope	*Demographic Analysis*
Product definition	Geographic market area
Geographic market	Population growth and trends
Project size	Elderly trends
Anticipated services	Key economic indicators
	Population forecast by market segment
Competition	
Existing products	*Need Assessment*
Compatibility of those products	Number of elderly choosing senior housing
Amenities of existing products	Income-qualified elderly
	Expected demand
Pricing structure of competition	Need forecast for product relative to existing supply

These tasks relate to congregate housing need. Similar steps would be required for each product identified because geographic market areas, population served, and need assessment methodologies vary depending on whether nursing care, hospice, housing, or outpatient services are being evaluated.[21, 22]

Site Analysis. During this step, the real estate specialist and developer will be searching for an appropriate site for the product. This process will continue through the assessment phase and may be refined

---

[21]American Association of Homes for the Aging, "Market and Economic Feasibility Studies," *Guidelines for Continuing Care Retirement Communities* (Washington, DC, 1984): 7–16.

[22]W. Donahue, M. Thompson, and D. Cowen, eds., *Congregate Housing for Older People,* (Washington, DC: International Center for Social Gerontology, Administration on Aging, 1977), DHEW Pub. No. 77-20284, 35–63.

and amended during master planning of the building. Site analysis consists of not only finding a desirable property at the right price, but also making certain that the site meets a variety of project criteria. Specific site criteria will vary from project to project; however, at a minimum, the criteria should include:

Cost (including improvements)
Location in relation to retail, residential, and commercial users
Access and transportation systems
Zoning restrictions or covenant restrictions
Neighborhood quality and type
Consumer acceptance
Size in relation to project needs
Topography and ease of development
Community support services and utility availability
Travel time and distance from primary user population
Potential for expandability
Environmental impact study requirements
    Wildlife and vegetation restrictions
    Open space requirements
    Utility impact
    Social and neighborhood compatibility
Clear title available[23]

Demand Evaluation.   In addition to the quantitative assessment of need, a project should also be concerned with whether the potential consumers desire the product. Demand evaluation is a process of surveying the expected clients of a project to determine if they see a need for the product, would desire to move in, and prefer certain services and amenities. It is also helpful to assess the attitudes of senior care givers and agency officials.

Information can be gained by personal interview, focus group sessions, mail survey, or telephone research. Regardless of approach, this step is extremely useful in assessing whether potential residents desire and would move in the project. If local clients have little interest or motivation, marketing will be very difficult.

A final result of the consumer survey is to identify preferred services,

[23]American Association of Homes for the Aging, *Planning Housing,* 16.

amenities, and design. Research in elderly attitudes toward housing indicates that opinions differ by age, income level, and location of residence. Therefore, seeking local input can save costly marketing and design errors. This process also begins developing the product image by alerting consumers to the proposed project.[24]

Program Definition and Project Scope. This step summarizes what will be provided. The statement should include the number of units and beds; the mix of units (e.g., one-bedroom versus two-bedroom, private versus semiprivate, subsidized or private pay); and the planned services and amenities (e.g., meals, social activities, transportation, health services, nursing care, rehabilitation, personal care, wellness programs, swimming pool, medication, golf, and tennis). Further, the program will define the type of function and quality level of each space.

Presenting program definition and scope of services fulfills multiple purposes. First, it will provide specific guidance to the architect and design team. Second, it will assist the financial feasibility consultant in projecting revenue and expenses. Third, it will provide a basis for the legal adviser to assess whether governmental or regulatory approvals are required or whether certain activities may be prohibited by law.

Legal and Governmental Issues and Approvals. The legal assessment provides a review of the requirements of governmental or regulatory agencies. It would include certificate of need, Medicare, Medicaid, health departments, and the Mental Health Commission. Further, the review will document necessary operational licenses or certificates, required zoning and building approvals, and mandatory environmental impact reviews.

Project Description and Restrictions. The final step in assessment is preparation of a narrative document that describes in detail the complete project and program of services, as well as the legal and regulatory restrictions or requirements for development and operation. This summary merely formalizes the results of the assessment phase and presents the findings in a format usable by architects, financial analysts, management, and marketing personnel.

[24]Worley, "Retirement Housing," 2–4.

Summary. The product analysis and assessment phase defines the project, determines if it is needed and desired by consumers, and identifies how it should be organized to meet legal and regulatory requirements. Population analyses, opinion survey, site analysis, and legal research form the basis of this phase. The results provide the framework for subsequent building design, financial feasibility, marketing, and management.

PHASE 3. PROJECT DESIGN AND PROGRAM PLANNING

The project design and planning phase translates the product, service package, and program into physical characteristics and cost. This phase is also commonly referred to as facilities planning and programming. Some of the steps in this phase are completed by the architect; others, such as functional workload and staffing analysis, by consultants; and still others, such as cost estimates, by the construction manager. The skills and capabilities of the architect and design team will influence the number of separate consultants required.

Project design and planning are characterized by specific but interrelated steps, as shown in Table 2-1. Each step is the building block for subsequent ones. Therefore, the timely completion of each step is important for the project to move forward on schedule.

Definitions. In order to make certain that all participants are speaking the same language, it is useful to define each step and the persons responsible for completion.

First, the steps in the facility planning process include:

Evaluation of physical facility (if a renovation project)
Functional assessment
Workload analysis
Staffing analysis
Preliminary equipment plan
Space plan
Master functional and space plan (building zoning)
Site plan
Preliminary cost estimate[25]

[25]Hardy, *Hospitals,* 32–33.

TABLE 2-4. Design and Planning Responsibilities

Project Design and Planning Steps	Primary Responsibility	Advisory Responsibility
Evaluation of physical plant (if applicable)	Architect	Owner
Functional assessment	Consultant or architect	Owner
Workload analysis	Consultant	Owner
Staffing analysis	Consultant	Owner
Preliminary equipment plan	Consultant	Architect
Space program	Consultant or architect	Consultant or architect
Master functional and space plan	Architect	Consultant
Site plan	Architect	All team
Preliminary cost estimate	Construction manager	Architect

Responsibilities. Table 2-4 identifies the persons who are primarily responsible for completion of each step. Where an individual has advisory responsibility, that is shown also.

Project Design and Planning Tasks. The following paragraphs describe the tasks associated with each project design and planning step.

Evaluation of Physical Facility. Because this step may not be required in all cases, a detailed discussion is not provided here. However, if an existing building is to be purchased or renovated, it will be necessary to conduct a complete evaluation of mechanical, electrical, and structural systems and to determine if spaces are adequate in size and location.[26]

Functional Assessment. This step defines all factors that affect the facility's efficient and effective operation aside from physical and architectural demands. Although no clear distinction exists between physical and functional assessments, the physical analysis usually relates to how the facility is constructed and the functional analysis to how it can be used, for example, is it "user friendly."[27, 28]

[26]Ibid., 73.
[27]Ibid., 77–79.
[28]Eric Smart, ed., *Housing for a Maturing Population* (Washington, DC: Urban Land Institute, 1983), 50–52.

The functional assessment has several basic objectives. These are to:

Achieve operational effectiveness

Ensure conformance with applicable codes, regulations, and standards

Optimize traffic flow

Optimize departmental relationships

Maintain flexibility and expandability for future needs

Segregate unlike functions and integrate like functions

Enhance circulation of visitors, staff, residents, and services

Enhance employee productivity

Maximize staff, resident, and visitor safety and comfort

A functional assessment is generally completed by reviewing current functional deficiencies in the case of an existing building, or listing a set of desired functional criteria in the case of a new building. The functional assessment for an existing building requires identification of departments and activities to be considered and interviews with key personnel. Topics to be discussed include attitudes, opinions, management, operating policies, staffing, anticipated changes in departmental operation, and existing and new equipment.

The following facts should be determined about each department:

Organizational structure	Traffic patterns
Number of full- and part-time staff	Materials movement
	Supplies and information movement
Hours of operation	Storage needs
Historical workload	Administrative requirements
Peak periods of operation	Work flow
Types of activity	Proximity needs relative to other
Special equipment	functions

It is helpful to prepare for each department or area a functional assessment narrative that describes the department, key operating issues, services provided, times of operation, and anticipated changes in operation. It should also detail key functional issues such as departmental relationships, staffing, equipment, organization of space, major work stations, and location constraints.

A functional assessment will include an analysis of building systems. It will also describe in detail how each department is organized and operates. Further, any special requirements for space, functions, activities, workflow, or traffic will be documented.[29]

When nursing care beds and housing are included in the same facility, the relationships described previously become quite complex. Further, if an existing facility is being converted from a nonhealth care to a health care use, then special codes and regulations need to be met.[30]

In the case of a new building, functional criteria must be established for each department. Based on design literature and experience in other institutions, functional criteria are operating characteristics that influence department location, size, and structure. However, no two organizations are exactly alike. Therefore, general criteria and experience must be modified to fit the needs expressed by managers and the planning team. Generally, the consultant begins with an optimal model in terms of size, location, and activity for a department. By interview, review of data, and on-site examination, the model is adapted to the needs of the individual facility.

In summary, the functional assessment attempts to answer questions such as: What activities will be in the building? How will activities be organized? How will security be maintained? How will activities be operated? How will functions be staffed? What supply systems are to be used? How will visitors, staff, and residents move within the project?

Workload Analysis. In the case of an existing facility, departmental workload analysis consists of documenting the historical volume of activity in each department and developing projections of future workload. In a new facility, projections will be made for each area. Each department or functional area has unique measures of workload. Generally, however, departmental workload is a function of residents, visitors, and the services program.

Workload projection is a key aspect of space determination since workload dictates staffing, equipment, and space needs. As a result, accurate workload projections are extremely important.[31]

[29]Ibid., 80–82.

[30]Michael Duffy and Victor Willson, "The Role of Design Factors of the Residential Environment in the Physical and Mental Health of the Elderly," *Journal of Housing for the Elderly* Vol. 2, No. 3 (Fall 1984): 43.

[31]Hardy, *Hospitals,* 88–89.

Staffing Analysis. The total number and type of personnel for each department or area should be determined. The identification of activities, work situations, and spaces is a function of staffing. As noted previously, workload influences staffing; and staffing influences activity, equipment, and space needs.

In order to predict the future staffing for each department, it is helpful to undertake the following procedures (as appropriate):

1. Assess existing staffing by department based on departmental interviews.
2. Calculate current staffing ratios compared to volume of workload for each department (for example, full-time equivalent staff per occupied unit, or work-hours per meals served).
3. Verify by comparison to industry standard and experience the appropriateness of current staffing levels and ratios.
4. Discuss and confirm staffing ratios and levels with members of the planning team.
5. Based on projected workload, calculate future staffing requirements by department.
6. Assess workstation and office requirements based on projected workload, management philosophy, and organizational structure.

The outcome of this process is documentation of full-time equivalent employees by type and number for each department, as well as identification and description of workstations and spaces needed by staff.

Preliminary Equipment Plan. It is important to identify basic equipment needs early in the planning process. The final product of the planning process, the building, is really a multifaceted piece of equipment. Its ability to do an efficient job and be adaptable to the ever changing needs of the users will be the long-term indication of the success or failure of the planning process.

In preliminary equipment planning, major pieces of necessary hardware will be identified. At times, this hardware dictates the characteristics of the space necessary to enclose it. Hard space areas that are equipment-intensive tend to be more expensive to build and more difficult to relocate. Examples of such areas in a health care setting are exercise rooms and recreational equipment, security system monitors, dietary facilities, building service areas, and emergency systems (such as generators).

Identification and examination of equipment needs early in the planning process permits establishing hard space requirements. Specific planning needs of these areas include the ability to expand in place, horizontal and vertical transportation links, service accessibility, and proximity relationships with other areas.

By first determining the requisites of equipment-intensive areas, the essentials for people-intensive areas (soft spaces) will follow. Soft space, being more adaptable, will tend to spin off the needs of the hard equipment spaces.

The measures necessary to complete preliminary equipment planning include the following:

Identify all departments and functions.

Based on interview process during functional assessment phase, develop a list of major pieces of equipment to be included in each functional area.

Compare equipment lists with industry standard for the function and area.

Review equipment lists with key administration or planning team members to verify accuracy of list.

Assess key functional features of each major piece of hardware in terms of users, traffic patterns, affinity to other activities, location needs, and size.

Document all major pieces of equipment and location by department.[32]

Space Plan. A space plan or program is a complete listing of each work area and room in the proposed facility and the number of square feet assigned to each room. It should also include a narrative description of the room's function, equipment, and furniture. Generally, the planning team can relate more easily to rooms, spaces, and workstations than to large blocks of square feet. Ultimately, the staff and managers' question becomes, where is the office, or storage room, or lounge? It is generally more efficient to move directly to this level of consideration.

The basis for assigning size (square feet) to each workstation is a combination of art, science, and experience. State, federal, local, and voluntary regulations govern much space allocation in health care facilities. These include minimum state licensing standards, and min-

[32]Ibid., 164–166.

imum requirements of construction and equipment for hospital and facilities, as well as safety regulations. In addition, operational needs imposed by accreditation, management approach, budgets, and medical and nursing practice influence the space determination process. However, for residential projects, little guidance exists in terms of regulatory standards or requirements.

In order to be most objective in this process of space determination, the consultant or architect should base all calculations on workload volume, staffing (type and number), equipment location and type, federal, state, and local standards, industry standards, and experience.

In developing a space program, the consulting team should provide a room-by-room listing of all areas to be included in the project. The specific size of each room (based on operational, equipment, and staff requirements previously examined) will be listed along with the number of each room type. These sizes represent the total net usable space (NSF) within each given room. To project departmental gross square feet (DGSF) and total building size (BGSF), various multiplier factors are used. These factors, developed over years of experience by architects and operators, identify the space required for other areas such as corridors, stairs, wall thickness, and mechanical spaces.

The formal space plan provides input to building design as follows:

1. It offers direction for the project architect to ensure all necessary spaces are included.
2. A listing of all available space can be used by the project planners to check that space requirements will be met.
3. When the total amount of net square footage and the departmental and building gross area have been calculated, preliminary construction cost estimating can be refined.
4. The space program can be used by the planning team to limit or expand the scope of the project to meet operational or budgetary requirements.

A complete and carefully prepared detailed space plan allows the planning team to verify many important aspects of the project without the costly trial and error process often encountered during the project design process.[33]

[33]Hardy, *Hospitals,* 112–115.

Master Functional and Space Plan. This step is a synthesis of data and ideas analyzed in the earlier planning steps. It will provide both narrative and graphic descriptions of the requirements of the planned facility. Among the issues to be addressed are:

Interdepartmental and intradepartmental relationships
Traffic flow (vehicles and pedestrians)
Vertical and horizontal circulation patterns
Operational concepts
Equipment requirements
Departmental space needs
Methods of obtaining flexibility and expandability, including phasing of the project
Schedules
Code evaluations

The master plan also will produce a narrative description and graphic representation for each department or function, including, besides the items in the preceding paragraph, the following:

Departmental activities	Staffing pattern
Services	Equipment
Key functional issues	Space required
Projected workload	

In addition, the master plan will produce a set of block drawings of the new facility.[34]

Site Plan. The site plan locates the buildings on the land in order to achieve technical, functional, and aesthetic planning criteria. It will be responsive to site restrictions, such as topography, street patterns, and zoning. Further, the plan will provide for efficient circulation of staff, visitors, and residents. Relationships among other site users, the neighborhood, and the community are addressed in site planning.

Detailed site planning, at a later stage, considers factors such as landscaping and site grading. However, it is important in this design

---

[34]Ibid., 92–93.

phase to have a clear and complete picture of building locations and sitework costs in order to produce a realistic cost estimate.

At this stage of analysis, site planning is especially concerned with utility availability and location. Cost of providing utilities, electricity, water, and sewer services may be prohibitive for some sites.[35, 36]

Preliminary Cost Estimate. The construction management specialist, who is either an outside consultant or a member of the architect and design team, will prepare preliminary cost estimates. Clearly, the accuracy of the cost estimate improves as the design becomes more detailed and specific. Most owners, however, are unwilling to wait until construction documents and contractor bidding have been completed to find out the construction cost. More importantly, waiting that long may force a redesign of the entire project if costs significantly exceed expectations. For these reasons, the construction manager is involved throughout the design process.

Cost estimates provide key data for subsequent financial analyses. Therefore, they should be as complete and accurate as possible. Required items are:

Land acquisition costs

Site improvement costs (including utilities)

Building construction costs

Major equipment costs

Fixtures, furnishings, and minor equipment

Heating and air conditioning systems

Architect and engineer fees

Other consultant fees, permits, and licenses

Insurance

Contingency fund

Construction draw schedule

Developer fees

Landscaping

Other development costs such as financing costs, other consultants' costs, and fees for financing will be added to this estimate by members of the planning team.[37]

[35]Ibid., 129–133.
[36]American Association of Homes for the Aging, *Planning Housing*, 16.
[37]Hardy, *Hospitals*, 33.

Summary. Project design and planning translates the product, program, and service package into physical characteristics and cost. The steps required include developing a functional plan, analyzing staffing and workload, producing a space plan, equipment plan, and master facility plan, arranging the building(s) on the site, and estimating the development cost. This phase requires input from the entire planning team, because design decisions determine cost and ultimately project feasibility.

PHASE 4. FINANCIAL FEASIBILITY

Determining the financial feasibility of a project is perhaps the most important decision faced by the planning team. In addition to answering the basic question of whether or not to proceed, the feasibility study may also indicate that the project needs modification in size or scope. Financial feasibility analysis answers the key question: Does the project produce the return on investment required by the owner?

Financial feasibility includes preparation of development and operating budgets for the proposed facility for a five-year period, accompanied by a statement of assumptions on which the financial statements are based.[38]

The budgets will serve as a guide for deciding the number of units to be built as well as the necessary rental fees or sales price for each unit.

The financial projections should include:

Development and operating cost projections

Development cash flow analysis

Development draw schedule

Identification of development costs by specific categories, such as land, building, equipment, professional fees, marketing budget, financing costs, contingency, legal, and accounting services

Operating revenues, monthly and cumulative, with five-year projections

Quarterly fill-up or sales schedule

Quarterly and annual operating expenses by department with five-year projections

Debt service calculation

[38]American Association of Homes for the Aging, *Planning Housing,* 17.

Cash flow projections for five years
Investment analysis and recommendation

In order to develop or analyze the financial model, the following
information is needed:

Physical Asset Costs	*Financing Costs*
Land	Total development cost
Site preparation	Financing mechanism
Building construction	Origination fees and points
Equipment (fixed and movable)	Interest and term of loan
Furniture and fixtures	

Professional Service Cost	*Type of Services and Units*
Architects	Unit mix and size
Engineers	Square footage (rentable)
Marketing	Square footage (common area)
Consultants	
Legal and accounting	Square footage (services)
Developer or manager fees	Meal service plan
	Housekeeping service plan
	Social service plan
	Shared services
	Nursing care plan

Chapter 4 provides a detailed analysis of financial feasibility.

PHASE 5. DEVELOPMENT AND CONSTRUCTION

The planning team should by now have a clear understanding of the
product being planned, how it functions, where it will be located, and
how much it will cost. The decision has been made to move forward,
and the architect has taken over the leadership role in this process.
This phase consists of a variety of design, technical, and construction
functions.[39] They include:

Schematic design	Design development
Outline specifications	Construction documents
Final equipment plan	Bidding
Revised cost estimates	Construction

[39]Hardy, *Hospitals,* 33–36, 154, 158–59, 170–74.

Schematic Design.   The single-line drawings of the proposed facility produced in this step identify each room and department, circulation and community spaces, and mechanical spaces. The design shows the location of all rooms and departments by level or floor and is based on the functional and space plans previously described.[40]

Outline Specifications.   This document defines the type and quality of construction and usually includes requirements and standards for such items as construction materials, structural and mechanical systems, interior finishes, roof, driveways, and hardware.[41]

Design Development.   The purpose of this step is to produce detailed drawings that expand upon the schematic design phase and define exact measurements for such items as doors, mechanical and structural spaces, wall, floor, and ceiling thicknesses, and equipment locations. These detailed drawings of each room and space provide data for revised cost estimates.[42]

Construction Documents.   These documents translate the entire planning process into sets of drawings and instructions that will guide the contractor in bidding and construction. Perhaps a major cause of cost overruns and disagreements during construction relates to these drawings and specifications. The greater the detail and accuracy of these materials, the less confusion and disagreement will occur. The construction documents show details of the building, equipment, finishes, size of each element, along with a detailed narrative of the standards to be followed for materials, equipment, and fixtures.[43]

Bidding.   If a bid process is used, the construction documents and specifications form the basis for contractors' bids. Poor quality documents and specifications lead to inaccurate and unreasonable bids. Therefore, the bidding step should be carefully coordinated with the preceding step. Responsibility for dealing with the contractors is generally best left to the architect. This individual, representing the owner, is better qualified to respond to technical questions of contractors regarding design and construction detail.[44]

[40]Ibid., 154.
[41]Ibid., 158.
[42]Ibid., 159.
[43]Ibid., 170–171.
[44]Ibid., 187–193.

Construction. Generally supervised by the architect or independent construction manager, this step ensures that the construction contract and the specifications are followed and that quality and cost are acceptable.

PHASE 6. MARKETING AND PROMOTION

The marketing of a senior adult community involves a wide range of activities targeted to persons age 65 and older as well as to their children. Marketing begins with a market survey and analysis prior to starting a project and continues during development. Once the project is operational, marketing is used to attract new residents. It is an ongoing process.

Marketing Coordination. A marketing coordinator should take responsibility for developing and conducting a comprehensive marketing plan as outlined in the following paragraphs. Marketing coordination consists of both plan development and implementation.

Plan Development. Preparation of a marketing and leasing plan, marketing budget, brochures and promotional materials, and selection of advertising and public relations professionals are included in plan development. The marketing plan consists of three phases: preconstruction, preoperational marketing, and operational marketing.

Implementation. Marketing plan implementation consists of setting up leasing or sales offices and models, hiring and training the leasing or sales staff, supervision and evaluation of leasing or sales functions, conducting personal sales presentations to civic and community groups, and implementation of cooperative agreements with local health care providers and businesses. Depending on the agreement, the last item may be a management responsibility during preoperations.

Marketing coordination is required during the period prior to construction through lease up. The staff consists of a marketing director (who may also serve as on-site project manager or resident services coordinator when the project opens) and leasing and sales personnel. In many cases, marketing is subcontracted out to a group specializing in senior communities until the facility is fully leased.

In addition, the project will have the following marketing expenses:

Advertising
Brochure and collateral materials

Leasing office staff, equipment, and operational expenses

Newsletter publication

Public relations

Special event presentations

Legal expenses in development of sales or lease contracts

These costs are paid from the project marketing budget, which should be a separate line item in the project pro forma. When the project is full, marketing becomes an expense item of the operations budget. Marketing functions consist of:

Developing the marketing plan and budget

Coordinating and training staff

Conducting presentations to community groups

Initiating agreements with local health care agencies and businesses

Identifying and selecting public relations and advertising firms

Reviewing and approving brochure and collateral materials

Conducting focus groups and opinion polls

Securing sales or leases on the project

PHASE 7. MANAGEMENT AND OPERATIONS PHASE

Although management is not usually thought of as part of the planning process, management personnel are key players. In fact, managers should be involved in development and preconstruction planning, pre-opening, and operations phases.

In the development and preconstruction phase, managers can assist in functional planning, financial projections, and project design.

The preoperational management phase will begin approximately six to eight months prior to the scheduled opening with development of a management plan and hiring of an on-site manager and resident services director. If health care is included, a nursing director should be hired before or at the same time as the director of resident services. To make the facility ready for opening, these individuals will:

Prepare management plan

Prepare social and activities plan

Prepare health care policies

Prepare or review maintenance plan

Prepare or review food service plan
Establish policies and procedures
Set up departments and activities
Begin staff recruitment and training
Establish and install accounting system
Identify and order initial inventory
Establish a project operating budget
Develop business systems
Establish bank accounts and utility accounts
Coordinate delivery of equipment and furnishings
Secure vendor contracts

Initial Management. This phase begins when the first tenant moves in and lasts until break-even occupancy is achieved. Primary tasks relate to the development and refinement of operating policies, systems, and procedures.

In this phase, the following specific tasks are conducted:

Continue recruitment and training of project staff
Implement management policies
Test and modify food service menus and serving systems
Verify inventory levels for all supplies
Implement and monitor financial and statistical systems
Refine budgets
Implement and revise social activities plan
Clarify communication channels with owner or sponsor and other members of management team
Review contracts for services

Ongoing Management. When break-even occupancy occurs, ongoing responsibilities will include day-to-day management. The continuing process will provide training, problem solving, financial analysis, and planning services. If management companies are used, both corporate and on-site staff will be involved.

If a separate management company is engaged, the following tasks should be performed by the corporate and on-site staff. With in-house management, many of these tasks are combined.

Corporate Staff

Provide consultation and support for all on-site staff

Provide quarterly training to on-site staff

Develop and monitor accounting systems

Develop and review operating policies

Provide statistical analysis of tenants—age, sex, income level, medical needs, hospitalizations, and nursing home use, in order to develop health care, management, and pricing policies.

Advise dietary staff regarding nutritional requirements of residents

Advise staff on health needs of and programs for tenants

Review productivity and adequacy of staff

Analyze and review expenses; prepare regular summary reports

Provide management back-up to on-site staff

Organize and recommend a preventive maintenance program for equipment

Provide planning, budget preparation, and personnel management assistance to on-site staff

Assist in preparation of annual operating, personnel, and capital budgets in conjunction with onsite staff

Advise on maintenance and repair contracts

Advise on social services programs

Advise on tenant opinion polls

Conduct performance evaluation

Analyze and prepare budget variance reports by responsibility center

Monitor state, regional, and national activities influencing project operation and viability

Recommend new programs and services based on planning and needs assessment in order to remain competitive

Evaluate pricing structure at least annually

Supervise and evaluate leasing activities

Coordinate ongoing marketing

On-Site Management.   The on-site project manager will have specific responsibilities in the areas of finance and budgeting, personnel, tenant relations, physical asset management, administration, and public relations.

Financial and budgeting responsibilities include collecting rents, making deposits, and maintaining accounting records; making required disbursements; working within a prescribed budget; and assisting in the preparation of annual budgets.

Personnel matters involve the recruiting, selection, promotion, and evaluation of all personnel. The on-site manager must also carry out personnel policies and provide leadership to the staff.

In the area of tenant relations, the manager must develop the philosophy and policies for tenant relations, meet with tenants regularly, supervise the resident services program coordinator, evaluate tenant attitudes, establish and use a tenant grievance procedure, and establish and carry out project rules and regulations.

Physical asset management is performed in cooperation with corporate staff and the designated representative of the owner. Together they must:

Solicit, analyze, and negotiate bids and contracts

Ensure proper maintenance of buildings and grounds

Maintain adequate insurance coverage

Analyze and evaluate utility costs

Conduct regular facility inspections

Develop and conduct a tenant repair request program in coordination with maintenance contract

Ensure the preventive maintenance program is in place and operating

Maintain inventory of plant assets

Administrative duties of the project manager are to:

Develop and maintain all files relating to the project, staff, and tenants

Develop and carry out policies and procedures to ensure smooth project operation

Prepare necessary daily, weekly, monthly, quarterly, and annual reports on turnover, utilization, workload, and staffing

Establish and maintain an emergency call and service program

Establish grievance system

Attend meetings relating to the project

Meet with community groups to ensure good public relations

Cooperate with the designated owner representative to ensure coordination of services

The project manager also assumes responsibility for some aspects of public relations. The manager must develop and carry out the leasing program after the marketing team responsibilities have ended. This entails promoting the project within the potential client community and developing programs and events to publicize the project.

Summary. Management is an ongoing process that begins during development prior to construction and continues throughout the life of the project. Management specialists play an important role in both design and operation. As a result, they should be members of the initial planning team.

CHAPTER SUMMARY

Seven major phases in project development have been identified as the planning process. Each phase is important to the success of the project and provides a building block for subsequent steps. These phases are:

1. Strategic thinking—positioning and organizing
2. Product analysis and assessment
3. Project design and program planning
4. Financial feasibility
5. Development and construction
6. Marketing and promotion
7. Management and operations

The following chapters describe these phases and discuss the process necessary for successful project development.

CHAPTER 3

PRODUCT ANALYSIS AND ASSESSMENT

RICCI IVERS CASSERLY

As described in Chapter 2, product analysis and assessment is Phase 2 in the planning process. The primary purpose of product analysis and assessment is to thoroughly evaluate the product or products that have been identified for development. Traditionally, this phase has been defined as market analysis or market feasibility, which encompasses need assessment and demand evaluation of a defined product. For purposes of this chapter, product analysis and assessment is defined as including market analysis, site analysis, and program definition.

The tasks included in this phase—product definition, market analysis, site analysis, and program definition and scope—are addressed in the following pages. The approaches used as examples for accomplishing the tasks serve mainly as guidelines or suggestions for the developer or sponsor. They should not be considered "How to do it" rules or processes. Instead they should be used as a basis or starting point from which to ask questions or to seek clarification from an individual who specializes as a consultant in the area of planning senior housing.

PRODUCT DEFINITION

The initial task in product analysis and assessment is to verify that the product or products identified in Phase 1 are accurate and agreed upon by the planning team. In determining the housing product, it is crucial for the project developer or sponsor and planning team to understand the highly segmented elderly market. Products will vary with regard to need for care and services, associated level of independence, and the type of living arrangement that will typically satisfy elderly needs and desires.

Older Americans are not a homogeneous group. Each individual ages at a unique pace and differs with respect to physical, socioeconomic, and psychological abilities, as well as needs for care and services. In order to accommodate these differences, individuals may require housing alternatives or a continuum of living arrangements.

An active, independent individual who has no physical limitations would most likely desire or demand the lifestyle of an independent environment that emphasizes recreational and leisurely living. In contrast, an individual who is frail and in poor health will likely have difficulty in performing activities of daily living and will need a housing arrangement that offers services and assistance.

It is useful, therefore, to think of housing arrangements in relationship to the different elderly market segments, typically based on needs for care and services and demand for a special lifestyle. Housing options are available to the elderly via a continuum ranging from fully independent living in traditional housing to fully dependent living in a nursing home (see Chapter 1).

Although it is useful to identify market segments in association with living arrangements and service packages, the continuum should not be used too rigidly. For example, the point at which an independent person needs or demands a congregate living environment is not clear. It appears that each individual bases that decision on his or her personal life situation and motivation. As a result, persons capable of independent living may choose congregate living for convenience or to avoid the burden of home management.

The number of housing alternatives available for the elderly has increased over the years. This is evidenced by a publication of the American Association of Retired Persons.[1] This book itemizes the following housing choices for the consumer: homes and apartments, mobile homes, condominiums, cooperatives, boarding homes, personal and residential care homes, congregate housing, homes for the aged, life care or continuing care facilities, retirement communities, home equity

---

[1] American Association of Retired Persons, *Housing Options for Older Americans* (Washington, D.C.: American Association of Retired Persons, 1984).

conversion, accessory apartments, echo housing, shared housing, and subsidized housing.

It is important then that the developers and sponsors understand which market segment of the elderly they want to serve and how best to accomplish this service. In doing so, a housing product can be defined according to level of living arrangement including:

1. Type of housing option, such as apartments, townhomes, cottages, single family homes
2. Service and amenity package
3. Age or functioning level of resident most likely to utilize services
4. Income level resident probably needs to afford defined product
5. Fee structure

MARKET ANALYSIS

Once the proposed product has been defined, the developer or sponsor knows the target market. The next step in product analysis and assessment is performing a market analysis for the defined product to:

1. Determine whether a need exists for the proposed product
2. Determine market demand for the defined product
3. Assist the developer in identifying the needs for other types of services not offered in the community
4. Refine the proposed product according to defined programs and project scope, including services and amenities and the number of units to be recommended, thereby establishing assumptions on which economic feasibility can be performed
5. Document market viability for lender approval
6. Use as a resource to justify any changes in zoning restrictions
7. Use in a prospectus for soliciting additional investors

The following pages describe the basic components of market analysis and how they relate to various living arrangements described in Chapter 1.

Basic Components of Market Analysis.   Market analysis consists of two basic components—quantitative analysis and qualitative analysis. The result of secondary research, quantitative analysis serves to determine product need and consists of defining the geographic market area, performing demographic analysis and competitor analysis, assessing need, estimating demand, and determining the number of units or beds needed.

Qualitative analysis, the result of primary research, serves to determine product demand by eliciting attitudes and preferences toward the proposed products using consumer surveys. Three types of primary research methods will be described: focus group and personal interview, telephone survey, and mail survey.

Quantitative Analysis

Geographic Market Area.   The first step in quantitative analysis is to define the total market area for the proposed project, that is, the geographic area from which the project developers or sponsors expect to attract their target market. The primary market area is that area from which a majority of the project residents are expected to originate (ranging from 80 to 90 percent), the secondary area is the remainder (10 to 20 percent).

Definition of the appropriate market area is crucial to meaningful market analysis. Narrowly defining an area may understate need. Conversely, creating too broad an area may overstate need.

When defining a meaningful market area, several factors must be considered. For example, physical or geographic barriers with respect to distance and travel times may distract the resident from relocating to an area. Also, attitudinal, social, cultural, or even religious barriers may exist causing individuals to not relocate. Elderly mobility trends with regard to immigration and outmigration patterns within an area must also be considered, as well as accessibility to health care, retail, and other amenities in the area.

In general, residents of service-oriented projects, such as congregate care, continuing care retirement communities, and personal care facilities will not travel extended distances from a current residence to relocate. In defining the geographic market area for nursing homes, particular attention must be paid to patient origin patterns of nursing homes in the area.

Definition of market area for independent living communities that cater to the young, active elderly can be difficult. Market areas tend to extend to a large region encompassed by intrastate and interstate boundaries.

Rather than simply relying on a map it is important to visit the community and get a feel for a realistic market area by interviewing community members.

In sum, market feasibility is only as good as the assumptions used to qualify the market area. It is recommended that final market area definition be agreed upon by both the project developer or sponsor and the project consultant.

Demographic Analysis. Demographic analysis is essentially performed to accomplish three broad goals:

1. To enable the developing or sponsoring organization to understand the historical and expected population, households, and economic trends of the total population in the geographically defined market area.
2. To enable the developing or sponsoring organization to understand the historical and expected population, households, and economic trends of the elderly population in general, and those of the target market (age- and income-qualified elderly)
3. To utilize this information in determining potential need and demand for the project

The identification of historical and expected trends in market area population and households in general, and those in the elderly population and households in particular, are of primary importance to any planning study for senior housing. Population characteristics such as age-specific growth rates will help determine the expected need for senior services. For example, if the area is expected to have a faster growth in the elderly population and households, the need for senior housing may increase in proportion to the expected growth in that age category.

An understanding of the economic characteristics of the elderly household population of the market area is also important in the determination of the demand for elderly housing, especially for facilities that are not government subsidized. Elderly population with a moderate to high income is a prerequisite for generating effective demand for private pay or nonsubsidized senior citizen housing. Any serious planning study for senior housing must look into the existing and projected economic characteristics of the elderly population in the market area of a proposed facility. In general, private pay senior housing serves the elderly population who have incomes exceeding $15,000 to $20,000 annually.

Before analyzing population and household trends, it is necessary to gather the most recent census data. Population estimates of the year under study and projections will be based on this census data. Depending on product definitions, it may be necessary to segment the elderly market by age. It is also useful to compare geographic market data to larger geographic areas such as county, state, and nation. In this way, it can be determined if the geographic market area is unusual or different from expected trends.

Economic Characteristics of the General Population.   There are several economic indicators that describe the economic strength of a geographic market area. At a minimum, demographic analysis should include median household income as evidence of economic status. Median household income is especially useful when it is used in comparison to other geographic levels or to determine, for example, whether or not an area is expected to maintain higher median incomes than the state or nation. Estimates of median household income are based on the most recent census. Private demographic firms provide estimates for the current year as well as projections. Further estimates may be obtained from local planning and economic development agencies or university-based planning centers.

Unemployment rates and building activity are additional useful statistics in determining economic strength of the market area. Local and state employment commissions and the U.S. Bureau of Labor Statistics can supply unemployment rates. Comparison of geographic market areas to larger geographic areas will demonstrate whether or not there is a positive economy and employment base.

Another measure of economic growth in the market area is commercial and residential building activity. A gauge for this activity is the number of new building permits issued for the area over a certain period; five years, for example. Useful information, ordinarily available from city building departments or real estate groups, includes the number of permits issued for commercial building, multifamily housing, and single family housing.

Population and Household Projections.   Population and household projections are available from a number of sources, based on information provided every 10 years by the U.S. Department of Commerce, Bureau of the Census. Governmental entities and private planning agencies predict population changes by a variety of methods. However, there is no certain and absolutely accurate methodology for predicting future population. The best approach is a reasonable estimate based on judgment, knowledge, sound reasoning, appropriate methodologies, interpretation, and selection of trends.

Agencies that produce projections perform updates each year. State and local planning bodies seem to be the best source of detailed population projections for larger geographic areas such as an entire city, county, or groups of counties. Private firms will provide population and household estimates for the current year plus a projection for the five-year period beyond the estimate. Private firms are often helpful because they are able to provide information for small geographic areas, such as groups of zip codes or census tracts that have been identified for the market area. It is important to obtain population and household projections from more than one source. The use of several data sources will enable the developer or sponsor to detect any differences in projections.

There are two sets of population and household projections relevant to demographic analysis: total population and households; and total elderly population and households, with an emphasis on the age segment specific to the project. Projections indicate if the population and households are expected to increase or decrease. Calculations of annual growth rates for a market area will determine just how much the population is increasing or decreasing. Annual growth rates should be calculated for those years that include the most recent census and the current year estimate. Growth rates should also be calculated for the years that include the current year and a five-year projection. Market area population and household projections and growth rates should be compared to larger geographic areas to detect any growth trends.

It is important to analyze at least two sets of data for the elderly population and households—one set for the total elderly population and households and one set for the target market with respective growth rates. In this way, comparisons can be made, and trends are identified. If possible, locate data for the elderly population and households that are segmented into not more than 10-year intervals.

Further comparisons of the projected elderly population and households of a market area may reveal some significant trends. These include comparisons of the total elderly population and households, and target market population and households (including elderly age segments), as percentages of the total population and households; and the total age-segmented elderly population and households (including the target market), as percentages of the total elderly population and households.

Income of the Elderly. The income level of elderly households is the most important determinant of their ability to demand a particular form of nonsubsidized or private-pay service housing. Each type of housing involves different payment mechanisms and pricing approaches.

Because different kinds of senior housing provide different levels of care and services, each developer or sponsor must set fees accordingly. The elderly generally should not spend more than 60 to 70 percent of their monthly income on a full-service adult congregate living facility. Only the elderly with incomes of approximately $35,000 per year or more could afford a rental of $2,000 per month.

Table 3-1 shows the income levels that would generally be required to support monthly rental or service fees for congregate services such as shelter, meals, transportation, and activities.

It is useful to determine what income level is required in order to screen qualified elderly for a proposed project. Estimates of the percentage of monthly household income that should be applied to rent, mortgage payments, or monthly fees can be used to do this. Finally, it is possible to identify the number of income-qualified elderly households living in the defined market area.

The percentage of monthly income that the elderly should be expected to spend on various housing arrangements is illustrated in Table 3-2.

Once the income levels have been identified for various types of housing, it is necessary to identify the age and income-qualified elderly in the market area that can afford the proposed housing. It is very useful to analyze this data with respect to various elderly age segments. For example, if it is discovered that the income levels of the targeted age segment would not support a private-pay moderate to upscale housing community, then the number of services and amenities may need to be altered to reduce monthly fees. This would allow the developer to adjust fees according to what the market can afford to pay.

TABLE 3-1. Yearly Household Income Required to Support Minimum and Maximum Monthly Rental For Congregate Housing

Annual Income	Minimum Affordable Monthly Rent— 60 Percent of Income	Maximum Affordable Monthly Rent— 70 Percent of Income
$10,000	$ 500	$ 583
15,000	750	875
20,000	1,000	1,166
25,000	1,250	1,458
30,000	1,500	1,750
35,000	1,750	2,042
40,000	2,000	2,333

TABLE 3-2. Percentage of Income Allowed for Different Housing Types

Housing Arrangement	Percentage of Monthly Income Allocated to Housing
Independent housing	
Rental (without services)	25–30
Purchase (without services)	30
Congregate housing	60–70
Supervised living or personal care	60–80
Nursing home (private pay)	80–90

Table 3-3 presents an analysis for a proposed congregate housing project in a sample market area. Data is presented for current year estimates and projections for five years beyond the current year estimate. (As with population projections, estimates for the current year and a five-year projection are sufficient.)

In the sample analysis, three different income level categories have been identified. By presenting the three income levels, it can be seen that although a large percentage of the target market (age 75 and over) earns or is expected to earn under $15,000, a considerable proportion of the elderly are currently earning or are expected to earn between $15,000 and $25,000. Maximum affordable monthly rents, using income-qualifying guidelines for these income levels, would range from $875 to $1,458 if 70 percent of monthly income were spent on housing.

For a small geographic area, private firms are best equipped to provide updates of age by income for the current year and projections for the five-year period beyond the current year estimate. With larger

TABLE 3-3. Income Distribution for Persons 65 and Over in the Market Area

Age	Year	Percent Earning Less Than $15,000 Per Year	Percent Earning More Than $15,000 Per Year	Percent Earning More Than $25,000 Per Year
65 and over	1980	67.4	32.6	13.2
75 and over	1980	76.5	23.5	8.3
65 and over	1988	46.9	53.1	28.1
75 and over	1988	58.7	41.3	18.9
65 and over	1993	38.8	61.2	38.0
75 and over	1993	49.6	50.4	27.3

areas of study, such as the county level, age by income data can be obtained using income levels from the most recent census as well as private firms. Depending on the census year, census information will be out of date for study purposes. One way to obtain a more recent income distribution is to adjust the census income levels for inflation and other economic changes that have occurred in the area under study.

Housing Characteristics.   Such housing characteristics as home-ownership status, housing values, and the approximate age of housing in a market area may serve as indicators of the type of housing that may be demanded. This information can be gathered from census reports. It may be possible to acquire current information from local realty associations, chambers of commerce, and planning centers in universities.

Housing values and the status of the real estate market can be contributing factors in the success of any retirement community. In depressed housing markets, prospective residents' delays in selling their houses can discourage them from moving into the retirement community. A depressed housing market can also reduce the amount of appreciated value the prospective resident will realize upon the sale of a home. When there is an opportunity to sell a home, however, the additional income could provide a prospective resident with enough income to qualify for housing.

Housing values are an important consideration in the determination of the location of a project, as well as an indication of whether the local elderly residents will be able to afford retirement housing prices. If, for example, the average housing value in a community is $50,000, but the developer wishes to command an entrance fee of $90,000, success in marketing the project might be difficult to achieve. Prospective residents would not find upscale rental housing particularly attractive in a low-income area.

A review of the years in which elderly homeowners moved into their homes may impact the need and demand for housing in a community. If, for example, a large number of elderly homeowners moved into their homes before 1950, this means that the homes are over 35 years old and may need increasing repairs and maintenance. Such endeavors can prove costly and stressful to any individual over time and might very well prove to be an impetus for moving into a facility.

Living Arrangements.   An analysis of elderly living arrangements may reveal other characteristics that impact need and demand for alternative living arrangements. Recent census information can be used as a base from which to determine this information. The percentage of elderly who are living alone is especially important to determine, for this group is likely vulnerable to social isolation and physical impairments. As a result, a large percentage of those age 65 and older, especially the older age groups, who live alone may be candidates for congregate living and personal care.

Additional Demographic Elements.   A good demographic analysis should contain, at a minimum, a discussion of the above characteristics for a defined geographic market. However, several other elements and considerations could very well enhance a market area analysis.

Especially in larger communities, some agencies collect information regarding mobility and migration patterns of various age groups. These statistics are particularly useful because they could indicate a source of potential residents if a large number of elderly have been immigrating over a period of time.

Children can have a major impact on the elderly housing market. It is generally well known that children of the elderly (especially the older, more frail, dependent individuals) play a key role in the elderly housing choice. An elderly individual who appears to be disqualified for housing may be qualified if income support by children and the proceeds from the sale of a home were added to the income base.

Elderly expenditure patterns should also be considered in the market analysis. The Bureau of Labor Statistics reports elderly expenditure patterns for larger geographic areas in the United States. Among items included in this report are food, housing, utilities and telephone, transportation, health care, and entertainment. All or some of these items are included in the monthly fees of a congregate, personal care, or CCRC facility.

Sources of Data.   Demographic analysis as one of the quantitative elements of market analysis is produced using secondary data sources such as the U.S. Bureau of the Census and private firms. Primary data produces the qualitative component of market analysis. This data is collected using such market research techniques as telephone, mail, or focus group surveys.

Competitor Analysis.   The broad goal of the demographic analysis is to determine the number of age- and income-qualified seniors who reside within the target market area. These individuals represent the prospective residents whom the developer needs to attract for the proposed project. The results of a demographic analysis, however, are only meaningful when used in conjunction with a competitor analysis.

Overall, the competitor analysis will determine what percent of the income-qualified residents of the target market are currently being served by existing facilities and could be served by any proposed facilities. The analysis should also provide a narrative summarizing the extent to which community-based support services are available. This analysis will enable the developer to estimate the degree to which the services, an *indirect* form of competition, may affect demand for housing.

The competitor analysis should answer the following questions:

1. Do any facilities in the target market currently offer housing to the elderly?
2. Does housing exist that caters exclusively to the elderly?
3. How do the facilities that cater exclusively to the elderly differ from one another? What types of housing products exist? What are the fee structures? How large is each facility? What types of units and numbers are available? How long has each facility been in operation and what is the current occupancy? What are some of the resident characteristics? From how far are they moving? Are there any age restrictions for admission to the facility? Are there waiting lists? What services and amenities, if any, are offered by the facility, and are these bundled (included in a monthly service fee or rent) or unbundled (purchased separately or à la carte)? Where are the facilities located?
4. Are the facilities catering exclusively to the elderly truly competitors of the proposed project? That is, do the facilities have similar attributes? Do they seek to serve the same age and income-qualified market and needs with regard to level of independence?
5. Are any projects currently under construction, and will they be competitor projects?
6. Are there any projects in the market feasibility stage?
7. To what extent are community-based services available?

A thoroughly investigated competitor analysis for retirement housing will answer these questions. If there is substantial competition in an area, it can be time-consuming. Not all of the information is easily obtained and in many cases requires a lot of creative research. The level of research effort must be taken into consideration in the market feasibility analysis budget. If there are limited research dollars, an analysis should answer most questions pertaining to existing facilities. Any information about projects under construction, specifically total units and target market, is useful.

Checklists 3-1 and 3-2 itemize possible services and amenities for a housing project and can be useful in competitor analysis of various facilities.

Table 3-4 (pages 112–113) demonstrates a sample competitor analysis of existing private pay senior housing. Identification of proposed competitors should be included in the analysis. The analysis presented here assumes that research has not uncovered any proposed housing.

The proposed project, for this example, is strictly a full-service adult congregate living facility. Proposed monthly rental rates range from $900 to $1500. Only three of the seven private-pay facilities (facilities A, E, and G, totalling 451 units) can be considered true competitors. Three facilities totalling 393 units (facilities B, C, and F) are comparable competitors by virtue of the services offered, although one (facility B) caters to a lower income population. Disregarding this facility leaves 303 comparable units.

If, to be conservative, all comparable facilities are considered along

CHECKLIST 3-1. Services Comparison

Services	Included in Monthly Fee	À la Carte	Comments
Congregate meals			
One meal			
Two meals			
Three meals			
Special diet preparation			
Health care			
Registered nurses on call			
Registered nurse onsite			
Nursing home onsite			
Intermediate			
Skilled			
Pharmacy			
Other			
Personal care			
24-hour security			
Van transportation			
Emergency call			
Housekeeping			
Weekly			
Other			
Laundry service			
Linens, weekly			
Personal			
Recreational and activity programming			
Utilities			

CHECKLIST 3-2. Amenities Comparison

Amenities	Yes	No	Amenities	Yes	No
Pool			Arts and crafts room		
Spa			Recreation lounge		
Parking, uncovered			Storage		
Parking, covered			Laundry facilities		
Beauty and barber shop			Central dining area		
Banking			Private dining area		
Postal services			Library		
Estate planning			Cable TV		
Financial planning			Exercise room		
Gift shop			Meeting rooms		
Convenience store			Central TV room		
Guest residence			Gardening area		
Woodworking			Greenhouse		
Walking path					

with the true competitor facilities, the total number for market share analysis is 754 existing units. Yearly incomes required to afford the units in this analysis range from $15,000 to $35,000 per year. It can be assumed then, that these facilities serve the same market segment as the proposed project; that is, those earning at least $15,000 per year. Market share analysis demonstrates that about 21 percent (754 units per 3533 age and income-qualified households) of total age- and income-qualified elderly are currently served or are needed to fill up competitor or comparable facilities.

Thus far, the discussion has been targeted toward projects that do not consist of a nursing care component, such as intermediate and skilled nursing home care, or personal care. Depending on the extent to which state agencies collect information, competitor analysis information for nursing homes is not too difficult to obtain, because they are state licensed and regulated.

Such information as age of facility, utilization data (occupancy), and days of care according to payor class (Medicare, Medicaid, private pay) are ordinarily available. Daily rate information requires field study, and collection of this data will depend on the research budget. For bed need determination, however, daily rate information is not necessary.

State agencies also regulate and provide information on personal care facilities. Generally, only the total number of licensed beds and the location of the facility are procurable from these agencies. Field-work will more than likely be needed to acquire utilization statistics.

In summary, competitor analysis determines the percentage of the age- and income-qualified elderly in the geographic target market currently being served or needed to fill up competitor facilities. Analysis also provides the developer with a comparison to use in marketing efforts and in further market research, such as consumer survey design.

Competitor analysis provides a framework for ongoing investigation, if the proposed project is determined to be viable. It allows the developer to uncover any unmet market needs and weaknesses and is a powerful tool in the development of strategy, thus enabling the developer to make the project market distinguishable from the competition.

Need and Demand Assessment Versus Market Penetration Rates. Thus far, three basic components of quantitative market analysis for a proposed project have been discussed: market area definition, demographics, and competitor analysis. Need and demand assessment is the last step in quantitative analysis. A few words must be said about how the concept of market penetration rates differs from need assessment.

Market studies typically bring the results of the demographic and competitor analyses together in the form of market penetration rates. They are essentially estimates of only potential *demand* or *desire* for the proposed project within the entire housing community, showing what percentage of income-qualified elderly must be attracted, given a specified number of units. If, for example, the proposed project will consist of 200 adult congregate living facility rental units, and demographic analysis indicates 2000 age- and income-qualified elderly, then the project must attract 10 percent of that group in the geographic market area to realize a 100 percent occupancy.

This analysis can be carried even further if there are existing or proposed competitor units in the geographic market area. If 100 units currently exist in the area, it would take 15 percent of the qualified elderly to fill up the proposed project and other competitor and proposed units. There are really no industry guidelines regarding required market penetration levels. Implied in market penetration is that with higher rates come higher risks.

The use of market penetration really assumes that all senior housing is 100 percent *demand* driven. Market penetration disregards need-driven elements that are inherent in adult congregate living, personal care living, and nursing home care. It is recommended to use need and demand assessment in determining market feasibility for a proposed project, rather than basing feasibility on market penetration. This procedure identifies the age- and income-qualified elderly target market that would *need* services and care, and in turn this group can be motivated to *demand* or desire housing. It is then possible to estimate the number of housing units or beds needed.

TABLE 3-4. Competitor Analysis for Existing Private Pay Senior Housing

Facility	Years of Operation	Number of Units	Type of Unit	Average Size (sq. ft.)	Percent Occupancy	Rent per Month Single	Rent per Month Double	Monthly Rent ($ per sq. ft.)	Endowment or Entrance Fee	Services and Amenities Included in Fee	Comments
A	1.5	40	Efficiency	390	70	900	1,150	2.31	No	Utilities, weekly maid service, 2 meals/day, scheduled transportation, nurse on call, nightly security, emergency call, library, chapel, activities, smoke alarm, sprinkler system	Congregate living/semiambulatory services. Available for additional fee: laundry, additional housekeeping, meal service, personal transportation, guest room, beauty/barber shop, coin-operated laundry, home health services
		105	1 Bedroom	426–520		1,150–1,300	1,400–1,500	2.69–2.50			
		10 / 155	2 Bedroom	629		1,400	1,650	2.22			
B	7 months		Apartments:		50				No	Activity center, emergency call, transportation, nurse on call, security	Independent or congregate living for ambulatory adults, no meals
		60	1 Bedroom	560		420	420	.75			
		3	2 Bedroom	900		525	525	.58			
			Cottages:								
		17	1 Bedroom	675		435	435	.64			
		10 / 90	2 Bedroom	900		525	525	.58			
C	N/A	8	2 Bedroom	1,100	85	700 +		.64	No		Independent or congregate living, rent depends on services purchased; located on campus that includes ICF nursing beds and custodial care

Facility	Yrs in Op. / Opens	No. of Units	Unit Type	Size (sq ft)	% Occ.			Ratio	Entrance Fee	Services	Comments
D	1.5	12	1 Bedroom	800	40	Condominium for purchase or rent 1 Bedroom: $64,500 2 Bedroom: 74,500 Rent N/A			No		Independent living, security, controlled access, medical alert system, plans for clubhouse and expansion to 35 units
		3	2 Bedroom	1,000							
		15									
E	16	120	1 Room w/ shared bath	N/A	75	600		N/A	No	3 meals/day, weekly maid service, utilities, security, and cable hook-up	Congregate living residence for ambulatory adults, dormitory living
			1 Room w/ private bath	N/A		625		N/A			
			2 Room w/ private bath	N/A		850		N/A			
			3-Room Suite, 2 persons	N/A		1,500		N/A			
F	20	81	Efficiency	264–472	99	698–835	1,166–1,303	2.64–1.76	27,200–39,700	1 meal/day, utilities, maintenance, 70 skilled nursing beds, scheduled transportation	CCRC. Waiting list. Additional amenities: beauty/barber shop, chapel, library, TV room, solarium, exercise room, lounge. Currently constructing skilled nursing replacement facility to include 90 beds
		149	1 Bedroom	540–866		855–1,255	1,212–1,693	1.58–1.41	45,400–72,300		
		65	2 Bedroom	736–1,310		991–1,615	1,459–2,086	1.34–1.23	62,400–88,000		
		295									
G	Opens in July 1989	176	Efficiency	300	0	775	975	2.58	No	3 meals/day, weekly maid/linen service, intercoms, scheduled transportation, activities	Congregate living
			Studio	408		875	1,075	2.14			
			1 Bedroom	460–504		975–1,100	1,175–1,300	2.12–2.18			
			2 Bedroom	600		1,500	1,700	2.50			

113

Approaches to Need and Demand Assessment for Senior Housing. The range of housing needs is generally described by the loss of capacity for self-care because of some chronic or acute condition. The services can be provided either in an alternative housing arrangement or in a home environment. In fact, a large percentage of elderly are cared for at home by friends or relatives without pay.

The need and demand for senior housing and nursing care depend on the level of functional disability, the support network of the individual, and the ability to pay. Individuals with high levels of disability and no home support are generally candidates for nursing home placement. Individuals with limited disability, but no home support, may be candidates for supervised living, such as personal care facilities.

An important factor in determining need and demand for senior housing is the informal support network available to assist the elderly on a daily or regular basis. Unfortunately, changing lifestyles, increasing longevity, and lack of services create problems for this network.

Family members have long been the primary source of assistance to elderly persons living alone. However, recent years have seen children moving to other locations for employment. Even when children are in the same community, often both husband and wife work and are not able to provide daily care.

Another often overlooked factor, the declining birthrate, has increased the ratio of dependent elderly to children. As a result, a family may have two or three elderly members, and one child for support.

Several approaches may be considered in estimating the number of individuals who need and demand moderately dependent, semi-independent, and independent housing arrangements. The ones presented here take into consideration the concepts of functional disability, ability to pay, and home or support networks. These approaches demonstrate how to arrive at the number of individuals who will likely need and demand housing as well as explain how to forecast need for senior housing units in relation to supply.

The approaches used to determine need for nursing home beds differ substantially from the ones used to determine other forms of senior housing. These issues as well as descriptions of methods of calculating bed need will be presented in a separate section.

Personal Care Housing—Moderately Dependent or Supervised Living. A useful approach in estimating need for this type of living arrangement is to estimate need based on studies that demonstrate an individual's ability or inability to perform daily living activities within specific age groups. These measures produce an index based on an individual's level of dependence with regard to specific functions. The National Center for Health Statistics has measured the prevalence of functional limitations for those noninstitutionalized individuals age 65 and older in 13 activities. Prevalence rates were calculated for 7 of the 13 activities, known as activities of daily living (ADLs) or personal care activities: bathing, dressing, eating, transferring, walking, getting outside and using the toilet.

The degree to which an individual has difficulty in performing activities of daily living is directly related to an individual's functional disability. The measure of difficulty encountered by some elderly in performing activities of daily living can give an approximate picture of those individuals who require moderately dependent or supervised living, such as provided in a personal care home or custodial home. Based on data from the 1984 National Health Interview Survey, the number of individuals age 65 and over having difficulty in performing personal care activities can be identified. Even though this population may have difficulty, not all will require assistance in performing personal care activities. Perhaps a better indication of the need for services found in personal care housing is the proportion of individuals who require assistance. This data is shown in Table 3-5. As one's age increases, however, the prevalence of functional limitations in some activities increases. If the elderly are segmented into age categories 65 to 74, and 75 and over, it can be seen that the difficulty in performing personal care activities and need for assistance increases with age.

Table 3-6 presents a sample analysis of an income-qualified population living in a geographic market area who would likely need per-

TABLE 3-5. Percentage of Elderly, Age 65 and Over, Who Receive Help in Performing Personal Care Activities

Level of Difficulty	Age				
	65 and over	65–74	75–84	80–84	85 and over
None	90.4	94.0	88.1	83.6	68.9
Help needed in performing personal care activities	9.6	6.0	11.9	16.4	31.1

Source: D. Dawson, G. Hendershot, and J. Fulton, "Aging in the Eighties, Functional Limitations of Individuals Age 65 Years and Over," Advance Data from Vital and Health Statistics No. 133, DHHS Pub. No. (PHS) 87-1250, Public Health Service (Hyattsvile, MD: National Center for Health Statistics, June 10, 1987): 7.

sonal care. The defined market area for this example is a county. This approach assumes the following:

1. Individuals likely to need personal care services will be the age 80 and over market segment.
2. Of the population age 80 and older, not all will receive personal care services. The persons who need such services will be those who have difficulty performing personal care activities and require assistance.
3. Not all persons who have difficulty in performing ADLs will receive care at a facility. Approximately 75 percent of the care received by noninstitutionalized disabled elderly is provided in the community by family and friends who are not compensated for their services. Another 5 percent of this population receive care provided by paid sources. It could be assumed that this 5 percent (plus 20% of the remaining noninstitutionalized disabled elderly) would likely be cared for in a facility, rather than at home.[2]
4. Only the income-qualified population age 80 and over who require personal care services will be able to afford private pay services. It is assumed that 60 to 80 percent of one's income will be spent for rent on a personal care unit. Income required to afford rent should be $15,000 or greater.
5. The number of income-qualified persons age 80 and over needing personal care equals the number of required units, assuming one person per unit.

TABLE 3-6. Personal Care Unit Need in the Market Area for Elderly, Age 80 and Older, with Income of $15,000 and More

	1988	1993
Number of elderly age 80 and over	7,915	9,800
Number of elderly age 80 and over having difficulty in performing personal care tasks and receiving help	1,800	2,245
Number of income-qualified elderly requiring personal care units	202	365
Less existing and proposed units	180	180
Net units needed	22	185

[2]House of Representatives, Select Committee on Aging, *Exploding the Myths: Caregiving in America,* January 1987, 5.

6. Any existing or proposed personal care units must be subtracted from the number of required units. In the example, 150 existing licensed units and 30 proposed units represent personal care service delivery.

The sample analysis indicates that an estimated 202 to 365 age- and income-qualified individuals would require personal care service between 1988 and 1993. By assuming one person per unit, this translates to 202 to 365 units. Subtracting existing units (150) and proposed units (30), to be conservative, demonstrates an estimated need for 22 to 185 units during the time period 1988 to 1993.

Congregate Housing (Semi-Independent Living). As stated previously, the National Center for Health Statistics measured the prevalence of functional limitations for those noninstitutionalized individuals age 65 years and older in 13 activities, 7 of which are known as activities of daily living (ADLs). The remaining 6 activities have been termed instrumental activities of daily living (IADL) or home management activities. These activities are preparing meals, shopping, managing money, using the telephone, doing heavy housework, and doing light housework.[3]

Congregate housing provides a range of home management and social services but stops short of providing personal care and medical related care. The prevalence of difficulty that the elderly have in performing certain home management activities and the number requiring assistance to perform these activities can give an approximate picture of individuals who require congregate housing services. Table 3-7 exhibits the percentage of those individuals who have difficulty and require assistance in performing home management activities closely associated with the ones provided in a congregate housing environment.

Congregate living, by virtue of services that may or may not be offered, is a hybrid containing need- and demand-driven elements. Not all who need services will demand them. Other arrangements may be made via coordination with agencies or relatives, permitting care at home. Demand is at best difficult to predict.

An estimate of market area demand is best accomplished using consumer surveys, which will be discussed later in this chapter. Another indicator of local demand may be elderly mobility trends, if ob-

---

[3]Dawson et al., "Aging in the Eighties," 3–5.

TABLE 3-7. Percentage of Elderly, Age 65 and Over, Who Receive Help in
Performing Home Management Activities

	Age			
Level of Difficulty	65 and over	65–74	75–84	85 and over
None	77.8	83.9	72.4	48.6
Help needed in performing home management activities	22.2	16.1	27.6	51.4

Source: Dawson et al., "Aging in the Eighties, Functional Limitations of Individuals Age 65 Years and Over," *Advance Data from Vital and Health Statistics* No. 133, DHHS Pub. No. (PHS) 87-1250, Public Health Service (Hyattsville, MD: National Center for Health Statistics, June 10, 1987): 9.

tainable. However, if local estimates are not possible, substitute measures may be used.

Substitute measures include the use of consumer survey results or other documentation that has been published, or the experience of the consultant. A recent survey conducted by the American Association of Retired Persons (AARP) on a sample of individuals age 60 and over indicated that about 10 percent are currently living in a retirement community or a senior building. The survey also revealed that when given 12 different housing options, 48 percent of respondents would consider congregate housing or a continuing care retirement community, respectively. Although these survey results are interesting, they should be cautiously used in predicting future housing selections of the elderly.[4]

Taking into consideration the survey results and the authors' experience, estimates indicate approximately 30 percent of those who may need housing will demand it. These estimates may be quite conservative for those age 75 and over because as previously suggested, the need for assistance in performing home management activities increases with age.

Table 3-8 presents an analysis of the need for congregate housing of an income-qualified population in a sample geographic market. The market area is identical to the one in the previous sample analysis for personal care. In general (or broad) terms congregate living environments will appeal to individuals age 65 and older. This approach as-

[4]American Association of Retired Persons, *Understanding Senior Housing, An American Association of Retired Persons Survey of Consumer's Preferences, Concerns and Needs* (Washington, DC: AARP, 1987), 5, 26.

TABLE 3-8. Private Pay Congregate Housing Need in the Market Area for Elderly, Age 75 and Older, with Income of $15,000 and More

	1988	1993
Number of elderly age 75 and over	14,848	18,500
Number of elderly age 75 and over having difficulty in performing home management activities and receiving help	4,910	6,119
Number of income-qualified elderly expected to need and demand congregate living units	608	925
Less existing and proposed units	754	754
Net units needed	<146>	171

sumes that typically, however, age 75 and over will choose this form of housing. Because it is difficult to predict how many elderly might in-migrate from beyond the service area, estimates of age-qualified elderly do not include this factor.

Further, not all the population age 75 and older will need congregate living support. Those individuals age 75 and older who have some difficulty in performing home management activities potentially need some form of assistance. It is also assumed for this example that 30 percent of those age 75 and over who are having difficulty and require assistance in performing home management activities would be interested in selecting congregate housing.

Only the elderly population earning over $15,000 per year will qualify for the proposed project in this example. The numbers of elderly who qualify at this income level may be considered conservative, because many of the elderly might sell their homes to move into a project, thus enhancing their buying power. Monetary support by children of the elderly is not taken into consideration in income qualifying. Any support from children or income from the sale of a home may make an income-disqualified elderly person an income-qualified congregate living resident.

In this example, the number of income-qualified elderly age 75 and over who need and demand congregate living equals the number of required units. An estimate of one person per unit is used because typically it is a single individual, age 75 and over, who chooses congregate living.

Finally, for the purposes of this example, any existing and proposed units comparable to the proposed product must be subtracted from the number of required units. In this example, there are 754 existing units (see Table 3-4) that are competitive and comparable to the proposed product. No proposed projects were found.

The analysis indicates that when using a conservative demand estimate of 30 percent the number of age and income-qualified elderly who are expected to need and demand congregate housing increases from 608 in 1988, to 925 in 1993. Assuming that one person will occupy each unit, the number of units needed will be 608 in 1988, and 925 in 1993. The number of units needed must be qualified with competitor and proposed units. Net units needed for the geographic area is negative for 1988 and positive (171 units) in 1993.

Fully Independent Living. By definition, fully independent living is *demanded* by all persons who do not require assistance with activities of daily living (ADLs) or support with home management.

Fully independent housing applies to the general housing situation of homes and apartments. The entire housing stock of a service area could, therefore, be available to the elderly or anyone else choosing to purchase or rent.

Considerable discussion has focused on the determination of housing for semi-independent and moderately dependent housing arrangements because each arrangement consists of complex approaches that include determination of need. The fully independent elderly constitute a solely demand-driven market. The developer is most likely familiar with the demand-driven housing market; determining demand for the fully independent elderly housing market is similar to assessing conventional housing projects.

Nursing Home Care. A highly specialized level of service rendered in an institutional environment, nursing homes provide around-the-clock care for individuals who require supervision, personal care, and medical assistance for chronic conditions. Because of the medical component, nursing homes must satisfy specific licensure standards and meet state and federal guidelines.

Most states regulate any facility that provides supervision, assistance, medical, and rehabilitative services on a 24-hour basis. The licensure levels most commonly associated with the long-term nursing home are intermediate and skilled care. The criteria for licensure are a function of the intensity of the service provided.

Only intermediate and skilled nursing care facilities qualify to participate in certification for Medicaid and Medicare reimbursement. Intermediate care facilities are distinguished from skilled care primarily by their residents' requiring less intensive assistance or fewer nursing hours per resident per day. Intermediate care residents also need less medical supervision. Skilled care residents experience a less stable medical condition, require more restorative nursing, and need more medical supervision than intermediate care residents.

Because nursing home residents require medical supervision and assistance, nursing home care is a need-driven market. Several methods can be utilized to forecast nursing care bed needs.

Nursing Bed Need Assessment. A careful evaluation of existing facilities is essential in determining whether additional nursing beds may need to be constructed. High occupancy rates in market area facilities may indicate a need for additional nursing home beds. It is particularly useful to gain an understanding of how current market area utilization levels compare to larger geographic areas. By comparing the market area with county and statewide occupancy levels, any substantial differences may be identified.

Local occupancies should also be compared to target occupancies that have been set by state planning agencies. The target occupancies are used by the state to forecast bed need for planning purposes. They are usually set to achieve a conservative estimate with reasonable utilization and vacancy. A comparison will show if there are any unusual differences.

Another indication of the level of need in the service area is the current average daily census (ADC) per 1000 population. This utilization statistic is produced by nursing homes in the market area. The figure is then applied to the 65 and older population to achieve an ADC rate.

The population age 65 and over is used because it accounts for a majority of nursing home patients. This premise is supported by preliminary data findings of the 1985 National Nursing Home Survey conducted by the National Center for Health Statistics. The findings showed that 88 percent of nursing home residents are age 65 and over. Of this total, 45 percent are 85 years and over, 39 percent are age 74 to 85, and 16 percent are age 65 to 74.[5]

Bed Need Projections. In general, state planning agencies, using a target occupancy, apply historical use rates in conjunction with forecasted population to predict bed need. These use rates are generally expressed as a ratio of patient days per 1000 population age 65 and

[5]Ester Hing, "Use of Nursing Homes by the Elderly, Preliminary Data from the 1985 National Nursing Home Survey," *Advance Data from Vital and Health Statistics* No. 135, DHHS Pub. No. (PHS) 87-1250, Public Health Service (Hyattsville, MD: National Center for Health Statistics, May 14, 1987): 2.

over, and as an average daily census per 1000 population. By developing statewide and county use rates, a forecast of total patient days and average daily census can be made; applying the target occupancy will identify the total bed need. State projections will serve as a gauge with which to compare bed need for the market area.

Another method is to average the use rates, utilizing the use rate for the market area and a larger area, such as a planning region. By averaging the rate of the market area and its respective planning area, any differences will be acknowledged. With all methods, in order to obtain net bed needs, the existing supply of nursing homes must be subtracted.

Consideration of Medicare's prospective payment reimbursement system may show that bed need projections will probably be insufficient. This system is expected to transfer a number of Medicare patient days and admissions from hospitals to skilled nursing homes.

The previous discussion of nursing home bed need assessment has oversimplified a very complicated process. It was designed to give the developer an overview of possible approaches. Individuals who are experienced in the field are best qualified to forecast nursing bed need.

Although nursing home care is a need-driven market, demand-driven methodologies using historical utilization rates have been presented. Demand methodology is limited because it is historical and reflects only facility availability. If facilities do not exist or are not acceptable, demand does not exist. It is further limited since it does not take into account a wide range of factors that affect the rate of utilization, including accessibility and appropriateness of the existing facility. A main weakness is that demand-based methodologies may not accurately reflect medical need for services because some current residents may have been inappropriately placed and do not need nursing home care and services.

In sum, the goals of quantitative analysis are to:

Determine the estimated numbers of age- and income-qualified elderly of the target market who currently reside and are projected to reside in the geographic market area, as well as assess the overall area with respect to demographic and economic trends (demographic analysis)

Identify the competition or comparable facilities currently serving the target market and determine what, if any, service gaps or unmet needs currently exist in the community (competitor analysis)

Adjust the results of the foregoing analysis to estimate need and demand for housing units or beds (need and demand assessment)

Qualitative Analysis. Two elements of the product analysis and assessment phase of planning have been identified and discussed: product definition and the quantitative component of market analysis. The conclusions derived from the quantitative analysis constitute just one component of the market analysis process. Qualitative analysis, using consumer research survey techniques, further validates these market conclusions. The analysis will help determine the marketability or demand for a product.

One way to determine marketability for a project is to seek the advice of the target market or potential consumer. The performance of qualitative analysis using consumer research surveys is important, especially considering the potential loss of millions of dollars if the project is built and then it is discovered that the market is not receptive to the project.

Properly performed, qualitative analysis should accomplish three broad goals.

First, qualitative analysis should educate the prospective consumer by providing information about the overall project concept. Many times individuals have preconceived ideas concerning retirement housing. They may equate it with an "old folks' home." After participating in a survey, the respondent may be able to dismiss these misconceptions and gain a further understanding of the concept.

Qualitative analysis should also gather opinions regarding attitudes and preferences toward specific aspects of senior housing with regard to design, services, amenities, fee structure, and payment mechanism. This research will allow the developer to test the assumptions made concerning consumer preferences. The results should influence program planning for the proposed project.

Finally, qualitative analysis helps to determine product demand, perceived need for retirement housing in the community, and the overall acceptability of the proposed project.

The completion of market analysis using both quantitative and qualitative analysis will provide additional information to reach a decision about proceeding with a project. Before a decision is made, however, the developer must understand the relationship between the two sets of results.

The developer may ask the question: Are the results of qualitative analysis of primary importance in my decision making compared to those in quantitative analysis? Both must be taken into consideration. If the demographics show that there is not a population to support a project, the answer is clear. Even if the demographics show that there is an overwhelming need, consumer research must be done. Should the results of the consumer research be weighed more heavily than the demographics? Demographics must be used as a screening device, but the results of consumer research, if properly performed, will also offer useful guidance. As an example, if only 300 income-qualified elderly live in a service area, but it is determined that 200 have expressed a serious interest in moving into a project, a developer might want to proceed with the project. The results of qualitative analysis are important to the decision of whether to build or not to build a project.

There are sources available that outline basic market research principles, as well as books on conducting consumer surveys. Such topics as survey development and design, sampling size, survey administration, and survey analysis are covered in detail.

Survey Methods. Two broad issues apply to all survey methods: obtaining lists to get a representative sample of the target population and survey design. Lists may be purchased or acquired from different sources, such as commercial firms and voter registration lists. It is important that these lists are up-to-date. An alternative method is to establish relationships with senior organizations and other groups that may have senior members, such as churches, synagogues, and civic and community groups. Once relationships are established, listings of members might be more easily obtained. Typically these member lists are under tight control by the organization.

Survey design involves length, wording of questions and instructions, and format or layout. Survey length is important and depends on the survey method selected. Also, lengthy surveys can become laborious and tiring for anyone. Survey layout should include easy-to-read print for aging eyes. Wording of questions and instructions should be concise and understandable. Surveys that include multiple choice answers should be written to promote ease of statistical analysis using computers.

The primary methods of conducting consumer research—telephone, mail, personal interviews, and focus groups—are discussed in the following paragraphs.

Personal Interviews and Focus Groups. Personal interviews involve one-on-one or face-to-face meetings and should occur in private settings rather than malls. Focus groups, considered a form of personal interview, generally consist of 10 to 15 individuals per session, with a session lasting from 2 to 2½ hours. Participants receive questionnaires and complete them with the help of a trained interviewer or moderator. As the moderator poses each question, the respondent provides an answer.

In some instances, focus groups are videotaped or recorded. This allows the developer or sponsor to observe group interaction and comments not expressed in a survey.

Several issues are relevant in using focus groups and personal interviews. The organization of focus group participants and personal interviews can be time consuming and create problems for the consultant who might be a stranger to a community. Again senior organizations may be very helpful, especially if incentives are given, such as donations to a group. The use of focus groups and personal interviews can be costly because of the extensive fieldwork and the number of interviews necessary to get a representative sample size.

Interviewer bias can also be a problem, especially when different interviewers are involved. Bias may result from the respondent's observations and perceptions of the interviewer or the way in which questions are presented, even with well-trained interviewers.

Both methods offer control in obtaining a response because the respondent's identity is known and there is an opportunity to establish rapport as well as clarify questions. It is also possible to utilize different forms of communication, such as diagrams and pictures, during personal interviews and focus groups. Longer questionnaires seem to work better with personal interviews and focus groups than in a mail survey approach.

Telephone Surveys. Telephone surveys are probably the quickest, but least reliable, way to obtain responses from a large sample size. Once an individual has been reached, there may be some hurdles to overcome in obtaining a response. Individuals may be leary of outsiders seeking personal opinions. As a result, interviews must be attentive to establishing initial rapport. Also, fewer questions must be asked. This method may not allow time for carefully thought-out responses and clarification of questions. Telephone surveys also may produce interviewer bias, although observable bias cannot occur; at times it is the surest way to obtain outrageous answers.

Mail Surveys. Mail surveys allow for longer questionnaires and for the respondent to work at his or her own pace in filling out the answers. There is no opportunity to clarify questions, however, and mail surveys do not provide any control in obtaining participant response and cooperation. The researcher must simply wait for a response. Low response rates are often caused by inappropriately worded cover letters that do not instill motivation or are perceived as junk mail. With mail surveys, the researcher may not always get a response from the intended respondent, as someone else, such as an adult child, may fill out the survey. Like the focus group or personal interview, the mail survey, properly filled out, provides documented evidence of demand for a project. Mail surveys can be considered the least costly of the methods, but there is a cost versus benefit trade-off. Even though mail surveys are relatively inexpensive, nonresponse rates may make a study very costly in the long run and the researcher can never be sure how well the respondent understood each question.

Sample Questions.   The best way to determine whether or not a project could be truly marketable and acceptable to a community is to ask the potential consumer. The survey respondents must be age- and income-qualified seniors. They may be currently living in homes, apartments, with relatives, or in competitor projects. The results should serve as a basis for future project planning by directly influencing decisions as to program definition and project scope, establishing the suitability of the site, indicating reasonable fee mechanisms, and demonstrating overall project need and demand.

Developers will reach their survey objectives in different ways, depending on the kinds of questions asked, the way questions are worded or presented, method of research, and method of analysis.

In order to determine survey objectives, the researcher needs to ask certain types of questions representing these categories:

Services and amenities	Fee structure
General design	Need and demand
Meals and dining	Demographics
Site preference	

The following examples of questions could be asked in any questionnaire.

Services and Amenities.   As previously discussed, a retirement community may offer a wide range of services and amenities, depending on the project. The questions should seek to find out just how important specific services would be to the respondent. In order to accomplish this, the developer or sponsor should provide the respondent with choices that deal with varying degrees or levels of importance. The following example demonstrates this kind of question.

Example: How important do you feel that each of the following services would be to you, if it were offered in a retirement community?

Service	Very Important	Important	Not Important
Housecleaning			
Beauty or barber shop			
Nurse on call			

General Design. Design questions may encompass a wide range of questions, from basic to detailed, including interior and exterior design. The developer or sponsor should ask what number of bedrooms the respondent prefers. A basic question may deal with unit type.

Example: In which of the following types of apartment units would you most prefer to live?
___Efficiency
___One bedroom, one bathroom
___Two bedrooms, one bathroom
___Two bedrooms, two bathrooms

A more detailed question may include unit size preferences.

Site Preference A site or several sites that have been considered suitable by the developer may or may not be suitable to the target population. A survey, at a minimum, should ask this question.

Example: If a retirement community were to be built in (specific location), would that site be:
___Positive
___Negative
___No opinion

Other site suitability questions may determine just how important a location is with regard to proximity to shopping, medical facilities, and cultural activities. Questions may deal with willingness to travel specific distances to a particular site, or whether or not it is important for the site to be located in a city, suburb, or rural area.

Meals and Dining. Questions that deal with meals and dining preference are highlighted as a separate category because so many other issues could be uncovered involving such issues as design and staffing.

A developer may only want to know how important central meals and dining are to the respondent or may want to find out just how many meals might be eaten daily in a central dining room. If, for example, respondents would prefer to eat two meals daily in a central dining room, this would give an indication of how to staff a central dining facility. Other design-related issues may deal with programming more space if private dining is preferred.

Fee Structure. A further indication of demand for a community is the amount an individual is willing to pay. The survey should ask the preferred type of payment mechanism (rental, entrance fee, or purchase) and how much the respondent is willing to pay for monthly rental or service fees, or for the purchase of a home. Further questions could ask why these choices were made and whether the respondent would prefer to purchase services as needed or have them included in a monthly fee.

Need and Demand. The developer or sponsor should determine if there is a perceived need for retirement housing in the community regardless of the respondent's level of interest, and if the respondent would be interested in moving to a retirement community and how soon. One example of how to determine demand for a particular project concept would be to ask the following question.

Example: Understanding that it is difficult to predict future needs for housing and related services, would you be interested in moving to a retirement community that provides (type of services) in:

    __One year
    __Two to three years
    __Four to five years
    __Six to ten years
    __More than ten years
    __Not interested at all

Other demand-related questions include variations of site preference and perhaps reactions to sponsorship of a facility. The type of developer or sponsor will, in many cases, influence a resident to move into a facility. Religious and government developers and sponsors are such examples.

Demographics.   Demographic questions will enable the developer to create a profile of survey respondents and will aid in interpreting survey results. Such demographic factors as age and income can be used to determine whether or not significant response differences exist within a survey group. Whether the respondent's current residence is owned or rented may influence preferences for payment mechanism.

At a minimum, the survey should ask age, income, gender, ownership status of current residence, and location of current residence by zip code. Optional questions could deal with perceptions of health status and activity limitations of the respondent. Responses can be cross-tabulated to determine if they affect need- and demand-related responses for housing.

Selecting the Consultant.   The previous discussion of the basic components of market analysis will prove useful in making the decision to hire outside consultants to perform this analysis. It is possible, of course, that the developer or sponsor will choose, and has the capability, to perform the analysis. However, most lenders require that the feasibility study be performed by an individual independent of the project who can conduct an objective analysis. The use of outside consultants provides additional expertise, lending more credibility to results.

The developer or sponsor must decide upon the firm to perform the analysis. Issues that need to be decided are should the same firm analyze market and economic feasibility, or should separate firms be chosen?

The most efficient approach is to choose a firm to perform both studies. A comprehensive economic feasibility report must be presented in the appropriate form to meet lender requirements. A preliminary economic feasibility analysis does not meet such requirements. The developer or sponsor needs to ask further questions: Can the firm that is to perform market analysis deliver a comprehensive economic feasibility study in a lender-approved format? and, if one firm does the marketing study and another does the economic feasibility, will each firm accept the other firm's results?

Cost considerations enter heavily into the process. A smaller, less well-known firm may be able to perform a quality study at substantially lower cost than a larger, more well-known firm. The developer sponsor needs to be assured that the lender will accept the lesser known firm's study. If not, initially lowered costs may now multiply.

Further, a single firm may not have consulting resources available to deliver both a quality economic analysis and a quality market analysis. All of these issues should be uncovered during the selection process.

The Selection Process.   Choosing a consultant is similar to choosing an employee. The firm should be reviewed and evaluated based on experience in the retirement housing field and references.

In the review process it is recommended that the developer ask several key questions. A sample study should be examined at the consultant's office, so that the developer or sponsor may become familiar with the consultant's work and the components of a study. Additional necessary information includes the range of costs and the time required to complete a study.

A list of past projects and staff credentials will indicate the experience level. References will verify such items as past projects per-

---

CHECKLIST 3-3. Selection of Consultants

History of Company

Number of years that company has been in business
Number of years that company has been in business of senior housing consulting

Organization of Company

Principal(s) of company
Expertise of principal(s)
Number of staff, background, and area of expertise, especially those who will be working on proposed project

Experience

Consulting expertise by facility type and number of projects
____Hospitals
____Nursing homes
____Retirement housing
_____Fully independent living retirement communities
_____Semi-independent living (adult congregate living)
_____Moderately dependent living (personal care facility)
_____CCRC (encompasses independent living, adult congregate living, and medical and nursing services)
_____Other
Level of consulting services (market analysis or economic feasibility) by facility
____Hospital
____Nursing home
____Retirement housing

---

formed, quality of work, the firm's ability to communicate effectively with the client, the firm's ability to complete past project tasks as set out in the proposal, and the firm's ability to complete tasks within the time and budget constraints identified in the proposal.

Checklists 3-3 and 3-4 illustrate the kinds of basic information that the developer or sponsor should acquire when reviewing firms that propose to conduct a market feasibility study.

Market Analysis Summary. Market analysis will enable the developer or sponsor to determine whether or not the proposed project is a viable concept for the proposed geographic area. The analysis will determine if there are sufficient age- and income-qualified residents to support the project. It is even more important to determine how realistic the demand is for a community. It is also essential to understand that the conclusions of the market feasibility study are based on assumptions and estimates that are subject to change and uncertainty. It is likely that some assumptions will not develop, and unanticipated events may happen. As a result, estimates may vary from actual results of the proposed project.

CHECKLIST 3-4. Projects Completed by Consultant that Resemble Proposed Project

Name of Project	Location	Person to Contact (address/phone)	Sample Questions	Yes	No
			Overall satisfaction with project performance		
			Effective communication between project manager and developer or sponsor		
			Ability to complete tasks of proposal		
			Ability to complete tasks within time constraint of proposal		
			Ability to complete tasks within budget constraints of proposal		

SITE ANALYSIS

Demographic analysis may indicate to the developer or sponsor and the planning team that a substantial market exists for the proposed project. If a site is unsuitable or perceived negatively by the target market, however, it is unlikely that a project will be very successful. Research should test consumer reaction to many questions about the proposed project, including the proposed site location.

Other issues besides consumer reaction must be considered by the developer in determining the suitability of a potential site. Location, accessibility to services and amenities, and features of the surrounding neighborhood serve as examples. Thoroughly researching and analyzing a proposed site prevents not only potential errors that contribute to developmental cost overruns, but also avoids the loss of multimillions on a project that would never be fully occupied. Cost of a site (and any necessary improvements), although important, is not the most important factor to study.

Site Analysis Issues.   Many issues must be considered by the developer or sponsor and the planning team regarding the suitability of a proposed site. A site located in the heart of a heavily populated target population will make it easier for residents to relocate and will enable them to maintain social, family, or religious contacts.

Access to public transportation, preferably located no more than one to two blocks away, will enable residents to be mobile, thus providing access to a wide range of places and activities. Shopping and other services such as libraries, places of worship, beauty and barber shops, a post office, and cultural activities (e.g., theatres, museums) should be located within walking distance or a short driving distance. Hospitals, medical centers and dental offices, and nursing homes should also be within walking or short driving distances. A site located near a hospital will provide the resident with assurance that emergencies will be resolved quickly.

The surrounding area must promote easy access to points of destination. Poorly maintained sidewalks and streets are a major inconvenience as well as an accident hazard. The site should be located near a major thoroughfare that permits easy access, identification, and visibility for residents, visitors, and employees.

The site should be located in a residental neighborhood or mixed residential neighborhood (one that includes single family homes, apartments, and other residences). The neighborhood should not only be visually appealing, but should promote security, with police and fire protection nearby, low crime rates, positive trends in property values, and overall stability.

A sometimes neglected but very important factor is the neighborhood's history, especially negative aspects. If the neighborhood had a heavy crime rate years ago, the perception still may be that the area has high crime, even though it is now safe. It may be difficult to turn around negative feelings in the minds of prospective residents.

The site should provide privacy and security, but should not seclude or isolate the elderly from other individuals and activities. A site that adjoins residential and nonresidential areas, such as light commercial areas, offering shopping and professional services, may be the ideal.

The topography of a site should be analyzed prior to purchase for specific factors that could affect overall development costs and operation of a project. Irregular land shape, slope of the land, location of flood plain and fault lines, and unusual terrain are among the physical features that must be considered.

A flat site is preferable to one that is steeply sloped, for example. A steep slope may require stairs that are difficult to negotiate, especially for those elderly who are less mobile. The slope of the site can also adversely impact project size. An irregularly shaped site will permit less units per acre than square or rectangularly shaped land. Particular attention should be made to the availability of any natural amenities such as lakes, walking trails, ponds, and streams. These may add to the appeal and marketability of a proposed project.

During the research process it must be determined whether utilities such as water, sewer, drainage, gas, electricity, telephone, and cable television are accessible and available.

The size of the site will influence project design. Mid- to high-rise buildings require less acreage as opposed to one- to three-level buildings, which are spread out. Size of the site should also be adequate for parking, future expansion, and privacy.

The site should be visually compatible with the community. High-rise living may be more compatible in the northern region of the United States than in the southern region. High-rise living in a neighborhood of single-family homes would not be compatible.

Familiarity with local planning and zoning ordinances and restrictions that would impact the environment is very important in the site selection process. The approval process may be very costly and is something for which the developer must be prepared. Such zoning factors that need to be researched are building height restrictions, density restrictions (the number of units allowed per acre), and parking space limitations. An awareness of any environmental restrictions concerning wildlife and vegetation is extremely important before making the purchase decision.

A positive attitude about a site location must be gleaned from the target population as well as from the surrounding community or neighborhood. A coalition of angry neighbors could very well turn around a sponsor's plan for building in their neighborhood.

PROGRAM DEFINITION AND SCOPE

Thus far, this chapter has provided the developer or sponsor with some suggested approaches for analyzing the proposed product. If the project is feasible, the next step is to further define the product by making decisions with regard to program planning; that is, to assess the product.

Several issues must be resolved during this phase. The number and mix of housing units (one bedroom, two bedroom, efficiency apartment units, condominiums, townhomes, single-family dwellings, private or semiprivate rooms) must be determined. It is also necessary to decide the type of health care and nursing services that might be provided on-site or provided via contractual relationships off-site. Consideration must be given to the intensity and level of services. Services that might be considered include: nurse on call, physician on call, emergency care, full-time nurse, infirmary, home health care, pharmacy, health promotion and wellness activities, intermediate and skilled nursing care, personal care, and rehabilitation. Also, it is necessary to identify the types of services and amenities that will be included.

A summary statement of program definition and project scope will serve planning team members as a basis from which to perform such tasks as economic feasibility analysis for financial consultant, facility design for the architect and design team, and assessment of legal, regulatory, and reimbursement issues with respect to the legal advisor.

CHAPTER SUMMARY

Product analysis and assessment consists of several tasks, each one building on the other.

1. Definition of the product(s) under study
2. Market analysis to determine whether there is a need and demand for the project by the target market population

3. Site evaluation

4. Assessment of the product

The approaches presented for completing each task, are, of course, not the only means of accomplishment. They serve as guidelines, or at least a starting point, from which the developer or sponsor may proceed.

The end product of this phase will be a working document that the architect, financial advisor, legal advisor, and marketing and management team members will rely on heavily as they proceed with the project.

CHAPTER 4

FINANCIAL FEASIBILITY

DIANNE B. LOVE and JAMES L. LAUGHLIN

INTRODUCTION

One of the most important aspects of the entire process of retirement housing is the consideration of the financial feasibility. Feasibility studies are viewed differently by the team members involved with a retirement development. During the planning stage, the feasibility study often becomes the major focus point in the development process. The question ultimately answered by the feasibility study, assuming it is prepared correctly, is whether or not a project is viable. Does it make sense to go forward—does it seem to work for the lender and the developer, as well as the residents?

A nonprofit sponsor looks to see that adequate income could be derived from a retirement development. A for-profit developer must be convinced that there is an appropriate amount of profit to warrant the risk. Depending on the type of product that the developer wishes to undertake, the feasibility study should highlight the initial or up-front risks as well as the long-term or ongoing risks that any form of retirement community may generate.

As an example, a continuing care retirement community (CCRC) has all the up-front risks of any other type of retirement community, but also has back-end risks associated with its health care facility. A developer or sponsor who ventures into a CCRC has a much higher likelihood of running into default problems than would a conventional multifamily housing developer.

The financial feasibility study is the second step in the evaluation process of a potential (proposed) project. The first step is the market feasibility study. (See Chapter 3.) The preliminary financial feasibility study, once the type of housing and the service package have been decided, determines whether the product can be provided at a price that the potential consumers are willing and able to pay, as well as whether the price will give the investors and/or developers the required return on investment. When it has been established that there is demand for the product at a price that provides a sufficient return after determination of all costs of the project, the final feasibility study is prepared.

PERSONS CONCERNED WITH A PROJECT'S FEASIBILITY

Several key individuals, some of whom are team members and some of whom are not, are interested in the financial projections of a development. Some of these key individuals include the developer, sponsor, investor, lender, resident, and regulatory agencies.

Developer or Sponsor. The for-profit developer is concerned with whether the return is worth the risk. Do the numbers illustrate that a project will generate the necessary cash to cover operational costs and debt service, and still have a sufficient profit to warrant the developer's risk in proceeding with the retirement community?

If the developer is a nonprofit sponsor, the feasibility study should show that sufficient compensation will be received to justify the risk taken by the sponsoring organization.

Investors. The investors are looking for long-term return and are very concerned with the risk capital that has to be injected into a project. It is not uncommon to require either the investor or developer to risk from $750,000 to $1.5 million up front to develop a CCRC. Investors look closely at pure cash on cash return. They will not be satisfied with tax incentives only because these have been reduced substantially by the 1986 Tax Reform Act.

Investors must be encouraged with realistic and positive financial study that establishes sufficient cash on cash returns, prior to any tax advantage.

Lender. The lender's interest in the feasibility study varies depending on that party's involvement in financing a project. Unless the developer or sponsor has a track record in retirement development, it is unlikely that a loan will be nonrecourse to the developer or sponsor. It is also unlikely that any lender will be willing to take any risks without sharing in some of the profit, either through points or participation in the profits of the retirement community.

Barring a strong record of market success, the developer will have to inject some amount of equity into a project. A transaction that does not require such equity is nearly impossible to negotiate. The developer or sponsor who decides to work in the field of retirement development needs a strong financial record, an excellent location, and a well-designed program to attract any lender.

A lender's interest in the financial study depends on when and where the lender becomes a part of the financial vehicle. A lender who is simply going to finance construction has an interest in the feasibility study that is very different from that of the lender who is going to be responsible for permanent financing of the project as well as construction.

In the first case, the lender may require no more than 35 percent to 50 percent presales for an entrance fee project, as an example, since construction financing is theoretically short-term. However, if the lender is going to provide permanent financing as well as construction financing, the presale or prelease requirement may be increased to as high as 80 percent to 85 percent before the lender will permit funding of the construction portion of the package. Lenders look for a debt service coverage ratio of 1.2 from the retirement developer.

Residents.   Residents are becoming more interested in the projected financial forecast, particularly residents who are planning to move into a CCRC. Many states require mandatory disclosure of certain financial information to the prospective residents, including the financial viability of the developer as well as the project.

Residents are becoming more sophisticated regarding their rights and need to know; developers, to achieve credibility, must provide sufficient financial information. The residents seek to determine whether their interests will be secured when required to pay an entrance fee deposit or a total entrance fee. If the entrance fee account is unsecured, the residents want to know who is guaranteeing the fees, and how the resident would receive a refund of the entrance fee if the developer or the project has financial problems.

More and more residents of CCRCs realize that they are equity partners. They will receive returns as will the developer, but they are certainly taking a risk through entrance fee payments.

Often too late, residents realize that even though information may have been disclosed, it was not disclosed properly, and that there are no guarantees that the project will work.

Regulatory Agency.   Twenty-three states have regulations applicable to CCRCs, and a few states have regulations in place concerning adult congregate living facilities (ACLFs).

The agencies want to know the project's likelihood of success. Some states require a detailed financial statement in the overall disclosure statement for a proposed project that is provided to a potential resident. They may also require that the information be reviewed by the appropriate regulatory agency before it can be given to the public.

Maryland, for example, has a detailed procedures book that stipulates what must be disclosed to prospective residents.

The regulatory agencies, and any state, county, and local laws applicable to a proposed development need to be addressed in the financial study. If, for example, the project is a CCRC, the increased costs associated with a CCRC due to state regulation need to be identified.

Even a rental project may be unworkable because of zoning, parking, density, set-backs, and other county and local regulations if the local jurisdictions cannot be persuaded to modify their current zoning or use restrictions. The preparer of the financial study must also address any proposed legislation that may impact the success of the development.

For example, a state may modify or eliminate the requirements that a retirement community must comply with the state certificate of need process. This may make it easier and more attractive for developers to develop CCRCs or life care communities in that state. This in turn may increase competition. Or, a state may be willing to allow construction and operation of as many beds as desired as long as the state is guaranteed that after five years there will be no state-sponsored patients in any of the beds.

If many rental projects currently exist in the state, the developer may find additional competition from rental operators who have sufficient land contiguous to the current site to construct a nursing facility that will become a competitor with the proposed CCRC.

PURPOSES OF FINANCIAL ANALYSIS

The financial feasibility study serves two basic purposes; to determine for the developer whether the proposed project can be expected to yield a rate of return equivalent to other projects of similar risk, and to assist the lender in determining the creditworthiness of the debt instrument. The investor and the lender are interested in an analysis of the risk of the project as well as the return on the investment. As with all investments, there should be a direct relationship between the risk of the investment and the return it generates. The greater the risk, the higher the expected return. For the lender, the higher the risk, the higher the risk component of the interest rate, and consequently the higher the interest rate on the debt instrument.

In evaluating the creditworthiness of a debt instrument, the lender must first determine whether to finance the project and then decide the terms on which to provide financing. The financial feasibility study is an essential component in the decision-making process. As part of this process, the structure of the financial instrument must be determined. How much equity will be required? What guarantees will be required? What will the interest rate be? The analysis of project risk will have a significant effect on the structure of the financing agreement. Thus, in order to evaluate the risk and the return of the project, information is required regarding the development cost; the cash flow generated by operations; the expected debt service cost; the structure of the entrance fees, if any; the cash flow from the project; and the management team. The financial feasibility study should also include management's assumptions in preparing the study, as well as the most likely scenario. In evaluating the creditworthiness of the debt instrument, the creditor will look at the security as measured by ratio analysis, the solidity of management, the completed demand study, and its comparability to similar studies.

Creditors, investors, residents, and regulatory agencies are primarily interested in cash flow analysis. They want to know if the project will generate sufficient cash to pay the operating expenses, the debt service, the debt service reserves, the reserve requirement for repairs and replacement and for future promised health care services, and any other reserves required either by law, by regulatory agencies, or by the bond indenture agreement.

CONTENTS OF THE FINANCIAL FEASIBILITY STUDY

Do not assume that anything that has been placed in the market feasibility study will be included in the financial feasibility study. Even though it may seem redundant, a developer should include in the financial feasibility study, in summary form, the conclusions and general descriptions of the market study. This information can help give a reader of the financial feasibility study a better picture of the overall project.

Many times the reader of a financial study does not receive the market study at the same time. To look at the numbers without having more in-depth analysis of the project places the reader at a disadvantage. The following information should be part of a financial study: a description of the project; information concerning the background of the developer or sponsoring organization; detailed information about the facility; and a comprehensive description of the resident programs.

Providing the market information in the financial feasibility study reduces the chance that the financial researcher misinterprets the market analysis and prepares inappropriate figures for the project. Otherwise the financial researcher may develop figures that go in one direction, while the architect and the market feasibility researchers plan a project that is completely different in concept, causing serious problems for the developer.

It also needs to be pointed out that most readers of a financial study will not have as complete an understanding of the product as the developer. Therefore, the feasibility study must stand on its own.

Description of the Project. The financial study should contain a synopsis addressing and highlighting the following:

The type of product
The number and type of units and nursing beds (if applicable)
The size of the units
The number of each type of units
Location of project

If the development is an existing project, the developer needs to explain why additional units should be added and the rationale for the mix of additional units and size of units. Because a retirement community is not a typical project for most readers of financial studies, it requires additional information in the feasibility study.

There will be many questions asked by the readers, which may not be the case for the typical multifamily financial study. Additional information should include an explanation of why the developer believes the product is a marketable concept. Such concerns as ease of filling units and evicting residents should also be addressed. In this section of the financial feasibility study the preparer needs to address how the developer plans to work with an 85-year-old widow who can no longer pay the rent. Will the developer terminate the lease and move her? Will the developer evict a resident in poor health, or one who is frail and aging? Is it possible to convince a court to remove the 85-year-old widow for nonpayment?

It is important to indicate how the developer plans to solve any negative issues. What, for example, are the location's special problems, if any? It is a good idea to include a small location map and site plan because the document will be reviewed by prospective residents and lenders or investors who may not be familiar with the location. Artists' renderings are beneficial as part of the exhibits to the financial feasibility study.

The preparer of the financial study should not duplicate a market study, but should summarize the pertinent information unique to the location, project, design, and segment of the population that the project plans to serve. It also is useful to describe why the developer believes residents in a certain segment of the market would wish to move into the community. What is the advantage of being a resident in a particular project? The highlights of the services and amenities need to be outlined, including such items as the level of food service, the number of times housekeeping is available, nursing service, and emergency call service.

STRUCTURING FEES, CHARGES AND RESIDENT CONTRACTS

Retirement housing arrangements generally are divided into two types: life care or continuing care retirement communities and congregate care or rental retirement facilities. Continuing care retirement communities require both the advance payment of an entrance fee as well as a monthly fee. The entrance fee may be refundable, either in total or in part, or nonrefundable.

Congregate care or rental facilities do not require the payment of an entrance fee, but charge a single monthly fee that is higher than for a CCRC. Also the term of the resident contract is for a shorter period of time than is the resident contract for a CCRC.

Whether the facility requires an entrance fee and a monthly fee or a monthly fee only, the total revenue generated from all sources must cover the total costs of the facility, including operating costs, repayment of debt (interest and principal), and all reserve requirements. Thus, the first step in determining the structure of the entrance fees and the monthly fees, is to determine the total cost of the facility.

This cost is a function of the services provided by the facility, the financing of the facility, the future health care services to be provided to residents free of charge or at a reduced rate, and the reserve requirements. Once the service package has been identified, the operating budget can provide the estimated cost of providing these services. The debt service requirement of the facility is provided by the development budget and the terms of the proposed debt instrument. The proposed resident contract will spell out the future services, such as life tenancy or nursing home care to be provided to residents at a reduced rate.

The cost of providing these services will be a function of the operating budgets of the health care facility as well as the expected utilization of these services. The expected utilization of health care services is a function of the actuarial evaluations of the mortality rate, the morbidity rate, the turnover rate, and the withdrawal rate of the individual facility. Actuarial rates for an individual facility are very difficult to forecast due to the small size of the population. Many CCRC facilities have experienced financial difficulties when the actuarial estimates have proven to be very different from actual experience.

Entrance Fees.   For CCRCs, entrance fees generally range from $20,000 to $350,000, with maintenance fees ranging from $400 to $2000 per month. The funds available to the facility for its cash requirements are a function of the level of entrance fees, the level of the maintenance fee, the investment income earned on the entrance fees, and the expected turnover of the apartments.

Entrance fees may be refundable, in which all or part of the entrance fee is refunded to the resident upon withdrawal from the facility or to the resident's family upon death of the resident. Even for fully refundable entrance fees, the facility usually charges a processing fee of 5 to 10 percent of the total entrance fee.

The entrance fee may be partially refundable, with the refundable portion decreasing over the time the individual is a resident of the facility. The third alternative is for the entrance fee to be nonrefundable.

Whether the entrance fee is refundable or nonrefundable, the facility has the use of the funds for at least the period of time the resident resides in the facility. This allows the facility to apply a portion of the entrance fees to reduce the amount of debt, and thus reduce its debt service costs. In addition, the facility will be able to earn investment income on the entrance fees, reducing cash needs.

For a CCRC, a portion of the entrance fee should also be used to fund the repair and replacement fund and the health care reserve fund. The repair and replacement fund provides for the repairs and replacement of the facility and equipment over the life of the project.

The health care reserve fund is used for the nursing home care and personal care promised in the resident contract. For life care facilities, the facility promises the resident a life tenancy in the apartment. During the resident's life, different levels of care will be required, resulting in differing levels of cost for the remainder of the resident's life. Resident contracts may offer a number of different options. Some provide for a specified number of free nursing home days, while others provide care at reduced rates.

Additionally, a portion of the entrance fee should be allocated to the refunding of the entrance fees upon the resident's withdrawal from the facility. The uncertainty of the actuarial estimates for individual CCRC facilities has resulted in the increase of rental projects.

Monthly Rental Fees. Congregate care facilities do not require the payment of entrance fees, but rather depend upon monthly rental fees for operations, debt service and reserve requirements. The monthly fees are generally separated into the base rental fee and the service fee. In fact, many lenders require that the monthly payment be broken out into the amount paid for shelter, called the base rent, and the amount paid for services, the service fee. Since the facility does not provide life tenancy, a health care reserve fund is unnecessary. However, a congregate care facility will incur costs for operations, debt service, and reserves for repairs and replacement of the facility and equipment. A portion of the monthly service fee must be set aside to provide for these requirements.

The service package may be offered either bundled or unbundled. On a bundled basis, the service fee should provide for the cost of providing the services and the base rent should provide for the development cost and debt service.

Whether the facility is a CCRC with an entrance fee plus a monthly fee, or a congregate care facility with a monthly fee only, the cash flow generated should be sufficient for all the costs of the facility. Theoretically, the entrance fee and the investment income should provide for the debt service, the health care reserve, and the repair and replacement reserve; the monthly fee should cover the operating cost. For a rental facility, the monthly fee must provide for all the costs of operating the facility.

Comparison of Rental Approach to CCRC Approach.   Only a few of the many advantages and disadvantages of rental projects are discussed here. With a rental approach it is not necessary for the resident to sell his or her current residence prior to relocating. The rental agreement usually requires only a 30-day notice by the resident prior to vacating a unit, whether or not the developer has been able to lease the unit again. This is often not the case for a resident of an entrance fee project, who can only leave once the unit has been remarketed.

Residents and adult children like the rental approach because there is no financial risk for the parents or the estate. More often than not there is no health care included in the facility, and therefore lenders have a "back door" should the community not work as an age-segregated development. Rentals are generally easier to market than facilities with entrance fees. Residents who have sold a home can often place the proceeds in a secure investment and cover the monthly rental from interest income.

The disadvantages of the rental project are not as numerous as the ones of the entrance fee, but there are still some. First, the monthly fee is generally considerably higher than that charged by an entrance fee facility, because there is no other source of funds to subsidize the debt and the operating costs. The ease of moving in and out of a project and the lack of financial penalties for moving out can create more frequent resident turnover. Greater marketing costs can be expected due to this turnover.

Most rental projects do not offer nursing beds as an option to the residents. The amount of health care assistance is minimal unless it is established under an insurance program or a developer contracts with a health care provider.

COMPONENTS OF FINANCIAL FEASIBILITY

The components of the financial feasibility study are as follows:

    Development budget
    Operating budget
    Cash flow analysis
    Pro formas
    Ratio analysis

The remainder of this chapter discusses these individual components of the financial feasibility study, as well as factors unique to the financial feasibility analysis of a retirement housing project. The final section of the chapter provides some guidance for selection of the preparer of the financial feasibility study.

Development Budget. The components of the development budget for a retirement project are similar to those of the development budget for any multifamily housing facility. The primary areas of difference will be in facilities that have a health care component subject to state regulation through the certificate of need process.

Although there is currently no review of capital expenditure requirement at the federal level, many states have certificate of need requirements for construction of health care facilities. Because state regulations vary, no specific discussion is provided regarding this process. Developers of projects with health care centers on site should contact the department of health and human resources in the pertinent state to determine whether the certificate of need regulation applies. If the state has such requirements, the developer should consult an expert in health planning and certificate of need regulation in that specific state.

Although the components or line items of the development budget for a retirement housing project will be similar to those of a multifamily housing project, many of the costs will be higher in order to address the specific needs of the residents and the additional services provided. For example, higher costs will be expected for construction costs, marketing costs, and start-up costs. The major cost components in the development budget are for land, land improvements, construction, development, and carrying charges.

A more detailed discussion of each of these classifications follows, as well as examples of development budgets for a retirement center and a health care center.

Land Costs. Such costs include the purchase price and all other costs incurred to acquire the land. Also included are any costs incurred during the holding period, between the time the land is purchased and the time it is placed in service. Additionally, any costs or expenses necessary to gain access, take possession, or put the land in its intended use are considered land costs. Costs that fall into this latter category include, but are not limited to the following:

Roads
Drainage
Land options

Water source

Inspection fees and permits

Soil engineering and testing fees

Necessary land grading, filling, clearing, or draining

Demolition of existing structures

Removal of buildings (less salvage value)

Any obligation assumed or payments made to discharge taxes, interest, or other expenses accrued at the time of purchase.

Land Improvements. Changes or additions to land that will deteriorate with the passage of time or use are land improvements; their cost includes all expenditures for labor, materials, and other costs associated with such improvements. Typical examples are sidewalks, paving, curbs, and sewer lines.

Construction Cost. All labor, materials, and other expenses to construct or acquire a permanent structure are considered construction costs. They include the cost of all structural and finish work, the installation of all furnishings and equipment, risk insurance, landscaping, and a contingency factor. Movable equipment, furniture, and fixtures may be included in this group or listed as separate line items. All fixed equipment and furnishings are part of the construction cost.

A developer could, for preliminary cost estimates, anticipate a $40 to $60 per-square-foot cost of construction for the residential space, and approximately $60 to $80 per-square-foot cost for the common or public areas.

Construction budgets need to include costs of the actual hardware for the facility for two categories. The first includes standardized items such as concrete, masonry, wood, plastic, insulation, doors, windows, glass, finishing, and accessories such as mailboxes. Items in the second category are generally found only in the retirement product; these include an emergency call system, left- or right-handed refrigerators, grab bars, easily operated blinds and draperies, community dining facilities, special equipment and furnishings, whirlpools, kitchen equipment, elevators, doors, security, spas, fixtures, phones, and grading.

Development Expenses. Fees and expenses other than the land and necessary construction costs are development expenses. These costs include, but are not limited to, the following:

Architectural fees	Advertising and publicity
Engineering fees	Lease-up expenses and site office
Consultant fees	costs
Financing charges	Certificate of need fees
Legal and accounting fees	Developer fees
Contractor's bonds	Start-up costs
Survey, permits, and title fees	Miscellaneous expenses

As a result of the longer fill-up periods, a retirement project will have higher advertising, marketing, lease-up, site office, and start-up costs than a standard multifamily housing facility.

Development costs are important because often items are overlooked or understated. Often developers who have not been involved with a retirement project understate the potential costs in determining if it makes sense to go any further with the project. Areas most often understated are the ones that would be considerably more than for a multifamily housing development.

Site identification is an involved process because of the consideration of various factors that will impact the success of the site for a retirement community. Such factors include location of hospitals, doctors, emergency and police services, nursing homes, shopping, and other items that would be included in a market criteria checklist.

Carrying Charges.   Such charges include the costs incurred during the construction period, including taxes and insurance during construction, loan interest on interim financing, and construction management.

The development budget is a line item listing of all the costs necessary to construct or acquire the facility broken out by major classification and by the timing of the expenditure. The latter item is necessary to predict the draw during the construction and lease-up period. The total of all the costs in the development budget provides an estimate of the amount of permanent financing required through either debt or equity financing. For entrance fee projects, a portion of the development cost may come from residents in the form of entrance fees.

Examples of development budgets for a rental retirement center, an entrance fee project, and a nursing home are provided in Tables 4-1 through 4-3.

TABLE 4-1. Development Budget for Rental Retirement Center

Description of costs			Months of Year			
	1	2	3	4	5	6
Land @ $6 per sq. ft.	2,090,880					
Equipment						
Furniture	6,667	6,667	6,667			
Fixtures						
Building @ $42 per sq. ft.	0	0	0	700,000	700,000	700,000
Construction mgmt.	10,000	10,000	10,000	10,000	10,000	10,000
Preop. consulting	15,000	15,000	15,000	15,000	15,000	15,000
Architecture and engineering	55,000					
Contingency	333	333	333	35,000	35,000	35,000
Marketing	25,000	25,000	25,000	25,000	25,000	25,000
Legal & accounting	13,333	13,333	13,333	13,333	13,333	13,333
Development fee	30,000	30,000	30,000	30,000	30,000	30,000
Origination fee	320,000					
Total monthly cost	2,966,213	100,333	100,333	828,333	828,333	828,333
Cumulative costs	2,966,213	3,066,547	3,166,880	3,995,213	4,823,547	5,651,880

Description of costs	12-Month total			Months of Year			
		13	14	15	16	17	18
Land @ $6 per sq. ft.	2,090,880						
Equipment							
Furniture	300,000	66,667	66,667	66,667	66,667	66,667	66,66
Fixtures							
Building @ $42 per sq. ft.	6,300,000	700,000	700,000	700,000			
Construction mgmt.	120,000	10,000	10,000	10,000	10,000	10,000	10,00
Preop. consulting	180,000						
Architecture and engineering	455,000						
Contingency	330,000	38,333	38,333	38,333	3,333	3,333	3,33
Marketing	300,000	25,500	25,500	25,500	25,500	25,500	25,50
Legal & accounting	86,000	1,000	1,000	1,000	1,000	1,000	1,00
Development fee	360,000	30,000	30,000	30,000	30,000		
Origination fee	320,000						
Total monthly cost	10,841,880	871,500	871,500	871,500	136,500	106,500	106,50
Cumulative costs	10,841,880	11,713,380	12,584,880	13,456,380	13,592,880	13,699,380	13,805,88

7	8	9	10	11	12	12-Month total
						2,090,880
46,667	46,667	46,667	46,667	46,667	46,667	300,000
700,000	700,000	700,000	700,000	700,000	700,000	6,300,000
10,000	10,000	10,000	10,000	10,000	10,000	120,000
15,000	15,000	15,000	15,000	15,000	15,000	180,000
						455,000
37,333	37,333	37,333	37,333	37,333	37,333	330,000
25,000	25,000	25,000	25,000	25,000	25,000	300,000
1,000	1,000	1,000	1,000	1,000	1,000	86,000
30,000	30,000	30,000	30,000	30,000	30,000	360,000
						320,000
865,000	865,000	865,000	865,000	865,000	865,000	10,841,880
6,516,880	7,381,880	8,246,880	9,111,880	9,976,880	10,841,880	10,841,880

19	20	21	22	23	24	Year 2 totals	24-Month total
						0	2,090,880
						400,000	700,000
						0	0
						2,100,000	8,400,000
						60,000	180,000
						0	180,000
						0	455,000
0	0	0	0	0	0	125,000	455,000
25,500	25,500	25,500	25,500	25,500	25,500	306,000	606,000
1,000	1,000	1,000	1,000	1,000	1,000	12,000	98,000
						120,000	480,000
						0	320,000
26,500	26,500	26,500	26,500	26,500	26,500	3,123,000	13,964,880
13,832,380	13,858,880	13,885,380	13,911,880	13,938,380	13,964,880		13,964,880

TABLE 4-2. Development Budget for a Continuing Care Retirement Community

			Months of Year 1			
Description	1	2	3	4	5	6
Costs						
Soil test & utility (water)		310,000				
Equipment: furniture, fixtures, & start-up						
Bldg/risk insurance	2,968,664	523,882	523,882	523,882	523,882	523,882
Landscaping						
Site development	955,767	955,767				
Professional fees (other)		400,000				
Architect fees	174,627	174,627				
Contingency	89,060	15,716	15,716	15,716	15,716	15,716
Marketing	30,000	30,000	30,000	30,000	30,000	50,000
Legal & accounting	40,000	0	0			
Other/start-up	3,335	3,335	3,335	3,335	3,335	3,335
Tax-exempt bond	1,884,000					
Operating capital	0					
Perm. origin. fee	0					
Working capital	0	0	0	0	0	0
Debt serv. reserve	3,209,890					
Total monthly cost	9,355,343	2,413,328	572,933	572,933	572,933	592,933
Cumulative costs	9,355,343	11,768,671	12,341,604	12,914,538	13,487,471	14,080,404
Bond proceeds	31,400,000					
Interest earned (7%)	0	128,594	113,816	109,688	105,536	101,359
Less interest payments (9.5%)		248,583	248,583	248,583	248,583	248,583
Net monthly cost	22,044,657	19,511,340	18,303,639	18,091,810	17,375,829	16,635,672
Number of occupied units		0	0	0	0	0
Occupancy (%)		0	0	0	0	0
Deposits	975,384	27,094	27,094	27,094	27,094	27,094
Less refunds						
Forfeited deposits						
Remainder	0	0	0	0	0	0
Total	975,384	27,094	27,094	27,094	27,094	27,094
Interest earned (7%)	0	5,690	5,881	6,073	6,267	6,461
Fees available	975,384	32,784	32,975	33,167	33,361	33,553
Cumulative	975,384	1,008,168	1,041,143	1,074,310	1,107,671	1,141,226

7	8	9	10	11	12	12-Month total
						310,000
						0
523,882	523,882	523,882	523,882	523,882	523,882	8,731,355
						0
						1,911,534
						400,000
						349,255
15,716	15,716	15,716	15,716	15,716	15,716	261,941
50,000	50,000	50,000	50,000	50,000	50,000	500,000
			20,000	20,000	10,000	90,000
3,335	3,335	3,335	3,335	3,335	3,335	40,020
						1,884,000
			0	0	0	0
					0	0
0	0	0	0	0	0	0
						3,209,890
592,933	592,933	592,933	612,933	612,933	602,933	17,688,004
14,673,338	15,266,271	15,859,204	16,472,138	17,085,071	17,688,304	17,688,004
97,041	92,699	88,331	83,937	79,401	74,339	1,075,240
248,583	248,583	248,583	248,583	248,583	248,583	2,734,417
15,891,196	15,142,378	14,389,192	13,611,612	12,829,497	12,052,819	12,052,819
0	0	0	0	0	0	0
0	0	0	0	0	0	0
27,094	27,094	27,094	27,094	27,094	27,094	1,273,418
					(191,013)	(191,013)
					52,400	52,400
0	0	0	0	0	0	0
27,094	27,094	27,094	27,094	27,094	(111,519)	1,134,805
6,657	6,854	7,052	7,251	7,452	7,653	73,291
33,751	33,948	34,148	34,345	34,546	(103,466)	1,208,097
1,174,977	1,208,925	1,243,072	1,277,417	1,311,962	1,208,097	

TABLE 4-2. (*Continued*)

Description	12-Month total	Months of Year 2					
		13	14	15	16	17	18
Costs							
Land & soil test	310,000						
Equipment: furniture, fixtures, & start-up	0					200,000	200,000
Bldg/risk insurance	8,731,365	523,882	523,882	523,882	523,882	523,882	523,882
Landscaping	0				193,041	193,041	193,041
Site development	1,911,534						
Professional fees	400,000						
Architect fees	349,255	139,410	139,410				
Contingency	261,941	15,716	15,716	15,716	15,716	15,716	15,716
Marketing	500,000	90,000	110,000	110,000	110,000	90,000	90,000
Legal & accounting	90,000						
Other/start-up	40,020	3,335	3,335	3,335	3,335	3,335	3,335
Origination fee	1,884,000						
Working capital							
Debt serv. reserve	3,209,890						
Total quarterly cost	17,688,004	772,343	792,343	652,933	845,975	1,025,975	1,025,975
Cumulative costs	17,688,004	18,460,347	19,252,691	19,305,624	20,751,599	21,777,573	22,803,548
Bond proceeds	31,400,000						
Interest earned (7%)	1,075,240	70,308	64,763	59,069	54,154	48,085	40,931
Less interest payments (9.5%)	2,731,417	248,583	248,583	248,583	248,583	248,583	248,583
Net monthly cost	12,052,819	11,102,200	10,225,037	9,283,589	8,243,185	7,016,712	5,783,085
Operational revenue & expenses							
Project 1 occupancy	0	0	0	0	0	0	0
Number of occupied units	0	0	0	0	0	0	0
Deposits	1,273,418	27,094	27,094	27,094	27,094	27,094	27,094
Less refunds	(191,013)						
Forfeited deposits	52,400						
Remainder	0	0	0	0	0	0	0
Total	1,134,805	27,094	27,094	27,094	27,094	27,094	27,094
Interest earned (7%)	73,291	7,047	7,248	7,447	7,648	7,851	8,055
Fees available	1,208,097	34,141	34,340	34,541	34,742	34,945	35,149
Cumulative	1,208,097	1,242,238	1,276,578	1,311,119	1,345,861	1,380,806	1,415,955

19	20	21	22	23	24	Year 2 totals	24-Month total
							310,000
			50,000	50,000	100,000	600,000	600,000
537,867	537,867	537,867	537,867	537,867	537,867	6,370,433	15,101,858
			93,625	93,625	93,625	860,000	450,000
						0	1,911,534
						0	400,000
						278,820	628,074
16,136	16,136	16,136	16,136	16,136	16,136	191,115	453,056
20,000	80,000					700,000	1,200,000
						0	90,000
3,335	4,643					27,988	68,008
						0	1,884,000
	500,000					500,000	500,000
	0					0	3,209,890
577,338	1,138,646	554,003	697,628	697,628	747,628	9,528,416	27,216,420
23,380,336	24,519,532	25,073,535	25,771,163	26,468,792	27,216,420		27,216,420
33,735	29,114	21,191	16,633	11,211	5,756	454,949	1,530,189
248,583	248,583	248,583	248,583	248,583	248,583	2,983,000	5,717,417
4,990,898	3,632,783	2,851,387	1,921,809	986,808	(3,648)		(3,648)
13	25	30	35	40	45	45	45
31	60	72	84	96	108	108	108
40,641	40,641	40,641	40,641	40,641	40,641	406,410	1,679,828
					(103,296)	(103,296)	(294,309)
					14,300	14,300	66,700
1,887,205	1,742,036	725,848	725,848	725,848	725,848	6,532,634	6,532,634
1,927,846	1,782,677	766,489	766,489	766,489	677,493	6,850,048	7,984,854
8,260	19,554	30,067	34,713	39,387	44,088	221,362	294,654
1,936,106	1,802,231	796,556	801,203	805,878	721,581	7,071,411	8,279,508
3,352,061	5,154,292	5,950,848	6,752,050	7,557,926	8,279,508		

TABLE 4-3. Development Budget for a Nursing Home

				Months of Year 1		
Description	1	2	3	4	5	6
Land						
Land Improvements	150,000					
Building construction		176,000	176,000	176,000	176,000	176,000
Movable equipment						
Consultants	50,000	11,818	11,818	11,818	11,818	11,818
Architects	77,440					
Other professional fees	50,000					
Marketing						
Contingency	0	8,800	8,800	8,800	8,800	8,800
Legal & accounting	25,000	10,000				
Start-up						
Perm. origin. fee						
Origin. fee	75,000					
Application fee	7,500					
Interim financing	0	3,443	5,106	6,703	8,313	9,935
Monthly totals	434,940	210,061	201,724	203,321	204,931	206,553
Cumulative	434,940	645,001	846,726	1,050,047	1,254,978	1,461,532

Operating Budget.   Operating budgets probably involve the most subjective evaluations made by a developer or the preparer of financial feasibility studies throughout the development process. The operating budget has major ramifications on the viability of a development. The operating budget is broken down into revenue assumptions and expense assumptions.

Developing a retirement community is not like developing a multifamily project; therefore, rent premiums for the most part do not exist. They are unrealistic in a retirement market. Rent level (the total monthly charge necessary to cover debt service and operating costs as well as profit) should be kept to no more than approximately 50 percent of the average annual elderly household expenditure, if possible. The market has experienced as high as 70 percent of the average annual elderly household income, but the closer the amount is to 50 percent of the elderly household income, the broader the market will be, and the easier it will be to market the product.

It is also suggested that the monthly charge for rent should be not more than 105 percent of the highest priced development in a given market area. Rent increases should not occur more often than once a year, even if month-to-month leases are involved in the project. If the

7	8	9	10	11	12	Total
						150,000
176,000	176,000	176,000	176,000	176,000	176,000	1,936,000
			100,000	100,000	200,000	400,000
11,818	11,818	11,818	11,818	11,818	11,818	180,000
						77,440
						50,000
		10,000	10,000	20,000	20,000	60,000
8,800	8,800	8,800	13,800	13,800	18,800	116,800
					25,000	60,000
			5,000	5,000	5,000	15,000
						75,000
						7,500
11,570	13,219	14,880	16,633	19,272	22,010	131,085
208,189	209,837	221,498	333,252	345,890	478,628	3,258,825
1,669,720	1,879,557	2,101,055	2,434,307	2,780,197	3,258,825	

leases are more than one year in duration, increases should be considered on an annual basis and tied to a national or regional consumer price index.

It is important to build in a sufficient amount of time in the operating budget for reaching 95 percent occupancy. The typical 200-unit project usually requires lease-up contingency for a cash shortfall for 18 to 36 months. It would not be inappropriate to anticipate another 50 percent to be more conservative in anticipating cash flow requirements of a developer.

A retirement housing facility has significantly higher operating costs as well as significantly higher revenues than a standard multifamily housing facility. The primary areas of additional revenues and costs are for the provision of support services. The level of both the revenue and the costs will be a function of the services offered by the facility. Another factor affecting the revenues and costs will be the way residents pay for the services—either on an à la carte basis or as part of a service package.

A retirement housing facility will have additional revenue from service income either through an additional monthly charge for purchasing a package of services, or from the purchase of individual services by residents. The additional operating costs for the facility will arise from the provision of such services as food service, social services or resident services, general and administrative costs, housekeeping and laundry, maintenance, health care, and depreciation.

The items of cost for the food service department include personnel, raw food, utilities, china and glassware, disposables, and other miscellaneous food services expenses. Utility costs may be included either in the departmental budgets or in a separate utility budget.

The social services or resident services department incurs costs for personnel, supplies, transportation, office supplies, health care professionals, and miscellaneous expenses.

General and administrative costs are personnel, advertising and marketing, security, insurance, property taxes, travel and entertainment, professional dues and publications, training and education, office supplies, consultants, management fees, telephone, and miscellaneous expenses.

Housekeeping expenses include personnel, cleaning supplies, small tools, laundry supplies, and miscellaneous expenses.

Maintenance department costs are personnel, supplies, small tools, landscaping, pool maintenance, garbage collection, exterminating, elevator maintenance, equipment maintenance contracts, and miscellaneous expenses.

Facilities with health care centers on-site incur additional expenses for the operation of the health care center. Generally the health care center has a separate budget with all the previously mentioned departments as well as departmental expenses for nursing care, physical therapy, occupational therapy, activity services, medical records, and all other costs associated with the operation of the center.

The facility will also have depreciation expense of the building, furniture and equipment, land improvements, and any other depreciable items. However, depreciation is an expense that does not require the payment of cash and is therefore not included in the cash operating expenses for the cash flow analysis. The facility should, however, establish a reserve for repairs and replacement that is funded on a regular basis.

Examples of the operating budgets for a rental retirement facility without a nursing home are provided in Tables 4-4 and 4-5.

The use of rules of thumb in developing operating budgets is extremely dangerous because both the service revenue and the operating cash are a function of the quantity and quality of the services offered and the packaging of the services, either bundled or unbundled.

During the lease-up phase of operations the facility will experience various levels of occupancy and consequently fluctuating demands for

**TABLE 4-4. Operating Budget for Rental Retirement Facility—
Variable Cost Summary**

Occupancy	20	46	50	75	95
Number of apartments	40	93	101	152	192
Food service	76,054	174,925	190,136	285,204	361,258
Social service	7,164	16,478	27,088	45,176	57,224
General and adminis-trative	40,537	93,235	101,342	152,013	192,550
Housekeeping	20,766	47,761	51,914	77,871	98,637
Maintenance	16,543	38,049	41,358	62,037	78,580
Total variable cost	161,064	370,448	411,838	622,302	788,249

services. This will result in different levels of revenues and operating
costs. The differing levels of operating costs occur because of their
uneven behavior. Some costs, such as the administrator's salary, are
the same regardless of the occupancy level. Others, such as raw food
costs or housekeeping labor costs, will vary directly with occupancy.

The classification of operating costs by behavior into either fixed
costs, which remain the same regardless of the level of occupancy, and
variable costs, which vary directly with occupancy, will facilitate the
preparation of the operating budget during the start up phase.

Table 4-6 provides an example of the food service department budget
in the fixed and variable format.

Some of the difficulty in anticipating operating costs arises because
the absorption rate that marketing will be able to obtain is unknown,
as well as the number of residents who will utilize meals, health care,
and extra housekeeping, once they are on-site. The operating budget
is the most subjective element in forecasting for a retirement project.

**TABLE 4-5. Operating Budget for Rental Retirement Facility—
Fixed Cost Summary**

Occupancy	20	46	50	75	95
Number of apartments	40	93	101	152	192
Food service	53,260	53,260	53,260	53,260	53,260
Social service	81,041	81,041	81,041	81,041	81,041
General and adminis-trative	364,812	364,812	386,812	386,812	386,812
Housekeeping	17,181	17,181	17,181	17,181	17,181
Maintenance	20,862	20,862	20,862	20,862	20,862
Total fixed cost	537,159	537,159	559,157	559,157	559,157
Total variable cost	161,064	370,448	411,838	622,302	788,249
Total cost	698,221	907,605	970,995	1,181,459	1,347,406

TABLE 4-6. Food Service Budget for Rental Retirement Center—Annual Costs

Occupancy	20	46	50	75	95
Fixed Cost					
Cook	24,053	24,053	24,053	24,053	24,053
Dining rm. mgr.	29,207	29,207	29,207	29,207	29,207
Total fixed cost	$53,260	$53,260	$53,260	$53,260	$53,260
Variable Cost					
Consultant/dietician	$1,053	$2,421	$2,632	$3,947	$5,000
Purchased services	0	0	0	0	0
Utilities	2,947	6,779	7,368	11,053	14,000
Raw food	$50,689	$116,586	$126,723	$190,085	$240,775
Personnel	17,715	40,745	44,289	66,433	84,148
China and glass	1,622	3,731	4,055	6,083	7,705
Disposables	1,014	2,332	2,534	3,802	4,815
Other	1,014	2,332	2,534	3,802	4,815
Total variable cost	$76,054	$174,925	$190,136	$285,204	$361,258
Total food service cost	$129,315	$228,186	$243,397	$338,465	$414,519

Further subjective elements, particularly for a CCRC, are age, unit occupancy (single or double), gender, and actuarial statistics in determining how many will need health care. Actuarial projections are an art as well as a science, and many communities have had financial troubles because the forecasts have missed their marks.

If a nursing facility is part of a CCRC, some items may generate extra income, such as oxygen; medication; wheelchairs; walkers; second and third meals; and physical, occupational, speech, and hearing therapy. The standard rate may or may not include the listed items; if not, the number of residents in the nursing facilities who will need ancillary services must be estimated.

Cash Flow Analysis. Once the development budget and the operating budget have been prepared, the next step is the cash flow analysis. During the construction and lease-up phase, the cash flow analysis should be prepared on a monthly basis. This is necessary in order to project the cash draw necessary during the construction and lease-up phase. Once stable occupancy has been achieved, the cash flow projections can be prepared on an annual basis. Most financial feasibility studies will include an annual cash flow analysis for a period of 5 to 10 years after lease-up.

The components of the cash flow analysis are as follows:

Cash draw for the development budget
Cumulative cash draw for the development budget
Cash flow from operations
Cash reserve requirements
Cash flow after reserve requirements
Cumulative cash flow after reserve requirements

Entrance fee projects will also include line items for entrance fees collected, entrance fees refunded, entrance fees forfeited, and income from investment of entrance fees.

Cash Draw for the Development Budget. The cash draw for the development budget represents the expected monthly cash requirements for development costs. Some development costs will have to be paid at the beginning of the project or at certain points during the project, whereas others will be incurred evenly throughout the construction phase.

The following development costs require cash payments during the first three to six months of the project:

Land and soil tests
Architectural, engineering, and developer fees
Contractor's bonds
Survey, permits, title, and origination fees
Certificate of need fees
Legal and accounting fees
Consulting fees for market and financial feasibility studies

Development costs requiring approximately even cash payments throughout the construction period include construction costs, construction management, preoperating consulting, marketing and advertising, and interim financing cost.

Development cost expenditures during the latter months of the construction period include furniture and equipment, start-up costs, permanent origination fee, and legal and accounting fees (these fees occur at the beginning and the end of the construction phase).

Cash Flow from Operations. The second section of the cash flow analysis is the operational revenue and expense cash flow. This section will have no dollar amounts until the construction of the facility is near completion; the amounts will increase beginning with the move-in phase. The components of this section include the occupancy of the facility in units and as a percent, the monthly revenue either in total or by source, the cash operating costs, and the net cash flow from operations.

Cash Reserve Requirements. The final section of the cash flow analysis is the reserve requirements section. The individual reserve requirements should be listed separately. Retirement facilities will generally have reserve requirements for debt service, repairs and replacement, future health care, refunds of entrance fees, and state mandated reserves.

The debt service reserve is generally a requirement of the bond indenture, obligating the borrower to establish a debt service reserve fund equal to the highest annual debt service payment during the life of the bond. This amount is generally funded from the bond proceeds. Additionally, the bond indenture and/or state regulations may require the funding of a reserve for repairs and replacement of the facility and equipment. Whether a legal requirement exists or not, the prudent management of a facility necessitates the establishment of a fund to provide for repairs and replacement of the building and equipment.

Facilities with health care centers on-site need to make provisions for the health care needs of the residents. For a life care center, the specific obligations of the facility are stated in the resident contract. For a rental facility with a health care center on-site, some provision needs to be made for residents who are unable to pay for their long-term health care needs. The average private pay nursing home resident exhausts his individual resources within 12 to 14 weeks of entering a nursing home. The facility will be responsible for providing the nursing home care until other means can be determined.

Many entrance fee arrangements specify the refunding of a portion of the fee under the terms of the contract. A reserve should be established for such refunds. The level of the reserve will be a function of the refundable amount of the entrance fee and the estimated number of residents likely to withdraw from the facility during the refund period.

State regulation of CCRCs varies. Some states require reserves to insure the financial viability of the facility or to assure the health care needs of residents. Developers and owners should contact the appropriate governmental department of the state to determine what, if any, reserves are required by law.

Operating Reserves.   More and more states require developers to have operating reserves before they can market and build CCRCs, and some state legislatures are considering mandatory reserves for rental communities. Cash flow from operations, less the total sum of all other reserve requirements, equals the net cash flow required for the month or year. The cash flow analysis also includes a cumulative cash flow calculation.

The operating reserve can range from one twelfth of the annual operating amount to the amount for an entire year. The reserve ensures that the facility will have sufficient funds to cover unanticipated operating costs or a shortfall if the occupancy rate runs below the anticipated schedule. The developer should consider establishing reserves for one year, whether mandatory or not.

Benevolent Reserve.   This reserve is often required by states for residents of CCRCs. It states that if residents can no longer pay the monthly assessments, they do not have to relocate because they already have paid a substantial amount in entrance fees. If, for example, a resident has financial difficulty and can no longer afford the monthly assessment, this reserve fund would cover the monthly amount.

The importance of establishing and funding adequate reserves cannot be overstated, even if they are not required in the state where a project is to be located.

PRO FORMAS

An essential component of the financial feasibility study, pro forma statements are projected income statements and balance sheets based on expected future transactions rather than on past occurrences. The usual pro forma statements are the statement of revenues and expenses, or income statement; the statement of financial position, or balance sheet; and the statement of cash flows.

Statements of projected revenues and expenses for at least a five-year period are included in the financial feasibility study. They are presented on an annual basis and generally include such statistical information as units available and occupancy rates, as well as projected annual revenues and expenses. The projection should cover the number of years necessary to include five years at stable occupancy. Table

TABLE 4-7. Income Statement for a CCRC ($ Thousands)

	Year 1	Year 2	Year 3	Year 4	Year 5
Earned entrance fees	700	1,400	1,470	1,544	1,621
Monthly maintenance	2,000	2,900	3,045	3,197	3,357
Nursing care	1,000	1,400	1,470	1,544	1,621
Ancillary services	200	300	315	331	347
Total revenue	3,900	6,000	6,300	6,615	6,946
Operating expenses	2,925	3,300	3,465	3,638	3,820
Operating income	975	2,700	2,835	2,977	3,126

4-7 is an example of projected revenues and expenses for an entrance fee project (CCRC); Table 4-8 depicts a rental project.

The financial feasibility study also includes the statement of financial position, or balance sheet, listing the projected assets, liabilities, and equity for the project at the end of the fiscal year. The only differences between the balance sheet for a rental project versus that for a CCRC project are that the CCRC balance sheet includes an escrow fund under assets and unearned entrance fees under liabilities. Projected statements of financial position are provided for the same time period as the statements of revenues and expense. Table 4-9 is an example of such a statement for an entrance fee project.

Statements of projected cash flow are also in the financial feasibility study. This statement lists the sources of cash and the applications or uses of cash on an annual basis. Statements of projected cash flow cover the same time period as the statements of revenues and expenses and the statements of financial position. An example of the projected statement of cash flow for an entrance fee project is shown in Table 4-10.

TABLE 4-8. Income Statement for a Rental Project

	Year 1	Year 2	Year 3	Year 4	Year 5
Base rent	1,800	3,000	3,150	3,308	3,473
Service income	1,500	2,500	2,625	2,756	2,894
Nursing care	1,000	1,400	1,470	1,544	1,621
Ancillary services	200	300	315	331	347
Total revenue	4,500	7,200	7,560	7,938	8,335
Operating expenses	3,375	3,960	4,158	4,366	4,584
Operating income	1,125	3,240	3,402	3,572	3,751

TABLE 4-9. Balance Sheet for a CCRC

Current Assets
  Cash
  Accounts receivable
  Raw food inventory
  Prepaid insurance
  Escrow account
Total Current Assets

Property and Equipment
  Building
  Accum depr-bldg
  Equipment and furniture
  Accum depr-equip
  Land improvements
  Land
Total Property and Equipment
    Total Assets

Liabilities and Equity
Current Liabilities
  Accounts payable
  Wages payable
  Notes payable
  Interest payable
  Security deposits payable
  Taxes payable
Total Current Liabilities

Long-term Liabilities
  Bonds payable
  Unearned entrance fees
Total Liabilities

Stockholders' Equity
  Paid in capital
  Retained earnings
Total Stockholders' Equity
    Total Liabilities and Stockholders' Equity

Ratio Analysis. A number of key ratios are used in evaluating the financial viability of a retirement housing project. These ratios are of interest to the creditors in measuring the facility's capacity to meet its debt requirements as they come due, and to the investors in evaluating the expected return on their investments. The most commonly

TABLE 4-10. Cash Flow Statement for a CCRC—Year 4

Revenue & Expenses	Year 3 Totals	37	38	39	40	41	42
				Months of Year 4			
Project 1 occupancy (%)		38	42	46	50	54	58
Number of occupied units		120	131	144	156	168	181
Deposits	1,679,828	33,868	33,868	33,868	33,868	33,868	33,868
Less: Refunds	(294,309)						
Forfeited deposits	66,700						
Remainder	6,532,634	725,848	667,780	754,882	754,882	754,882	754,882
Total	7,984,854	759,716	701,648	788,750	788,750	788,750	788,750
Interest earned (7%)	294,654	48,297	53,011	57,413	62,349	67,313	72,307
Fees available	8,279,508	808,013	754,658	846,162	851,098	856,063	861,057
Cumulative		9,087,520	9,842,179	10,688,341	11,539,440	12,395,503	13,256,560
Monthly revenue, 1.312 per unit	592,186	157,496	171,986	188,365	204,745	221,125	237,504
Less operating cost	613,261	112,860	115,485	118,451	121,418	124,385	127,352
Less management fee	29,609	7,875	8,599	9,418	10,237	11,056	11,875
Net cash flow before depreciation	(50,684)	36,761	47,902	60,496	73,090	85,683	98,277
Interest expense @ 9.5% 31,400,000							
Cash flow after debt serv.	(50,684)	36,761	47,902	60,496	73,090	85,683	98,277
Cumulative	(50,684)	(13,923)	33,979	94,474	167,564	253,247	351,524

used ratios are times interest earned, debt service coverage, break-even point, margin of safety, internal rate of return, and cash on cash.

Times Interest Earned.   The times interest earned ratio measures the ability of the project to meet its interest obligations. The higher the times interest earned ratio, the greater the probability of the project being able to make interest payments as they come due. The times interest earned ratio is calculated by dividing the earnings (before interest expense and income tax expense) by the annual interest expense. Because interest expense is tax deductible, the calculation uses earnings before payment of income tax.

Debt Service Coverage.   The debt service coverage ratio measures the ability of the project to generate sufficient cash to make the annual debt service payments as they come due. The debt service payment includes both the principal and the interest payment. Again, the higher the debt service coverage ratio, the lower the risk of the project not being able to make its debt service payments. The debt service coverage

43	44	45	46	47	48	Year 4 Summary	Cumulative Summary
62	66	70	74	78	82		
193	206	218	231	243	256		
33,838	33,868	33,868	33,868	33,868	33,868	406,410	2,086,238
						0	(294,309)
						0	66,700
754,882	754,882	754,882	754,882	754,882	754,882	8,942,451	15,475,085
788,750	788,750	788,750	788,750	788,750	788,750	9,348,861	17,333,714
77,330	82,382	87,464	92,575	97,716	102,887	901,043	1,195,697
866,080	871,132	876,213	881,325	886,466	891,637	10,249,904	18,529,411
14,122,639	14,993,771	15,869,984	16,751,309	17,637,775	18,529,411		
253,884	270,263	286,643	303,023	319,402	335,782	2,950,218	3,542,403
130,319	133,285	136,252	139,219	142,186	145,153	1,546,365	2,159,626
12,694	13,513	14,332	15,151	15,970	16,789	147,511	177,120
110,871	123,465	136,059	148,652	161,246	173,840	1,256,342	1,205,657
						0	0
110,871	123,465	136,059	148,652	161,246	173,840	1,256,342	1,205,657
462,395	585,860	721,919	870,571	1,031,817	1,205,657		1,205,657

ratio is calculated by dividing the annual cash flow and interest expense by the annual debt service required payment (annual payment for both principal and interest).

Break-even Point. The break-even point is the occupancy level necessary to have the revenue generated from the project cover both the fixed cost of the project and the variable cost of the facility at that level of occupancy. At all levels of occupancy less than the break-even occupancy, the facility will lose money. At all occupancy levels greater than the break-even occupancy level, it will earn a profit. The break-even point is calculated by dividing the annual fixed cost of the facility by the difference between the average revenue per unit and the variable cost per unit. The break-even point is generally expressed as a percent occupancy of the facility.

The break-even point is a function of the relationship of fixed costs to variable costs. As a general rule, the larger the percentage of fixed cost of the total cost of the facility, the higher will be the break-even point. The reverse is also true. The higher the percentage of the total costs that are variable, the lower the break-even occupancy. Thus, the break-even occupancy of the facility can be lower by making greater use of variable costs as opposed to fixed costs.

Margin of Safety. The margin of safety is a measure of the risk of the investment or loan. The lower the margin, the greater the risk of the project not being successful. The margin of safety, which is the difference between the expected stable occupancy level and the break-even level of occupancy, measures how much occupancy can decrease without the project incurring a loss. This margin is a function of the expected stable occupancy level and the break-even occupancy level. Therefore, the relationship between the facility's level of fixed cost and variable cost is important.

Internal Rate of Return. Of particular interest to investors is the internal rate of return of the project, that is, the discount rate that equates the net present value of a stream of cash flows, including the initial cash outflow, to zero. The internal rate of return represents the true interest yield of the project. In evaluating investment opportunities, investors compare the internal rate of return of specific projects to the rate of return available on other projects of similar risk. The project with the highest relative internal rate of return is chosen for investment. The required rate of return by an investor is a function of the risk of the project as well as the cost of capital to the investor.

Cash on Cash. The cash on cash return before taxes often ranges between 8 and 15 percent. Cash on cash measurement is arrived at by dividing income before taxes by the amount of investment capital injected by a developer or investor. By way of example, if the before-tax profit from a retirement community equals $500,000 and the amount of equity invested by a developer equals $5 million, the cash on cash return to the developer would be 10 percent. However, projects have been developed with a cash on cash return of as low as 3 percent and as high as 20 percent.

CRITERIA FOR GO/NO-GO DECISIONS

The final decision whether or not to proceed with the development of the retirement housing facility will be based on an evaluation of the project's security as measured by ratio analysis, the complete demand study, the experience and strength of the management team, and the comparability of the financial feasibility study to studies of similar facilities.

In the ratio analysis, the developer or lender is looking for a break-even point of 65 to 70 percent once the project is up and running. Debt service coverage of at least 1.2 times and preferably 1.3 will be expected. The internal rate of return looked for will depend on the location of the facility and the risk of the project. The developer or lender will generally expect a higher internal rate of return for a retirement housing facility than for an office building due to the additional risk involved.

For developers who have had successful experience with retirement communities, lenders will normally require the developer to inject 20 percent equity. For developers without a proven record, an equity position of up to 40 percent may be necessary.

SELECTING A FINANCIAL FEASIBILITY CONSULTANT

When selecting a financial feasibility consultant, the development team should evaluate the reputation, experience, and qualifications of the consulting firm. The reputation of the firm should be analyzed in terms of previous studies performed for retirement housing facilities. References should be obtained from clients who have successfully developed similar projects. Questions need to be answered regarding the individual who will actually be preparing the study. What experience and training does the individual have in the areas of real estate development, health care, and the elderly?

CHAPTER SUMMARY

Financial forecasts attempt to demonstrate a project's financial viability as simply as possible, even though many would say after reading a report that it is anything but simple to follow. Financial feasibility studies do not have to be difficult in an attempt to impress the reader. The financial analysis should show whether there is sufficient cash flow to provide for the development costs, including construction expenses, initial operating losses during fill-up, operating costs, debt service, reserve requirements imposed by debt agreements or other state requirements, and adequate return to the sponsor or the developer.

CHAPTER 5

SURVIVING THE MINEFIELD: LEGAL IMPLICATIONS IN THE DEVELOPMENT OF RETIREMENT HOUSING PROJECTS

KEITH D. KIRSCHBRAUN

INTRODUCTION

A retirement community requires substantial capital investment, the devotion of considerable time and effort, and carries with it significant risk to the developer. The risk associated with the retirement housing project can be managed by appropriate planning. The developer increases the likelihood of a successful community by plotting a course through the minefield of issues and problems involved in retirement housing before the project is ever actually developed.

This chapter identifies certain legal issues that should be considered in the initial planning phase of the retirement community project. The issues addressed include general legal considerations in the organization of retirement housing ventures, unique considerations in business relationships involving tax-exempt and for-profit entities, and liability considerations in the organization and operation of the community. It is impossible to address all of the legal considerations in the development of such a project. For example, the chapter will only tangentially refer to the tax issues that must be considered. However, the goal is to provide the developer with insight into the myriad legal issues likely to be confronted.

ORGANIZATION OF RETIREMENT HOUSING VENTURES

The development of a retirement housing project should not precede consideration of the legal issues that consistently arise in such an undertaking. The organization of the development entity itself, zoning considerations, the regulatory implications of providing health care or other assistance to elderly residents, and liability considerations are among the various legal issues that should be analyzed before development so as to effectuate the goals of the participants. If these issues are not addressed at an early phase in the project, adjustments to the legal structure and physical project may have to be made at substantial cost, or the project may no longer be feasible.

This section will address certain legal considerations in the development of a retirement housing project. By necessity, the analysis will focus on a limited number of issues in this complex area. Generalizations are difficult when so many of the issues involve the laws of 50 states; however, the discussion in this section will attempt to provide insight into select legal issues in retirement housing.

Creation of a Development Entity.   Although numerous factors should be considered in the selection of the legal entity for development of the project, this discussion will focus on the impact of risk and control in the decision-making process. The impact of federal and state securities laws will also be briefly addressed.

Basic Legal Structures.   There are three basic legal structures that may be utilized for a development entity involving the ownership of a retirement housing project: a general partnership, a limited partnership, and a corporation.

Most states have adopted the Uniform Partnership Act (UPA) to govern general partnerships. Pursuant to the UPA, a partnership is an association of two or more persons to carry on as co-owners a business for profit.[1] All partners in a general partnership are general partners and have the right to participate in management decisions.[2] The partnership agreement, however, may delegate certain of the day-to-day management decisions of the partnership to a managing general partner. As a general rule, all partners are able to bind a partnership within the course of partnership business. However, a partner who

[1] Uniform Partnership Act § 6 (1914).
[2] *Id.* § 18.

lacks authority to act for the partnership does not bind the partnership through his or her actions if the person being dealt with knows that the partner lacks such authority.[3]

Although the general partnership provides a mechanism for equal control over the retirement housing venture, it also requires the participating partners to assume the risk. All partners are jointly and severally liable for wrongful acts or omissions of any partner made in the ordinary course of business.[4] Joint and several liability also extends to breaches of trust by a partner. Pursuant to joint and several liability, a partner may be sued personally and individually for the entire partnership liability arising from such acts. Partners are jointly liable for all the debts and obligations of the partnership.[5]

The transfer of a partner's interest to another does not, absent agreement of the other partners, entitle the assignee to participate in management of the partnership, but merely entitles him or her to the profits from that interest.[6] A general partner's share in profits is determined by the partnership agreement.

In contrast to the general partnership, a limited partnership permits apportionment of management and risk based on the participant's desired level of involvement. Unlike general partnership statutes, limited partnership statutes often vary significantly.

The Revised Uniform Limited Partnership Act (RULPA), although not as widely followed as the UPA, provides a basis for comparison. The RULPA provides that a limited partnership involves two or more persons, with one or more general partners and one or more limited partners.[7] The general partner or general partners are responsible for the operations of the business. A limited partner does not exercise such control. In fact, if the limited partner becomes involved in the control of the business, he or she may become liable as a general partner.[8] In general, a limited partner is not personally liable for partnership debts and obligations beyond the amount of the limited partner's contributions. Thus, although the limited partner is not able to exercise a coequal right of management with the general partners, he or she is able to avoid the full scope of liability of a general partner.

A limited partner's interest is assignable to the extent permitted by

---

[3]*Id.* § 9.
[4]*Id.* § 15(a).
[5]*Id.* § 15(b).
[6]*Id.* § 27.
[7]Revised Uniform Limited Partnership Act § 101 (1976) (as amended in 1985).
[8]*Id.* § 303.

the partnership agreement.[9] The limited partner's share in partnership profits is governed by the partnership agreement.

If the only consideration involved in structuring the organization of a development entity venture were liability, the corporation would almost invariably provide the best shield from liability for all participants. A corporation may be organized on either a for-profit or nonprofit basis pursuant to state law.

A for-profit corporation is owned by its shareholders. The shareholder's ownership interest is not an interest in the corporation's assets themselves; instead, it is a derivative ownership of assets through the ownership of corporate stock. That stock is generally transferable, although restrictions may be placed on transferability.[10] Shareholders participate in corporate profits through dividends paid on a per share basis. A nonprofit corporation is not typically owned by anyone, although control over its activities may be vested in members of the corporation. Members are typically not entitled to share in profits of a nonprofit corporation and may be prohibited from such participation by state law.

A for-profit corporation that maintains its corporate identity will generally limit the shareholder's risk to his or her investment in the corporation. The corporation must maintain its identity as a distinct "person" and not function as the alter ego of any individual involved in the corporation. If that identity is not maintained, the shareholders risk possible piercing of the corporate veil and individual liability. A shareholder in a properly maintained corporate entity will generally not be held liable for the debts and obligations of the corporation.[11] However, this characteristic of a corporation is applied in varying degrees depending on the state. A nonprofit corporation should also be careful to maintain its corporate identity in order to insulate its members from similar liability risks.

Management of a corporation is typically vested in a board of directors.[12] Shareholders of a for-profit corporation may indirectly participate in the management of a corporation through the ability to vote for directors.[13] Members of a nonprofit corporation may be entitled to exercise similar control. Therefore, although day-to-day management is vested in the board of directors, the shareholders or members may maintain the authority to change that management if it proves to be unsatisfactory.

[9]*Id.* § 702.
[10]Revised Model Business Corp. Act § 6.27 (1984).
[11]*Id.* § 6.22.
[12]*Id.* § 8.01.
[13]*Id.* § 8.03.

If corporate organization is chosen for the development entity, the developer will usually choose a for-profit corporation, rather than a nonprofit corporation. The rationale for this is fairly straightforward. The mere creation of a nonprofit corporation pursuant to state law does not entitle the corporation to federal income tax exemption or, in most instances, state tax exemption. Tax exemptions usually require further qualification based on organizational and operational requirements designed to insure dedication of the organization to specific charitable purposes. These requirements will be further discussed later in this chapter. Unless the developer intends to dedicate the assets of the organization to a charitable purpose, the for-profit corporation should generally be utilized.

In structuring a retirement housing project, different considerations may affect the choice of legal entity. The choice will vary from project to project depending on the goals of the particular participants. This reflection of the participants' goals can be illustrated by the following example.

Mr. Jones is an apartment developer who is about to enter into his first retirement housing venture. The retirement community will be a rental project that will not require the payment of an entrance fee, but will provide a limited package of services in addition to the apartment unit itself, such as laundry, housekeeping, and an optional meal package. Assume that in the first instance, Mr. Jones's primary goals are to obtain additional investors and maintain control over the developing entity. Based on these assumptions, Mr. Jones's attorney may suggest the use of a limited partnership in order to obtain capital from investors who in return obtain interests as limited partners. If Mr. Jones already controls an adequately capitalized development company he may wish to use the company to serve as general partner of the limited partnership. The corporation may provide Mr. Jones with some insulation against personal liability as a general partner in the limited partnership. Through this mechanism, Mr. Jones is able to control the partnership as general partner, and the limited partners are able to participate as investors with limited risk. Although recent changes in the tax laws have reduced the tax benefits available through investing in partnerships, the partnership may further particular investors' goals by providing them with the mechanism to obtain qualifying tax deductions, because a partnership is treated for tax purposes as a pass-through entity.

Assume in the second instance, that Mr. Jones desires to build a similar project, but this time with different goals. He is primarily concerned with limiting the liability of all of the participants in the venture but still wishes to have the development entity primarily responsible for operating the retirement community. Mr. Jones's attorney may in this instance suggest that a corporation be established as the development entity in which Mr. Jones and his associates would participate as shareholders. If the number of participants is limited and involves only individuals as investors, the attorney may also consider the feasibility of filing for Subchapter S status[14] with the Internal Revenue Service in order that the shareholders may obtain tax results similar in many ways to those of a partnership.

Finally, in the third instance, assume that Mr. Jones has the same goals as in the first example, but has the additional goal of limiting the involvement of the limited partnership in the actual operation of the retirement community. Mr. Jones wishes to permit a few select associates to participate with him in the development of a management entity to operate this prospective retirement community and other retirement communities. Because in this instance the management entity is not anticipated to provide any tax benefits to the individual investors, and management services often involve significant risk of liability, Mr. Jones's attorney suggests that he utilize a management corporation to contract with the limited partnership for management of the community.

Whether participating in the development of a relatively simple rental project without an entrance fee, or the development of a continuing care retirement community offering the full range of services to the elderly, the individual goals of the participants must be analyzed in determining an effective legal structure. The failure to recognize individual goals in favor of a cookie-cutter approach to organization may deprive the participants of benefits that could otherwise be obtained.

Securities Implications.   The sale of stock in a corporation, interests in a limited partnership, or any other security, must comply with federal and state securities laws. The development of retirement housing communities often involves securities implications.[15] The developer typi-

---

[14]26 U.S.C. §§ 1361–1379 (1982 & Supp. II 1984, Supp. III 1985, Supp. IV 1986).

[15]Although this particular section addresses implications in the formation of the development entity itself, it is also important to note that the Interstate Land Sales Full Disclosure Act of 1968 provides a number of disclosure and recordation requirements for sales of certain types of land. The Interstate Land Sales Act was designed to curb abuses in the sale of undeveloped land to purchasers in other states. Similar to the application of the securities laws, there are exemptions to the applicability of the Interstate Land Sales Act itself and to the application of registration and disclosure requirements provided therein. 15 U.S.C. §§ 1701–1720 (1982 & Supp. II 1984, Supp. IV 1986).

cally seeks the infusion of outside capital in order to provide sufficient resources for the project and to reduce the developer's own dedication of funds. If the investors lack control over the project, the interest purchased may well be considered an investment contract and, therefore, a security.[16]

The Federal Securities Act of 1933 (the Act) was designed to prohibit fraud by requiring that all relevant information be disclosed to a prospective investor. This disclosure philosophy is implemented through the requirement that the distribution of securities be registered. The Act makes it unlawful to use interstate commerce or the mails to sell certain securities unless the sales have been registered or unless there is an available exemption from registration.[17]

The Securities and Exchange Commission has promulgated various registration statement forms on which to register securities transactions. Under the Act, the issuer of the securities is required to disclose all material information, including the risks associated with an investment. Generally, the registration statement must disclose, among other things, financial statements and information, management's discussion and analysis of the issuer's financial condition, a discussion of the business, and information relating to management and certain security holders.

As mentioned, there are exemptions from federal registration requirements. The registration process is often complicated, costly and time-consuming. A developer may find that the project can be structured in order to take advantage of an exemption from the registration process. However, the Act and rules promulgated by the Securities and Exchange Commission limit the scope of securities offerings that may qualify for such exemptions. Certain types of securities and certain transactions are specifically exempted by the Act.[18] Additionally, certain securities and transactions are exempted under rules promulgated by the Securities and Exchange Commission pursuant to specific authority granted by the Act.[19] Generally, an exempt security is exempt only from the Act's registration requirements. Provisions of the Act prohibiting fraud apply whether or not the securities involved are exempt from registration requirements.[20]

An example of a statutory exemption from the federal registration requirements is the intrastate exemption. The Act specifically exempts

---

[16]15 U.S.C. § 77(b)(1) (1982).
[17]*Id.* § 77e.
[18]*Id.* §§ 77c(a), 77d.
[19]*Id.* §§ 77c(b), (c).
[20]*Id.* § 77q.

from the registration requirements any offer or sale of securities made exclusively to residents of a single state, as long as the issuer resides in or is incorporated in the same state and does business in that state.[21] No resales may be made outside the state for a period of at least nine months after the date of the last sale.[22]

In those instances in which the developer anticipates obtaining the necessary investors through a local offering, consideration should be given to structuring the offering to meet the intrastate exemption to the federal registration requirements. Depending on the factual circumstances though, the sale of securities in connection with interstate land sales may affect the ability of the issuer to claim the intrastate exemption.

As previously mentioned, the Securities and Exchange Commission has also promulgated rules exempting certain securities and transactions from federal registration requirements. In 1982, the Securities and Exchange Commission promulgated Regulation D, which includes exemptions from federal registration requirements for three categories of limited offerings. The subject exemptions do not focus on whether or not an offering is conducted intrastate. Instead, these limited offering exemptions revolve around the amount of the offering and the number and characteristics of the investors involved. These are the three categories of limited offerings: (1) offerings of less than $1,000,000 by certain issuers in a 12-month period[23]; (2) offerings by any issuer of less than $5,000,000 in a 12-month period to an unlimited number of accredited investors plus 35 additional persons[24]; and (3) offerings of any amount by any issuer to an unlimited number of accredited investors plus 35 sophisticated persons.[25] The manner in which *accredited investors* and other terms are defined, along with general considerations that must be met for any offer and sale under Regulation D are further outlined in the Securities and Exchange Commission rules.[26] However, even though these limited offerings are exempt from federal registration requirements, the rules do establish requirements for notifying the Securities and Exchange Commission of Regulation D offerings.[27]

State securities laws also regulate the sale of securities. State se-

[21]*Id.* § 77c(a)(11).
[22]17 C.F.R. § 230.147 (1988).
[23]*Id.* § 230.504.
[24]*Id.* § 230.505.
[25]*Id.* § 230.506.
[26]*Id.* §§ 230.501, 230.502.
[27]*Id.* § 230.503.

curities legislation and regulations should be examined carefully because they vary from state to state. Although the federal securities laws emphasize disclosure, some states actually regulate the terms of the offering. It should also be noted that an exemption from registration under the Act does not assure exemption under the laws of the state in which the offering is made. Therefore, registration or qualification in the state will be necessary unless the offering is accomplished in a manner that qualifies for a limited offering or other exemption under the state's laws. In addition, persons involved in the offering may be required to register as brokers or dealers.

Zoning. A fundamental principle in any real estate development project should be to research the existing zoning for the property to be purchased or developed. This is especially true for a retirement housing project. Retirement housing often is not a contemplated use of a zoning authority's existing classification system. Rezoning, obtaining an exception or variance, or the creation of special zoning districts may be required in a particular jurisdiction.

In the absence of a zoning ordinance that provides for special districts for senior citizens, a typical problem is that a planned retirement housing project does not fit neatly into any of the existing zoning classifications for some municipalities. For this reason, the retirement housing project developer needs to be somewhat versed in the techniques of preparing and presenting a rezoning application.

Every rezoning request begins with the desire for a land use opportunity unavailable under the present zoning for the land; the first step is to define this goal precisely. It may be very specific, such as to build a two-story retirement housing apartment project for which the architectural plans have been completed; or it may be very unspecific, such as to provide the possibility for a multiservice retirement community in a development yet to be planned. In any case, the landowner's requirements must be identified with regard to the basic development characteristics: uses, building area, height, and building location on the site.

A zoning request should accommodate the land use goal, with sufficient flexibility for reasonable alterations, but no more. To seek more than the landowner wants or needs burdens the zoning request with unnecessary baggage that may jeopardize the result. Zoning practitioners have found that generally, all else being equal, the greater the development rights requested, the more difficult the case.

Almost always, there are several possible ways to achieve the desired change in development rights. For example, assume that a developer has land zoned to accommodate a two-story apartment housing project of 200,000 square feet. The developer however wants to build a four-story, 200,000-square-foot apartment project, restricted to retirement housing. Most jurisdictions allow at least three alternatives.

First, the developer can simply request a variance as to the height of the apartment structure. Second, he or she might request a rezoning to the next level of building development, say, one allowing 10 stories at 500,000 square feet of development. Then, to eliminate the unnecessary (and very possibly, opposition-producing) size, the developer offers a deed restriction limiting the development to 200,000 square feet and four stories. A third possibility is to apply for zoning referred to in different jurisdictions variously as a planned development, planned unit development, or planned development district, through which all the development standards are defined to meet precise needs. In each case, the zoning request hits the target, but one may offer practical advantages. The board or commission charged with variance authority might be more sympathetic to a proposed retirement housing project than the rezoning decision makers, or the planned development vehicle may enjoy particular favor with local government. What is important is that the alternatives be identified and compared for overall desirability.

Obviously, a retirement housing developer will not be effective without a thorough familiarity with the zoning code of the city for which the project is planned. The zoning alternatives for a land use goal cannot be identified without knowledge of the zoning classifications and the development rights allowed by each; nor can a case be best directed without knowledge of the procedural rules governing applications, notices, hearings, and decisional rights and requirements. The zoning process and applicable ordinances should be carefully researched prior to purchase of the land in order to determine whether or not there will be significant obstacles to development of retirement housing.

It is not uncommon that a desired rezoning will create a problem rendering it unacceptable from a planning or political standpoint, but the remedy is readily within the landowner's means. In such a case, the zoning request may include a binding commitment to take the remedial action. A typical example involves rezoning that will increase traffic around the site. A large retirement housing project may be planned for a street system that can generally dispatch the traffic satisfactorily, except for an intersection without a signal at the location of the project. A $25,000 traffic signal would more than make up for the added traffic, but the city has no plan to supply one. If the problem threatens the request and the new zoning is worth the $25,000 expense, the retirement housing applicant may seek an accommodation that makes occupancy conditional upon the landowner's funding the new signal. Sometimes, gratuitous dedications of land within the zoning request area for street or other public purposes may solve potential problems; other times, such offers may merely embody public advantages that offset the undesirable effects of a zoning change. In every case, the goal should be to alleviate problems that cannot be avoided. Conditions requiring the landowner to make affirmative contributions can be written in the form of deed restrictions prohibiting a building permit until the requested affirmative action is complete, or they can be accomplished through restrictions contained in a planned development request.

The developer needs to recognize, however, that even after the desired zoning classification is obtained, governmental authorities may attempt to restrict the use of such property through rezoning. An example of this occurred in Illinois.[28] A landowner had initially applied to rezone property so that a nursing home on the property would be a conforming use and enlargement and improvement of the property would be allowable. The Zoning Board of Appeals of Cook County held a hearing on the application during which local municipalities objected to the zoning change unless the landowner executed a restrictive covenant running with the land for 25 years. The covenant was executed and a restriction imposed that the property be used only for the purpose of a nursing, convalescent, and/or retirement community until the expiration of the 25-year period. Rezoning approval was recommended by the Zoning Board of Appeals and the Cook County Board of Commissioners adopted the recommendation.

The property owner subsequently undertook the investigation of a possible retirement housing project. Cook County approved the plans for the construction of a prototype retirement building on the property and issued a building permit. The prototype was built, and the owner subsequently proceeded to pursue plans for a nursing and retirement housing complex. The owner's architect inquired into obtaining a permit but was informed that an action compelling issuance of the permit would have to be filed or that an opinion would have to be obtained from the state's attorney to determine whether the proposed development was proper under the zoning classification. The state's attorney

[28]*Pioneer Trust and Sav. Bank v. County of Cook*, 71 Ill. 2d 510, 377 N.E.2d 21 (Ill. 1978).

ultimately issued an opinion that the proposed construction of a retirement community would not violate the terms of the restrictive
covenant. The opinion indicated that a factual matter would exist as
to whether or not the construction was in fact a retirement community.
After the opinion was issued, the property owner reapplied for a building permit but was once again refused because of an anticipated change
in the comprehensive zoning plan. The Cook County Board of Commissioners subsequently amended the Cook County zoning ordinance,
which resulted in a reduction of the number of permissible units per
acre on the owner's property from 17.4 to 8 units per acre.

The trustee of the property filed an action in court seeking to compel
the issuance of a zoning certificate and a building permit. The plaintiff
agreed that a property owner has no right in the continuation of a
zoning classification; however, the owner argued that he had substantially changed his position over a period of a decade in reliance upon
the zoning classification.[29] Ultimately, on appeal, the property owner's
position was upheld. However, the property owner was required to
pursue the case through the Illinois Supreme Court for a project that
had been in essence previously approved by local zoning authorities.

An additional alternative that may be available in some jurisdictions is the creation of a zoning classification for the elderly or retired.
Zoning laws that create special districts for the elderly have been
attacked on constitutional grounds. However, zoning for the elderly
has previously been found to be constitutional where designed to meet
an existing housing need of the elderly.[30] The creation of a special
zoning district for the elderly would also have to be consistent with
the specific legislation authorizing zoning.

In summary, the most common zoning problem will be that a planned
retirement housing project does not fit within the existing classification
scheme and that rezoning, or obtaining an exception or variance, will
accommodate the project. The creation of special zoning districts may
also be an option.[31]

---

[29]*See Id.* at 510–524, N.E.2d at 21–27.

[30]*Taxpayers Ass'n of Weymouth Township v. Weymouth Township,* 71 N.J. 249, 364
A.2d 1016 (1976), *cert. denied and appeal dismissed,* 430 U.S. 977, 97 S.Ct. 1672 (1977).

[31]In a project for the conversion of apartments to cooperatives or condominiums, the
developer should also investigate possible state and local laws or ordinances restricting
conversion. Special state statutory provisions may provide additional limitations where
the conversion involves apartments rented to the elderly. See generally *River Park
Tenants Ass'n v. 3600 Venture,* 534 F. Supp. 45 (E.D. Pa. 1981). The federal government
has also expressed concern with regard to condominium and cooperative conversion
projects and enacted the Condominium and Cooperative Abuse Relief Act of 1980, which
promotes notice of conversions and affects certain self-dealing contracts and leases. 15
U.S.C. §§ 3601–3615 (1982).

Regulatory Implications of Providing Health Care or Other Assistance to Elderly Residents. The provision of health care or other assistance to elderly residents may involve significant regulatory compliance issues. Health care capital expenditures may be reviewed pursuant to certificate of need or Section 1122[32] programs. Continuing care or life care retirement communities may be subject to state registration and certification requirements. The provision of health care in the retirement housing project may require state licensure. The treatment of Medicare and Medicaid patients will necessitate compliance with the Medicare and Medicaid program requirements. Additionally, providers of health care may find themselves faced with illegal remuneration and fraud and abuse issues at both the federal and state levels.

Certificate of Need and Section 1122 Review. The federal government at one time promoted the concept of health planning as a means for controlling the cost of health care. The idea was to encourage states, through participation in federal funding, to establish health planning programs for approval of certain capital expenditures for health care facility development or for the expansion or termination of health care services. The review would consist of a determination of the need for the project. The certificate of need and Section 1122 programs arose from this federal design. If a retirement housing venture involves development of a health care facility, or includes a health care facility as a venturer, the issue arises as to the reviewability of the venture in states with certificate of need or Section 1122 programs.

Certificate of need is implemented pursuant to state legislative action, although it was originally promoted through federal legislation.[33] The states first implemented certificate of need review pursuant to federal design, but over time they have tailored the review process to their own perceived goals. State certificate of need laws typically cover capital expenditures made by or on behalf of a health care facility that exceed a stated minimum. Additionally, capital expenditures associated with changes to a health care facility may be reviewed. These changes may include certain increases or decreases in bed capacity, redistribution of beds among various categories, or the relocation of beds from one physical site or facility to another. A substantial change in services may also subject the expenditure to review. A health care facility typically includes intermediate care and skilled nursing facilities, as well as hospitals.

---

[32]§ 1122 of the Social Security Act, 42 U.S.C. § 1320a-1 (1982 & Supp. I 1983, Supp. II 1984).

[33]National Health Planning and Resources Development Act of 1974, 42 U.S.C. §§ 300k–300t-14 (1982).

Certificate of need review usually involves an application and hearing process with the opportunity for area health care providers and other interested persons to object to the project. Certificate of need review requires that the applicant demonstrate need for the capital expenditure. Need is usually based on demographic and economic factors, taking into account the existing sources of care in the service area. If a certificate of need review is required but not obtained, the prospective health care provider may be sanctioned for proceeding with the project. Sanctions may include injunctions to preclude the violator from further development of the project, the denial or revocation of a license to operate the health care facility, and additional civil or criminal penalties.

Section 1122 of the Social Security Act was enacted to assure that federal funds appropriated under the Medicare and Medicaid programs were "not used to support unnecessary capital expenditures made by or on behalf of health care facilities which are reimbursed under" such programs.[34] Implementation of Section 1122 review was accomplished through agreement between the state and the federal government, and the activities which were subject to Section 1122 review and the review process itself were similar to certificate of need review. A health care provider could lose Medicare and Medicaid reimbursement for costs related to the capital expenditure that it could have claimed if Section 1122 approval had been obtained. However, the Section 1122 program is likely to be of less concern in the future since federal funding for the program was halted during the preparation of this chapter.

The federal government in recent years has reduced its commitment to health planning review. Some states have repealed or are considering repeal of such programs, while others have permitted programs to "sunset," or lapse, where the enabling legislation expired at the end of a designated period. However, many states still have some sort of capital expenditure review program.[35] Therefore, any prospective provider of health care should determine the scope of health planning review in the states in which projects are planned.

State Regulation of Continuing Care or Life Care Contracts. In many states, retirement communities that offer continuing care or life care contracts are regulated.[36] Regulation of continuing care retirement

[34]42 U.S.C. § 1320a-1(a) (1982).

[35]*See, e.g.,* Ga. Code Ann. §§ 31-6-40 through 31-6-50 (Supp. 1985 and 1987).

[36]*See, e.g.,* 40 Pa. Cons. Stat. Ann. §§ 3201–3225 (Purdon 1988 Supp.). A survey of state statutes conducted during the summer of 1987 identified 23 states with legislation addressing the provision of continuing care or life care. To some extent the number of states is arguable since the type of regulation may vary from state to state.

communities (CCRCs) generally developed in response to some widely publicized failures by CCRCs, which resulted in significant hardships to elderly residents. State regulation of CCRCs is intended to provide for some security for elderly persons seeking continuous care.

Developers will find varying approaches to regulation of continuing care contracts. This is reflected in the variety of agencies charged by the state legislatures with the responsibility of regulating continuing care contracts. Depending on the states in which the developer operates, he or she can expect to deal with one or more of the following: departments or divisions of insurance, social services, aging, public health, securities, commerce, housing and urban renewal, community affairs, or human resources. The number and variety of agencies involved provides insight into the approach of each state legislature to the continuing care issue. Some legislatures view the continuing care issue as an insurance issue, some treat it as a health issue, some treat it as an investment issue, and others treat it as an aging issue.

The nature of the legislation itself can differ. Legislation may focus on insuring the solvency of continuing care communities, insuring full and accurate disclosure to prospective and current residents, or may address both of these concerns. In any event, the developer should become familiar with existing legislation, along with any proposed legislation or regulation.

CCRC legislation can significantly affect the planning for a project that involves continuing care. Depending on the state, a certificate of authority or permit may be required before a continuing care contract can be solicited or executed. An application for a permit or certificate of authority may require the preparation and disclosure of substantial information, such as ownership of the applicant, reserve funding or security, affiliations, prior business experience of the applicant or manager, determination of rates, financial projections, and a description of the financing. The state may also require that the contract contain specific provisions and provide specific rights to the resident. The developer may be required to maintain escrow accounts for entrance fees and/or reserve funds in an attempt to protect the financial condition of the community from mismanagement or inaccurate financial projections. States may also provide for authority to assume control over financially troubled CCRCs. Residents may also be afforded liens against the CCRC in some states as a further protective measure.

Some states may expansively interpret the statutory definition of a continuing care or life care contract or community to regulate some communities that might not have considered themselves subject to regulation. The states may look to the contract language itself for indications of a continuing obligation to the resident. One example of

the potential for broadened interpretation is provided by a case in
Pennsylvania.[37]

A nonprofit corporation operating a retirement community appealed
an order of the Insurance Commissioner that classified the entity as a
continuing care provider subject to the provisions of the Pennsylvania
Continuing Care Provider Registration and Disclosure Act. The retirement community consisted of a skilled and intermediate care nursing home and independent living area. The residency agreement provided for an entrance fee of $79,000 to $85,000 for the right to occupy
an independent living facility. Residents also paid a monthly maintenance charge of $200 to $250, which covered certain building maintenance and consultation with a nurse. A communal dining room was
provided where the residents could purchase meals at their discretion.
The community health care facility was operated on a fee-for-service
basis with residents of the facility being charged at the same rate as
nonresidents. The residency agreement also provided: "Health center
facilities and residential living will continue to be available to a resident even if he, she or they are financially unable to pay such charges,
provided that resident provides documentation . . . of such financial
inability to pay."[38] The entrance fee itself was used 40 percent for
endowment, 40 percent for development, and 20 percent for depreciation or major improvements. After development of the community, the
nonprofit corporation's board of trustees intended to designate 80 percent of all entrance fees for endowment with no portion of the fee
reserved for the care of the individual.

The Insurance Commissioner determined that the retirement community had promised to provide board, lodging, and health services to
its residents for life in return for the entrance fee and that the residents
had a reasonable expectation that they would receive such services for
the remainder of their lives regardless of their ability to pay.[39]

The nonprofit corporation contended that it only furnished lodging
in return for the entrance fee and that meals and medical care were
provided on a fee-for-service basis. The retirement community argued
that it was a fee-for-service provider instead of a continuing care community. The residency agreement contained a statement that the
agreement was not intended to constitute an undertaking or contract
to care for the resident for life.

---

[37]*Moravian Manors, Inc. v. Commonwealth Ins. Dep't,* 521 A.2d 524 (Pa. Commw. Ct.
1987).

[38]*Id.* at 525.

[39]*Id.* at 526.

The Commonwealth Court of Pennsylvania affirmed the Insurance Commissioner. The statute itself had defined continuing care as "[t]he furnishing to an individual, other than an individual related by consanguinity or affinity to the person furnishing such care, of board and lodging together with nursing services, medical services or other health-related services . . . in consideration of the payment of an entrance fee with or without other periodic charges."[40]

The court determined that the statement disclaiming continuous care was eroded by other contractual provisions. Another contractual provision indicated that health center facilities and residential living would continue to be available even if the resident was unable to pay. The court stated that it was "not persuaded that the Act is applicable solely to life-care providers and that fee-for-service providers, such as petitioner, are beyond its scope."[41]

State Licensure.   Licensure requirements may affect the desirability of providing certain types of care in a retirement housing venture. Personal care, skilled care, intermediate care, home health care and adult congregate living are among the categories that may be licensed by a state authority. Compliance with licensure requirements is often cumbersome. States typically require significant structural conformity and compliance, and also regulate the policies for care at the facilities.

The effect that licensing standards may have can be illustrated by an example in which a developer with experience in housing has purchased a hotel for conversion into a retirement community. The developer does not need the entire complex for independent living units and has decided that it would be a good idea to use a significant portion of the building for nursing care. The developer purchases the hotel and begins renovation to accommodate the retirement community. During renovation, he learns of the state's licensing standards for nursing beds. Review of the licensing standards indicates that certain changes would have to be made to the basic structure of the facility, such as widening the hallways, which would destroy the economic feasibility of converting a portion of the facility to nursing beds. The result is that the developer has bought more than he can use.

Medicare and Medicaid Program Requirements.   If the retirement center will include the provision of health care services or beds for which reimbursement is expected under government programs, the developer

[40]*Id.*
[41]*Id.* at 527.

should become familiar with the reimbursement system. Subject to certain limitations, the Medicare program provides, pursuant to Title XVIII of the Social Security Act, reimbursement for the provision of care in a skilled nursing facility.[42] Medicare does not, however, cover care provided in an intermediate care facility. The Medicaid program is a joint state and federal program established pursuant to Title XIX of the Social Security Act. Federal law requires states participating in the Medicaid program to provide coverage for skilled nursing care to certain classes of qualifying beneficiaries.[43] States are currently also permitted but are not required to provide coverage for intermediate care services to eligible beneficiaries.[44] Effective October 1, 1990, the distinction between the coverage by the Medicaid program for skilled nursing care and intermediate care will be eliminated. Consolidated coverage will be provided for nursing facilities.[45] The potential Medicare and/or Medicaid provider should not anticipate receiving payment from such programs at a level comparable to payment received from private patients. In fact, the provider may find that payment in some instances is inadequate to compensate for the care of Medicare and Medicaid patients.

The conditions of participation under the Medicare and Medicaid programs should also be considered before development of the center. To participate as a provider of services in the Medicare and Medicaid programs, the facility must obtain certification through the Health Care Financing Administration of the United States Department of Health and Human Services. In order to obtain certification, the nursing facility must comply with conditions of participation. As with state licensure, the conditions of participation may impose significant requirements upon the provider of care.[46] The conditions of participation for nursing facilities under the Medicare and Medicaid programs include physical as well as operational requirements.[47]

[42]42 U.S.C. § 1395d(a) (1982).

[43]*Id.*, §§ 1396a(a)(10)(A), 1396d(a)4.

[44]*Id.*, §§ 1396a(a)(10)(A), 1396d(a)(15).

[45]Omnibus Budget Reconciliation Act of 1987, Pub. L. No. 100-203, § 4211(f), (h) (1) and (6), 101 Stat. 1330-205; 206 (1987).

[46]The Omnibus Budget Reconciliation Act of 1987, Pub. L. No. 100-203, §§ 4203(a), 4213(a), 101 Stat. 1330-179, 180, 1330-213, 214, 216 (1987), provides for possible civil money penalties for failure to comply with the Medicare or Medicaid conditions of participation.

[47]42 C.F.R. §§ 405.1101–405.1137, 442.200–442.202, 442.250–442.254, 442.300–442.346 (1987).

Federal and State Fraud and Abuse and Illegal Remuneration Prohibitions. Additional federal and state laws impact the provision of care in a retirement housing community. Care providers are subject to civil and criminal sanctions for certain activities that are considered improper under federal or state law. These improper activities may arise in the context of filing false claims or even through an attempt to provide incentives in structuring participation in the profits of the enterprise. Effective October 1, 1990, civil monetary penalties may be assessed against anyone who knowingly and willfully certifies, or causes another individual to certify a material and false statement with regard to a nursing facility resident assessment under the Medicare or Medicaid programs.[48]

Health care providers are subject to substantial penalties for the submission of prohibited claims for reimbursement under the Medicare or Medicaid programs.[49] For example, if a provider knows or has reason to know that a service was not provided as claimed, the provider could incur significant sanctions beyond mere denial of reimbursement. The Medicare and Medicaid contract may be jeopardized by the violation and the provider subjected to monetary penalties.[50] The provider may also be subject to criminal prosecution for Medicare or Medicaid fraud and abuse, which currently includes a fine of up to $25,000, five years in prison, or both.[51]

The provision of services to patients receiving certain government assistance results in additional restrictions on the provider. Illegal remuneration statutes prohibit the knowing and willful soliciting, receiving, offering, or paying, directly or indirectly, of any remuneration in return for referrals of Medicare or Medicaid patients, or patients receiving assistance under the Title V Maternal and Child Health Services Block Grant Program or Title XX Social Services Block Grant Program. The prohibition further extends to the furnishing of any item or service reimbursable under those programs, or for the purchase, lease, or order of any good, facility, service, or item reimbursable under the programs.[52] The effect of these statutory provisions is to eliminate what may seem a normal business arrangement in which coventurers

---

[48]Omnibus Budget Reconciliation Act of 1987, Pub. L. No. 100-203, §§ 4201(a)(3), 4211(a)(3), 101 Stat. 1330-160, 161, 162, 1330-182, 184 (1987).
[49]42 U.S.C. § 1320a-7a (1982 & Supp. III 1986).
[50]*Id.* § 1320a-7.
[51]*Id.* § 1320a-7b.
[52]*Id.*

receive profit based on their contribution of business to the venture. However, Congress has proscribed payments for the referral of such patients. The statutes impose federal criminal sanctions that currently include a fine of up to $25,000 per violation, or five years in prison, or both. Governmental authorities are examining certain arrangements in the health care industry to determine whether or not the arrangements were intended to induce referrals of such patients.[53]

States may also have their own illegal remuneration statutes which impose civil and/or criminal penalties.[54] Additionally, some states have commercial bribery statutes that impose obligations upon certain persons acting in a fiduciary capacity.[55] In such a state, if a participant in the retirement housing venture is found to have a fiduciary or other special relationship with regard to the residents or patients of the retirement center, the person with the fiduciary relationship may be subjected to commercial bribery charges if he or she agrees to accept a benefit in order to influence him or her to act in a certain manner with regard to the resident or patient. The person offering the benefit, or agreeing to confer the benefit, may also be subject to penalty. Thus, in some states a fiduciary who refers a beneficiary to a facility for care and is paid for the referral may be subject to commercial bribery charges. Some states permit the resident or patient to consent to the payment for referral and absolve the fiduciary of any violation.[56]

UNIQUE CONSIDERATIONS IN BUSINESS RELATIONSHIPS INVOLVING TAX-EXEMPT AND FOR-PROFIT ENTITIES

The Effect of the Venture on a Nonprofit Entity's Tax-Exempt and Public Charity Status.
The retirement housing industry has historically involved nonprofit, tax-exempt institutions. For-profit involvement in retirement housing and retirement communities is a fairly recent phenomenon. The presence of the tax-exempt entity in retirement housing has presented, and is increasingly presenting, situations in which tax-exempt and for-profit organizations are entering into business relationships. These relationships can prove mutually beneficial.

---

[53]*See United States v. Greber,* 760 F.2d 68 (3rd Cir. 1985), *cert. denied,* 474 U.S. 988, 106 S. Ct. 396, 88 L.Ed. 2d 348 (1985); *United States v. Hancock,* 604 F.2d 999 (7th Cir. 1979), *cert. denied,* 444 U.S. 991 (1979).

[54]*See, e.g.,* N.M. Stat. Ann. §§ 30-41-1 through 30-41-3 (1978).

[55]*See, e.g.,* Tex. Penal Code Ann. § 32.43 (Vernon 1974 and 1988 Supp.).

[56]*See, e.g.,* Tex. Penal Code Ann. §§ 32.43, 1.07(a)(9) (Vernon 1974 and 1988 Supp.).

The mere fact that one entity is tax-exempt and one entity is for-profit does not necessarily mean that they are incapable of a working relationship. There are limitations on the scope of permitted activities between tax-exempt organizations and for-profit entities which must be carefully observed in order to preserve the tax-exempt entity's exempt status and possible tax benefits to the developer. However, understanding these limitations will permit the developer to effectively work with tax-exempt organizations.

Why should the for-profit entity spend the time to develop such an understanding? In light of the changes in the tax laws resulting from the Tax Reform Act of 1986, it may be difficult to attract the affluent individual investor to a retirement housing project. Additionally, tax-exempt financing has been curtailed. The equity required to finance a project has also increased. Developers must find alternative sources for equity and for increased revenue once a project is completed. Tax-exempt entities may be one source because they have long been involved in health care and retirement projects. A prospective developer of a retirement housing project should, however, have some familiarity with the unique considerations involved in entering into a joint venture[57] with a tax-exempt entity.

Who are the tax-exempt entities that might be interested in a working relationship with a for-profit entity? The list includes hospitals, universities, churches, governmental units, nursing homes, home health agencies, and retirement communities. Why would any of these entities be interested in a joint venture with a for-profit? Tax-exempt entities have missions to pursue. In order to pursue such a mission, the tax-exempt entity needs the funding to achieve its goals.

Tax-exempt entities are facing significant pressures and are interested in alternative sources of revenue. Charitable giving is down, and tax law changes may further discourage donations. A university may face sagging enrollment but has land available for use. Churches are concerned about living conditions and care arrangements for elderly members. A governmental unit may have land that could be utilized to provide housing for its citizens and revenue to the governmental unit. Nursing homes serve elderly patients and may perceive retirement housing as a natural adjunct to their endeavors. Home health agencies are also heavily involved with elderly patients and already provide services to such patients in their homes. Hospitals are seeking

---

[57]The term *joint venture* is used in the general sense to reference a working relationship among the parties and not in the technical, legal sense of a general partnership formed for a specific purpose.

additional revenue sources. Reimbursement programs, such as Medicare and Medicaid, have implemented systems that often reduce compensation for care of beneficiaries under those programs. These systems also tend to reward the hospital for discharging the patient to alternative sources of care, such as a skilled nursing facility in a retirement community.

What does the developer need to know about the tax-exempt entity? Typically, a tax-exempt entity receives its exemption pursuant to Section 501(c)(3) of the Internal Revenue Code.[58] An organization must follow the procedures for obtaining recognition of federal tax-exempt status if it is to achieve such status. Incorporation as a nonprofit corporation pursuant to state law is insufficient by itself. The entity must meet both organizational and operational tests to qualify. A Section 501(c)(3) organization must be organized and operated exclusively for exempt purposes. It is important to note, however, that if an organization is empowered or engages only insubstantially in activities that do not further its exempt purpose, its exemption will not be denied or revoked.[59]

Among the organizational requirements for a Section 501(c)(3) exempt organization is that the organization must limit its purposes to one or more exempt purposes, such as religious, charitable, scientific, literary, or educational purposes.[60] The organization must dedicate its assets to an exempt purpose, must not devote more than an insubstantial part of its activities to influence legislation, and the organization must not participate or intervene in any political campaign on behalf of any candidate for public office.[61]

Operationally, the organization must engage primarily in activities that accomplish one or more of its exempt purposes. Providing retirement housing and supplying hospital care are examples of types of activities that may qualify for exemption if certain conditions to insure their charitable nature are met.[62] Importantly, a tax-exempt organization must not permit its net earnings to inure in whole or in part to

[58]26 U.S.C. § 501(c)(3) (1982).

[59]Treas. Reg. § 1.501(c)(3)-1(b)(1)(i)(b), 1.501c(3)-1(c)(1) (as amended in 1976).

[60]26 U.S.C. § 501(c)(3) (1982); Treas. Reg. § 1.501(c)(3)-1(d)(1)(i) (as amended in 1976).

[61]26 U.S.C. § 501(c)(3) (1982); Treas. Reg. § 1.501(c)(3)-1(b)(3)(i) & (ii), (b)(4) (as amended in 1976).

[62]Rev. Rul. 72-124, 1972-1 C.B. 145; Rev. Rul. 64-231, 1964-2 C.B. 139; Rev. Rul. 61-72, 1961-1 C.B. 188; Rev. Rul. 69-545, 1969-2 C.B. 117; Rev. Rul. 83-157, 1983-2 C.B. 94.

the benefit of private shareholders or individuals, and it must serve a public, rather than a private, purpose.[63]

A tax-exempt organization may in reality be taxed on certain of its income. The gross income derived by an exempt organization from any unrelated trade or business regularly carried on by it, less exemptions and allowable deductions, is unrelated business income subject to taxation.[64] An organization that has substantial unrelated business income may jeopardize its exempt status.

A tax-exempt entity desiring to participate in a joint venture with a for-profit entity is therefore subject to limitations on its activities, or it will possibly jeopardize its exempt status. Tax-exempt organizations are facing increased scrutiny from federal, state, and local taxing authorities, and from the private business sector itself, which often perceives the tax-exempt organization as a competitor.

A tax-exempt organization may also be subject to certain additional requirements if it qualifies as a public charity, or nonprivate foundation, under the Internal Revenue Code.[65] For an organization to qualify as a public charity it will need to meet certain control or support tests, which involve the demonstration that it is organized to benefit another specific type of public charity or that its sources of funding meet particular tests.[66] Public charity status may be important to an organization in order to avoid requirements of private foundations concerning taxes, recordkeeping and reporting. Participation by a public charity in a joint venture may affect its ability to meet public charity tests.

If the tax-exempt entity is a political subdivision of the government,[67] state constitutional and statutory restrictions may also affect its ability to participate in joint ventures. A state statute may limit or prohibit a governmental entity from owning an interest in a for-profit entity or from loaning or contributing anything of value to a for-profit entity. Restrictions may also apply to the extension of credit by the governmental entity to the venture.

What are the possible ways in which a business relationship can develop between a tax-exempt entity and a for-profit entity? The pos-

---

[63]26 U.S.C. § 501(c)(3) (1982); Treas. Reg. § 1.501(c)(3)-1(d)(1)(ii) (as amended in 1976).

[64]26 U.S.C. §§ 511–514 (1982 & Supp. III 1985, Supp. IV 1986).

[65]26 U.S.C. § 509(a) (1982).

[66]*Id.* § 509(a)(1)-(3).

[67]Income accruing to governmental units is subject to exemption under federal law pursuant to I.R.C. § 115.

sibilities include participation and ownership in general or limited partnerships, corporations, and through contractual arrangements such as leases, management contracts, and service agreements. Each of these arrangements, however, involves a degree of risk to the tax-exempt entity and may also result in adverse tax consequences to the for-profit entity. It is therefore important to both entities that any relationship be carefully considered and structured. In many instances, a tax-exempt entity will seek a private letter ruling from the Internal Revenue Service in order to obtain a determination as to the effects of the proposed transaction. A response to the private letter ruling may take some time to obtain, therefore, the timetable for the request and response should be built into the project.

A tax-exempt organization participating in a partnership will be examined to determine whether it is serving a charitable purpose, and the venture itself will be examined to determine whether the arrangement permits the exempt organization to act in furtherance of the purposes for which exemption has been granted. The inquiry is particularly important where the tax-exempt entity is to serve as a general partner because the Internal Revenue Service perceives a possible conflict between a tax-exempt organization's duty as a general partner to further its other partners' interests and the pursuit of the tax-exempt entity's own exempt purpose.[68] A tax-exempt entity participating as a partner in a partnership may also be subjected to unrelated business income tax which, if substantial, could jeopardize its exempt status.[69] Dividends received by tax-exempt shareholders, however, are generally exempted from unrelated business income tax.[70]

In many instances, a for-profit organization related to a tax-exempt entity may participate in the joint venture. The participation of the for-profit entity may help to insulate the tax-exempt entity from jeop-

[68]*See* Priv. Ltr. Rul. 7820058 (Feb. 17, 1978) in which the Internal Revenue Service indicated that a proposed transaction involving a Section 501(c)(3) organization as a managing general partner in a limited partnership organized to own an apartment complex for low-income senior citizens would jeopardize the Section 501(c)(3) exemption. *But cf.* Priv. Ltr. Rul. 8418129 (Feb. 2, 1984) in which a tax-exempt organization's participation as managing general partner in a limited partnership to own a rehabilitated building for low-income elderly and handicapped persons was found permissible. Private letter rulings do not have precedential value and may not be cited as authority. They are determinative only with regard to the entity requesting the ruling based on the facts presented. However, they provide some indication of the Internal Revenue Service's position with regard to particular issues.

[69]Treas. Reg. § 1.512(c)-1.

[70]*Id.* § 1.512(b)-1(a).

ardizing its tax-exempt status and from liability arising from the venture itself. However, the Internal Revenue Service will examine the relationship between a tax-exempt entity and related for-profit entities to determine whether the for-profit organization's activities should also be attributed to the tax-exempt entity.

From the for-profit developer's perspective, before implementation of a joint venture (e.g., a partnership or lease) with a tax-exempt entity, the effect of tax-exempt use should also be considered. The use or leasing of property by a tax-exempt entity may affect the tax benefits to the property's owners. Tax-exempt use property must be depreciated under an alternative system pursuant to federal tax law. Tax-exempt use property is recovered over a longer recovery period than other property of the same class, and antiabuse provisions are designed to prevent the use of partnerships or other pass-through entities to structure transactions to avoid restrictions on depreciation deductions.[71]

From the tax-exempt entity's perspective, a management contract with a for-profit entity as manager of the tax-exempt entity's facility may also be problematic. This is especially true if the tax-exempt entity has used tax-exempt financing to build the facility. A management contract for tax-exempt financed property must be carefully structured in order to preserve the tax-exempt status of the bonds.[72]

CONTRACTING WITH ELDERLY RESIDENTS

The elderly deserve a clear and concise contract explicitly defining the terms and conditions of their stay in the retirement community. The developer should recognize, as a matter of self-interest, that contract terms may be construed against the developer and contractual disputes may irreparably injure one's reputation in the industry.

There are a number of forces, often conflicting, that will affect the manner in which legal documents are prepared for retirement community projects. The terms that the various documents involve should attempt to reconcile these competing interests. The need to effectively market the community and the attorney's own desire to protect his or

[71]26 U.S.C. § 168(g), (h) (1982 & Supp. II 1984, Supp. III 1985, Supp. IV 1986).

[72]*See* Rev. Proc. 82-14, 1982-1 C.B. 459 which provides operating guidelines for issuance of advance rulings by the Internal Revenue Service that facilities are not used in the trade or business of a nonexempt person within the meaning of I.R.C. § 103 when the facilities are to be managed by a nonexempt management company. As part of the Conference Report to the Tax Reform Act of 1986, Congress has directed the Treasury Department to liberalize those guidelines.

her client often result in a tug-of-war between the marketer and the lawyer. Marketing should be conducted in a responsible manner with an understanding of the legal implications of misrepresentation, and the lawyer should be cognizant of the marketing implications of the drafted agreements.

Other forces may prescribe the terms and conditions of the agreements. State statutes and common law affect every form of retirement community and the relationships between the owners, operators, and residents of the retirement community, whether through condominium statutes, cooperative statutes, landlord-tenant relationships, licensor-licensee relationships, statutes governing CCRCs, contractual law, or other forms of statutory or common law. These laws may vary in effect, from indirectly affecting the terms of the agreements to actually prescribing the terms of the agreements.

The financing arrangements involved may also result in prescribed conditions. Lenders, whether private institutions or government agencies, have an interest in protecting the strength of their loan. Partners in investments have similar concerns with regard to the strength of their investment.

The document preparation process should be sensitive to all of the conflicting forces involved in development and operation of the retirement community. Documents prepared for one project may be completely inappropriate for another project. As much care should be given to their preparation as to any other facet of the development of the community.

The following discussion will focus briefly on some of the more common arrangements for development of a retirement community. The discussion will attempt to provide insight into the basic attributes of the relationships created and, in some instances, focus on particularly critical issues in the drafting of contractual provisions.

Condominium Sales.   Each of the states has statutes governing condominium ownership. Typically, a declaration of condominium is filed by the developer pursuant to state statute. The information to be included in the declaration is specified in the applicable statute. Such information may include a legal description of the land on which the improvements are to be located, a general description of each condominium, the number of condominiums and their size, a description of the common elements and recreational facilities, and each condominium's interest in the entire condominium project. The declaration may set forth the conditions under which a condominium may also be sold, leased, or otherwise devised.

In the case of a retirement housing project consisting of condominiums, the declaration of condominium often includes a covenant or limitation relating to occupancy of the condominium by the elderly. The validity of such age restrictions in condominium projects has been upheld in many jurisdictions.[73]

The developer sells each unit pursuant to a sales contract identifying the terms of sale along with the legal description of the condominium itself. The purchaser receives fee title to the unit pursuant to the unit deed providing for the location and size of the condominium transferred. Additionally, the purchaser receives an undivided interest in the common elements, such as hallways, parking areas, and recreation facilities. The purchaser usually pays both a mortgage and a monthly maintenance fee for the common property.

In addition, an owners' association is typically incorporated pursuant to articles of incorporation and bylaws to manage the property. Often, the condominiums are managed by the developer until a certain percentage of the units are sold, whereupon the owners' association is vested with management authority. The owners' association may elect to exercise its management authority or contract with a manager or management company to provide management services. An owners' association is typically governed by a board of directors. The owners' association often has rule-making powers and may promulgate restrictions that bind condominium unit owners. The owners' association may be able to dictate the use of the condominium premises and to specially assess charges for unexpected repairs or maintenance of the property.

The elderly resident will have the rights and obligations of an owner of the condominium and will correspondingly be able to transfer that ownership interest to another qualifying resident. The development entity may through this vehicle limit its own continued involvement in the operations of the community.

Cooperative Sales. Another device that has been used to market living units to the elderly is cooperative housing. A cooperative is often organized as an association or corporation by a developer pursuant to

---

[73]See, e.g., Preston Tower Condominium Ass'n v. S.B. Realty, Inc., 685 S.W.2d 98 (Tex. App.-Dallas 1985, no writ); White Egret Condominium, Inc. v. Franklin, 379 So. 2d 346 (Fla. 1979).

state law either to acquire a real estate project of the developer, or to contract with the developer for construction of the project. The cooperative usually purchases the entire property and arranges for its financing. The cooperative itself owns the property and, if mortgage financed, the mortgage covers the entire retirement housing project.

A key distinction between cooperatives and condominiums is that shares are sold in the cooperative to those individuals who will occupy the dwelling units.[74] The shareholders own an interest in the cooperative; whereas, in a condominium project the purchaser acquires title to the condominium itself. Regardless of the actual amount paid by the shareholder for his ownership interest in the cooperative and for the right to occupy a particular unit, each shareholder usually receives only one voting share in the cooperative itself.

In addition to the ownership interest that the shareholder acquires in the cooperative through the purchase of stock, the shareholder enters into a proprietary lease of the unit itself. This proprietary lease provides a mechanism for retiring debt service of the cooperative and meeting operational costs for the community itself. The occupant often makes payment of his or her proportionate share of mortgage, maintenance, and certain other expenses on a monthly basis similar to a standard lease. The agreement should provide the flexibility to adjust payments periodically, as determined by the board of directors of the cooperative, in order to meet changing conditions in the community itself.

The owner of an interest in a cooperative may find it more difficult to divest his or her interest than the owner of a condominium. Cooperative organizational documents tend to have more restrictions on the transferability of an interest in the cooperative. Sale of the shares in the cooperative may be subject to the approval of the cooperative's board of directors. Through this restriction and age restrictions on the transfer of shares, the elderly nature of the community may be preserved, although such limitations may extend beyond a determination of age alone. For example, the sales price may also be predetermined or subject to limitations.

The elderly resident is provided with an equity interest in this form of retirement community; however, it is in the cooperative entity itself

---

[74]The sale of shares or interests in the development entity itself should be distinguished from the sale of shares in the cooperative. Whereas the sale of shares in a development entity has significant state and federal securities implications, the sale of shares in a cooperative may not even involve the sale of securities or investment contracts under federal securities laws. *See Grenader v. Spitz,* 537 F.2d 612 (2nd Cir. 1976).

and not the real property. The shareholder is also provided the right to occupy a particular unit in the community owned by the cooperative. The developer is permitted to limit his or her continued involvement in the operation of the retirement community. The developer may participate in management or the provision of services to the community after development, or alternative arrangements can be made with a management company experienced in the provision of care to the elderly.

Rental Agreements. A retirement housing project that merely contemplates leasing apartments to the elderly should specify that the unit itself and no additional services, or specified limited services, are being provided. The term of the lease, security deposit, and rental payment due should be clearly stated along with the manner in which rent increases and refunds of the security deposit will be made. The developer should also clearly state restrictions on subletting and assignment in order to avoid the potential occupancy of the project by younger populations.

Realistically, most developers will find that they cannot market the rental property without providing additional services to the elderly. Emergency call systems, meals, nursing care, and laundry and cleaning services are just a few of the variety of services that may need to be provided in order to make the community attractive. The standard rental agreement does not contemplate the provision of such services. Therefore, if such services are to be provided, the developer needs to consider the effect they will have on the pricing structure and the terms of the rental contract.

The rental agreement should clearly define and limit the landlord's responsibilities in return for the payment of the specified rent. Those services that the landlord intends to provide as part of the rental fee should be clearly stated and limited. All other services should be excluded specifically from the rental fee itself. The tenant should be clearly informed as to the availability of, and the fees and payment arrangements for, any additional services.

The relationship between the owner and elderly resident is a landlord-tenant relationship, and subject to the state laws governing such arrangements. State laws typically address a number of leasing matters, such as inspection and repair, the return of security deposits, entry by the landlord, eviction of the tenant, subletting by the tenant, harassment, change of ownership, withholding of rent, retaliation, security devices, interruption of utilities, and tenant exclusion. Often, statutory provisions will require bold type or underlining before a landlord may enforce a particular lease provision.

The landlord-tenant relationship provides the elderly resident with ownership of a leasehold interest in the apartment. The resident will have a limited term for which he or she is obligated to pay rent; however, this also permits the landlord to periodically increase the cost to the resident through upward adjustments of rental rates.

In contrast to the sale of condominiums or transfer of property by a developer to a cooperative, the lessor is likely to have a continuing relationship with the elderly resident, although the lessor may contract for the provision of certain management functions or the provision of additional services, such as housekeeping and food service, which the community may offer.

Resident Agreements.   As previously indicated, resident contracts for CCRCs may be subject to state regulation. If so, such contracts should be carefully drawn in light of applicable statutory and regulatory requirements. In some instances the form of the agreement, or specific terms, may be prescribed by state law.

The resident agreement should allow the CCRC to adjust to new conditions in the marketplace and to provide for capital needs. Originally, resident contracts assumed certain responsibilities for the resident for life, including skilled nursing care. The CCRC originally assumed this responsibility in return for the assignment of all of the resident's property. This evolved into the payment of an initial endowment or entrance fee, and monthly maintenance fees. The fees were often not subject to increase. Due to the failure of a number of CCRCs, CCRCs have restructured the resident contract.

The following discussion will focus on the attributes of the resident agreement. Often, the attributes discussed may also be found in ancillary agreements or policies associated with the resident agreement. The developer should exercise care to ensure that significant requirements upon the resident are, in fact, binding upon the resident.

A resident agreement should indicate that the resident has limited rights with regard to his or her stay in the community. The agreement should indicate whether it creates any kind of interest in the property of the community. Usually, the resident agreement will merely provide for the right to occupy the unit and receive the services provided pursuant to the agreement.

The timing, amount, and method of payment of the entrance fee should be clearly stated. Initially, life care contracts often provided that the entrance fee was not refundable, but current CCRC resident contracts often provide that the entrance fee is either fully or partially refundable. Since the refund of all or part of the entrance fee may be substantial, it may be prudent to indicate that the refund will occur when the owner receives an entrance fee from a new resident of the vacated unit. If the refund is to be dependent on a sliding scale based on the period of time the resident occupied the unit, such scale should be clearly established.[75]

The monthly service fee itself should be agreed to; however, there should be flexibility for the provider to increase the fees. The agreement should also identify any applicable restrictions and/or monthly fees for additional residents of the unit. The services provided in exchange for the monthly maintenance fee should be clearly identified in the agreement. Additional services available to the residents on a fee-for-service basis or other payment arrangement should also be clearly delineated.

The scope of health services provided under the resident agreement must be carefully defined. Those health care services provided on site and through the monthly service fee should be identified. For example, current resident contracts may limit the amount of nursing care provided before additional fees for such care are imposed or may provide that nursing care is solely provided on a fee-for-service basis.

The manner by which temporary or permanent assignment to the health care facility at the community is determined should be stated. The agreement should also address the transfer of the resident from the community health care facility to a higher level of care outside the community and the responsibility for the cost of such care.

The physical health expected of the resident upon occupancy of the unit should be stated. Responsibility for furnishing and maintaining the furnishings in the unit should be identified. The policy on alterations to the unit and the ownership of automobiles and pets should be included. Additionally, the ability of the staff of the community to enter the unit in the event of an emergency or for maintenance should be provided for.

The community's policy with regard to financial ability of the resident should also be stated. Often the resident represents that he or

---

[75]The tax effects of entrance fees to the owner and resident should also be considered in drafting the resident agreement. If the entrance fee could result in taxable income to the resident, consideration should be given to proper disclosure of that effect. If the development of a loan in lieu of all or part of the entrance fee is considered, state and federal laws regulating CCRCs and lending practices should be examined in structuring the terms of the loan.

she has sufficient income and assets to pay for lifetime occupancy. The resident also typically agrees not to impair his or her ability to meet the financial obligations of the contract without the consent of the owner. The agreement should also address any health insurance requirements for the resident.

In many instances, in order to make the community attractive to the resident, the agreement provides that in the event the resident becomes unable to meet his or her obligations and cannot obtain assistance from other sources, the CCRC will continue to provide care to the resident upon certain conditions. These conditions typically include that the resident did not misrepresent financial ability and did not impair ability to pay, that the resident exhausted available resources, and, in some agreements, that the owner determines that its financial condition will not be adversely affected by continuation of the care. Caution should be exercised in drafting such provisions in states that regulate continuing care or life care contracts. A community that may not consider itself subject to such regulation may, in fact, be considered a CCRC due to a provision assuring continuous care.[76] However, from a marketing standpoint, the need for such a provision may outweigh the regulatory consideration.

Conditions for termination of occupancy of the unit should be identified. These terms should describe rights of termination of both the owner and the occupant. Breach of the agreement, interference with or threat to the health and safety of other residents or staff, and failure to comply with community policies may be some of the events upon which the owner could terminate the agreement. The effect on a resident of the death of a coresident, or termination of residency by a coresident of the unit should also be addressed. The terms under which the resident will physically vacate and remove his or her possessions should also be developed in the agreement.

In states where it is permissible, the agreement should clearly indicate that it is subject to and subordinate to all mortgages and security interests affecting the property of the community and that the owner may freely assign the agreement. If the agreement may be rescinded by the resident within a particular time period, conditions of that rescission should be identified.

The residence agreement provides the elderly resident with the right to occupy a dwelling unit and reserves the ownership of the unit itself to the developer or other entity to which the developer sells or leases the community. The elderly resident is provided with assurances of a

---

[76]*See Moravian Manors, supra,* footnote 37.

certain level of health care and other services, but the resident agreement should permit the CCRC the flexibility to ensure the continued financial viability of the community. The owner of the CCRC must expect a continuing, lasting commitment to caring for the needs of the elderly resident through its own facilities or by contracting or arranging for the provision of required services.

Admission Agreements. If the retirement community includes an intermediate and/or skilled nursing facility, the developer will need to become familiar with patient rights and will need an admission contract that clearly sets forth the terms by which the patient is to receive care in the nursing complex. The admission agreement will be governed in many significant respects by the laws of some states,[77] and by federal law if the nursing facility provides care to Medicare or Medicaid beneficiaries.

The admission policies of nursing facilities have been and will continue to be affected by nursing home reform legislation. Effective October 1, 1990, nursing facilities participating in the Medicare or Medicaid programs must not require residents to waive their benefits or give assurances that they are not eligible or will not apply for benefits under Medicare or Medicaid. As of that date, nursing facilities must also not require that a third party guarantee payment to the facility as a condition of admission or continued stay.[78]

The Medicaid program will further require, effective October 1, 1990, that a facility may not charge, solicit, accept or receive, in addition to any amount otherwise required to be paid under the state's Medicaid plan, any gift, money, donation, or other consideration as a precondition of admission or continued stay.[79]

The federal conditions of participation for the Medicare and Medicaid programs establish standards for patient rights in skilled nursing and intermediate care facilities.[80] These conditions must be met if the facility is to provide care to Medicare or Medicaid beneficiaries. Generally, the facility must maintain written policies regarding the rights and responsibilities of patients. These policies and procedures must be made available to patients. Each patient must be fully informed, before

[77]See, e.g. Cal. Health & Safety Code §§ 1599–1599.4 (West 1988).

[78]Omnibus Budget Reconciliation Act of 1987, Pub. L. No. 100-203, §§ 4201(a)(3), 4211(a)(3), 101 Stat. 1330-160, 168, 1330-182, 193 (1987).

[79]Omnibus Budget Reconciliation Act of 1987, Pub. L. No. 100-203, § 4211(a)(3), 101 Stat. 1330-182, 193 (1987).

[80]42 U.S.C. §§ 1395x(j), 3027, 1396a, 1396d (1982 & Supp. II, 1984, Supp. III, 1985); 42 C.F.R. §§ 405.1121, 442.311, 442.320 (1987).

or at the time of admission, of these rights and all rules governing patient conduct and responsibilities. These policies should be acknowledged by the resident in writing along with any amendments to the policies. The regulations establish that the patient must be fully informed in writing of all services available in the facility and of the charges for these services, including charges for services that are not paid for by Medicare or Medicaid. This information must be provided before or at the time of admission and on a continuing basis as changes occur.

The patient's rights extend to controlling his or her medical condition and treatment and include being informed of his or her medical condition by a physician, unless medically contraindicated, being afforded the opportunity to assist in planning the care and treatment, and being afforded the opportunity to refuse certain treatment. The patient must also be encouraged and assisted to exercise personal rights, as a patient and as a citizen, and to voice grievances and recommend changes at the facility.

In drafting the admission contract, it is important to recognize that these regulations restrict the ability of the facility to transfer or discharge a patient. The transfer or discharge must only be for medical reasons, the patient's welfare or that of other patients, or nonpayment, unless prohibited by the Medicare or Medicaid programs. The patient should also be given reasonable advance notice to insure orderly discharge or transfer. Effective October 1, 1990, the Medicaid program will require a participating nursing facility to establish and maintain identical policies regarding transfer, discharge, and the provision of services required by Medicaid, for all individuals regardless of source of payment.[81]

The patient's financial affairs are also provided protection. If the facility manages the patient's funds, the facility should be prepared to account to the patient for those funds and must preclude commingling of a patient's funds with funds of the facility or of any other person except another patient.

Patients are protected from abuse and restraints by the regulations that place conditions upon such restraints. The patient must also receive confidential treatment of personal and medical records and must be afforded additional privacy rights. The patient must be able to freely associate and correspond and to participate in social, religious, and community group activities. The patient generally retains the right to

[81]Omnibus Budget Reconciliation Act of 1987, Pub. L. No. 100-203, § 4211 (a)(3), 101 Stat. 1330-192, 193 (1987).

control and use personal possessions as space permits, and the patient must not be required to perform services for the facility.

The admission contract itself should be easily understood. The policies and procedures of the facility and the agreement should clearly establish the patient rights required under federal and state law. The facility should also state clearly those permissible situations under state and federal law under which the patient's rights are limited by other considerations.

LIABILITY CONSIDERATIONS

The specter of liability is a formidable one for the retirement housing developer. Liability may arise through the necessary and numerous contractual relationships that flow from the development and operation of a retirement community. For example, typically there are a number of contractual arrangements with lenders, contractors, architects, attorneys, lessees, managers, and residents.

Further liability may attach through allegations of tortious conduct on the part of the owner or operator of the retirement community. Torts are acts or omissions for which a person may be held liable regardless of whether there is a contractual relationship between the person committing the wrong and the person who has suffered the injury. Torts include, without limitation, assault, battery, false imprisonment, intentional infliction of emotional distress, trespass, conversion, defamation, invasion of privacy, negligence, and certain activities that the law recognizes as creating liability even without fault.

As previously discussed, state and federal statutory requirements may also have civil and/or criminal liability implications for the developer. For example, securities laws impose disclosure requirements on the offering and prohibit improper solicitations and fraudulent activities. The following discussion will address selected areas of concern for the retirement housing developer.

Liability Considerations in Contracting with the Elderly. The nature of the relationship between the operator of the community and the resident will affect the obligations arising under the contract. As previously indicated, the condominium and cooperative arrangements create a buyer-seller relationship. The sales contract may contain representations and warranties on the part of the seller that are considered inducements for the purchase of the property by the buyer. Misrepresentations by the seller or the failure to disclose certain defects in the property may result in liability to the seller.

The development of a rental project creates a landlord-tenant relationship between the lessor and elderly resident and, correspondingly, imposes obligations on the landlord and tenant pursuant to state law. Many states impose a significant burden on the landlord. The failure of the landlord to meet its obligations may result in significant financial consequences, because a state may impose damages by statute for such failure.

The development of a CCRC is often not intended to provide an ownership interest to the resident; however, it does create a contractual arrangement. Depending on the state and the language of the agreement, courts in interpreting the resident agreement may also apply certain principles of licensor-licensee and landlord-tenant relationships in trying to define the obligations of the parties.

The admission agreement creates a contractual arrangement for the provision of health care to a patient. It also creates a provider-patient relationship that imposes obligations on the health care provider, whether or not they are reflected in the contract itself.

A number of the considerations for contracting with the elderly have previously been discussed in this chapter. The significance of those considerations often directly relates to the potential liability of the operator of the community. The party drafting a contract is often tempted to use vague, general language in an attempt to permit various interpretations of the contract. The apparent hope is that if the language is broad enough any desired interpretation may be made. However, a principle of contract law that is often applied to the interpretation of a contract is that the contract should be interpreted against the party drafting it. Thus, the retirement community operator should not hide behind language subject to various interpretations, because a court may interpret the provision in favor of the elderly resident. This is not to say that certain contingencies should not be built into the contract. The contract should permit adjustments for changing conditions.

A concise, clear contract will facilitate marketing of the retirement community. However, the advertising materials and contract used for the retirement community should be carefully examined to insure that they do not promise more than they can deliver. The temptation to incorporate effusive descriptions of the services provided into the contract itself should be guarded against, although the contract can be drafted in a marketable manner. Otherwise, the developer may create warranties without intending to do so. Representations with regard to the services to be provided at the community should be carefully considered. The developer may face charges of breach of contract or misrepresentation if he or she later decides against providing services promised to be provided or fails to provide them in the manner described in the contract or marketing literature.

Considerations in Designing and Caring for the Elderly Resident. The retirement housing developer must be cognizant of the potentially fragile nature of the market being sought. Design and construction of the housing project must take into account the particular needs of the elderly resident and visitor. Failure to do so may create a liability trap.

Since the developer is marketing to a population that can be more susceptible to injury, courts may impose a greater duty of care on the design and construction of the premises. This greater duty may be reflected in the court's interpretation of the services promised through the contract itself, or through the application of tort law theory, such as negligence. A retirement community houses the elderly resident, and it should be expected that other elderly persons will visit the community. If an elderly visitor is injured when climbing up a poorly designed stairwell, the court may find that the design was inadequate in light of the expected use. A court might find the same flight of stairs adequately designed for other purposes.

The addition of the service function to the retirement housing package will also generally increase the potential liability of the provider. This is particularly true if the retirement community includes the provision of health care services. The assumption of responsibility for the health care of the community's residents may naturally result in issues concerning the quality and level of that care. These issues may arise in a number of contexts. A retirement community that provides skilled care, for example, may face issues as to the quality of nursing care, the appropriateness of the prescription and dispensing of medication, and the extent to which the patient's condition is monitored. The developer who endeavors to enter the health care field should recognize the associated risks.

Responsibility for Liability. The individual or individuals who are involved in developing the retirement community should be concerned about their own potential for liability. As previously discussed, this potential should be considered in the organization of the development entity because the type of entity chosen may affect the extent to which the individual's own assets may be exposed. Further, even if the choice of entity is a corporation, care must be taken so that the corporation is not treated as an alter ego of the individual, so that the corporate veil is pierced and individual liability results.

The various interrelationships involved in the development of the retirement community may also cause liability implications to the developer that seem illogical on their face. The developer may be charged with responsibility for a number of other contracting parties. For example, if construction of the community is defective, the owner may be charged with negligently selecting or supervising the work of the contractor. Similar allegations may be made if the owner leases the facility to another operator or enters into a management agreement. The owner should therefore carefully select those persons with whom he or she does business, require appropriate indemnification by the contracting parties, and the maintenance of appropriate insurance by such parties. Such insurance should, to the extent possible, also include the developer as an insured party.

The developer must also recognize a possible responsibility to co-owners. A partner has a fiduciary relationship with other partners and must not breach that fiduciary duty. Similarly, a director on a board of directors has a fiduciary responsibility to the corporation and its shareholders. These fiduciary relationships are essentially positions of trust requiring the partner or director to act with care and prudence, and in the best interest of the partnership or corporation, and not to act in self-interest to the detriment of the partnership or corporation.

The retirement community operator should implement risk management systems that will continually assess the potential for liability and methods for correcting potential causes of liability at the retirement community. The responsibility of the entity for the actions of its employees also demands that procedures be developed to reduce the risk of employee mistakes in the operation of the community.

Of course, a crucial element in the liability scenario is the maintenance of adequate insurance coverage. A program should be developed for monitoring and reevaluating such coverage periodically.

CHAPTER 6

MARKETING AND SALES

JAMES L. LAUGHLIN and S. KELLEY MOSELEY

INTRODUCTION

This chapter discusses the role of marketing in the development and operation of a retirement community. It addresses basic principles of marketing, but more importantly points out the special issues in marketing to seniors. Because the market comprising senior housing and senior consumers is relatively new, more speculation than experience exists concerning it.

The Meaning of Marketing. Marketing has changed over the past several years and is no longer thought of only as face-to-face selling and advertising. The definition has broadened significantly to include research, planning, and public relations as well as the typical selling functions. It includes all of the activities needed to transfer products, goods, or services from the producer to the consumer.

Marketing has a strong consumer orientation. It identifies consumers' needs, develops products and services to satisfy those needs, and creates demand for the product or service. Norman McMillan, in his book *Marketing Your Hospital,* identified marketing as simply: "Finding out what people want and giving them more of it and finding out what people don't want and giving them less of it."[1]

---

[1]Norman McMillan, *Marketing Your Hospital* (Chicago: American Hospital Publishing, Inc., 1981), 4.

Although marketing, particularly market research, uses the scientific methods of social and behavioral science, it cannot identify or control all of the variables affecting consumer behavior. It is, therefore, primarily an art rather than a science and relies more on skilled, experienced individuals making reasonable decisions than on scientific theories and laws. This is particularly true in selling to seniors due to the relative newness of this older group as a marketing target.

Closely related to economics, marketing draws upon the well-known economic concepts of utility, demand and supply analysis, marginal revenue, and diminishing utility. It creates time, place, and possession utility (usefulness) by motivating consumer behavior. Marketing means having a product when people want it, where they want it, and on terms that they are willing to meet.

Marketing also draws from the social sciences, including psychology, sociology, and statistics. These fields provide insight into individual and group behavior as well as give guidance on sampling, probability, and statistical analysis.

The marketing function in retirement housing interacts with all other functions, such as design, development, financial management, and operations, in areas relating to sales volume, cost, and profit. Conflicts between marketing and other functions may arise, especially between management and marketing. It is essential that marketing promises what management can deliver or unhappy clients will soon result. This situation occurs when the sales staff, in their zeal to fill up a community, describe the services to be offered in somewhat unrealistic terms.

Why Is Marketing Needed?   Although the need for marketing may seem obvious, that is, to increase sales, it has broader implications.

Developers who do not listen to consumers will generally fail.

Conversely, those who do listen and respond to consumers will find increased market acceptance.

Society will increasingly demand that senior housing developers be responsive to elderly needs.

Retirement housing communities serve the needs of the elderly; unless they are sensitive to those needs, they have little purpose.

Marketing Functions.   Marketing encompasses several identifiable steps or functions. These include determination of the product, the target market, the price, the location, and the methods to promote the product.

Although without clearly understanding these elements, a senior housing developer is unlikely to be successful, there are no universally correct answers for handling the issues. In fact, different communities and products will require different mixes of the same elements. In some situations, a low-priced product within a local market is appropriate. In others, a higher priced product with a regional market area is the selected mix.

Marketing elements do not operate in a vacuum. The characteristics and goals of an organization and the forces operating in the external (legal, political, economic, social, and demographic) environment will significantly affect the product, target market, price, location, and method of promotion. As an example, assume that a developer, Mr. Smith of Mega Real Estate, decides to construct a luxury retirement community with all services, including a continental restaurant and a skilled nursing home, in Westchester County. He has thus defined the product, the location, and in a practical sense, the price. A luxury facility, which implies high prices, also defines the promotion methods because individuals who can afford such a facility are not likely to buy from an advertisement in the classified pages.

Often these kinds of decisions are made within the first weeks of creating the idea of a retirement development without independent assessment of the external environment and organization's goals. These forces might redefine the product, price, location, and promotion strategy.

Assume that Mr. Smith hires a consultant to advise on his proposed project. The consultant's report advises Mr. Smith of the following:

Westchester County has an elderly population of 3,000 persons.

The average elderly household income is $12,000 per year with 10 percent earning over $20,000.

Six other moderate to upscale projects either exist or are planned for the community.

The state nursing home planning agency has established a moratorium on any new construction of nursing care beds.

Clearly, the outlook for Mr. Smith's luxury retirement housing product is not encouraging. However, he presents the idea to his board of directors. The board, after listening to the presentation, concludes that luxury retirement housing is not consistent with the company's mission as a builder of low-cost homes. Further, the chairman does not believe that Mega Real Estate Company has the in-house knowledge or expertise to carry out such an expensive project. Mr. Smith is depressed because he has already invested $100,000 of company funds in the project.

This scenario describes how both external and internal forces can directly affect the selection of the product, price, location, and promotion method for retirement housing. Research and analysis are required prior to defining the product to be developed. Guidelines for avoiding costly mistakes are provided in the following pages.

Summary. Marketing consists of all of the activities needed to transfer goods and services from the developer to the consumer. Because the behavior of consumers, especially senior consumers, is not well documented, marketing is a complex task. It includes defining the product, determining if a market exists, identifying an appropriate price, assessing where to locate the product, and finally, deciding on methods of promotion.

UNDERSTANDING THE SENIOR CONSUMER

An Overview of Consumer Behavior. Prior to considering the senior consumer, it is helpful to develop an awareness of general consumer behavior by examining the motivation and psychology of individuals. Although the reasons for consumer behavior are sometimes unclear, this analysis will aid in understanding why certain products or services are chosen by consumers.

Economists would suggest that there is a clear and direct relationship between the price of a good or service and the quantity purchased. If the price of an item is increased, fewer consumers will purchase it, if the price is decreased, more items are purchased. This simplistic view ignores consumer attitudes, income, and competing goods and services.

More realistically, consumers are influenced by their attitudes, habits, needs, and desires. If every individual in society were completely different developing advertising and marketing strategies would be difficult. Fortunately, most members of society are not hermits or rugged individualists. Societal influences cause individuals to tend to follow patterns of their peer groups. One such group has gained public attention by being classified as yuppies (young, urban, upwardly mobile professionals). Yuppies exhibit very similar buyer behavior. They purchase BMWs and certain name-brand clothes, eat at "in" restaurants, live in professional neighborhoods, and shop at the "right" stores.

Knowing these facts about yuppie group behavior should make it easier to assess the expected buyer behavior of this group.

Unfortunately, determination of consumer behavior is not quite that straightforward. Buying motives flow from the buyer's impulses and desires, and these change during a person's lifetime. Anyone who has studied management or psychology is familiar with Abraham Maslow's discussion of the motivation of human behavior.[2] Essentially, Maslow suggests that individuals must first satisfy their basic needs before they can address higher order needs. These needs, in order from basic to higher, include:

1. Food, shelter, clothing, and sex
2. Safety and security
3. Social sense of belonging and love
4. Status and self-esteem
5. Self-actualization, or achievement of full potential

Clearly, this hierarchy has some validity—a starving man is not overly concerned with the status of his position, his car, or carpet colors in his house.

These needs may motivate buyers. This means that a purchaser of goods or services will act based upon such factors as status, fear, and physical requirements. More often in American society, the motivation to purchase is based on weighing emotional versus rational factors. Emotional factors are ones that satisfy the senses, such as touch, taste, or sight; they may also appeal to desires for prestige, status, pleasure, and enjoyment. Rational motives are more practical and include economy, dependability, safety, durability, convenience, quality, and value. In addition, consumer behavior is influenced by other factors—age, sex, income, culture, ethnic heritage, group membership, social class, and brand loyalty. Moreover, people are influenced by the opinions and attitudes of others, such as members of a peer group or prominent personalities. A celebrity who claims to use a product leads others to believe that they will be like the celebrity if they purchase the product. For the elderly, the opinions of children also influence certain buying behavior.

Market Segmentation. Of primary interest, given all these motives and influences, is how to successfully target a market to a particular

[2]A. H. Maslow, *Motivation and Personality* (New York: Harper, 1954).

consumer. One method is to classify consumers into groups based on observed buying behavior. Examples include:

Price-sensitive groups who base purchases on thrift and economy comparison

Emotion-sensitive groups who base purchases on symbols and images that promise satisfaction

Brand-loyalty buyers who purchase familiar products because of image, prestige, value, convenience, or price

The rationale for segmenting consumers into groups is that no single product can meet the needs of all consumers, but it is possible to define a product that meets a particular group's preferences. Market segmentation can be seen in many products. For example, bathroom tissue doesn't come in just one style, but in several—flowered, or abstract prints, white or colored paper, scented or unscented varieties. Another example is Coca-Cola, which is marketed as "Classic," regular "Coke," cherry-flavored, diet, caffeine-free, and diet caffeine-free. These choices address the desires of defined groups of consumers.

To properly segment, it is necessary to determine the needs, wants, or desires of the target group. These consumers are then classified into categories, such as price sensitive, emotion sensitive, or brand loyal. Other classification methods include:

Social class (lower, middle, or upper)

Education (less than high school, high school, college)

Age (young, middle-aged, elderly)

Life cycle (child, adolescent, unmarried young adult, newly married, full nest, empty nest, survivor)[3]

Although all of these factors influence consumer behavior, this discussion highlights the behavior of persons over 65 years of age.

First, the elderly are not a homogeneous group, but their behavior does differ from that of younger persons. According to the Bureau of Labor statistics, those over 55 years spend less on clothes and shelter than younger Americans. However, they spend a great deal more on health care. Interestingly, those over age 75 spend the least on all items except health care.

---

[3]Patrick Murphy and William Staples, "A Modernized Life Cycle," *Journal of Consumer Research* (June 1979): 12–22.

It is unrealistic to define the retirement housing market as all persons over the age of 65. The market segment under age 75 is quite different from the over-75 age group; thus segmenting the seniors market is extremely important. For analyzing seniors' buying behavior, appropriate segments are:

Age (55 to 70 years, 70 to 79 years, over 80 years)
Sex
Annual income (less than $15,000, $15,000 to $25,000, over $25,000)
Geographic region (Northeast, Southeast, South, Midwest, Far West, Northwest)
Religion
Race or ethnic origin
Social class (lower, middle, upper)

The marketing goal is to develop a product that meets the needs or desires of a particular segment. The elderly, who are motivated by many of the emotional and psychological factors pointed out earlier, seek safety or security, as well as social interaction. Moreover, adult children are motivated to provide or seek a safe, secure, and stimulating environment for their parents. It is important to be aware of the involvement of children in motivating the elderly to select senior housing. Children often make the initial contact in order to gather information, especially for nursing home or personal care selection.

The Senior Consumer.   What factors motivate senior consumers? Like other consumers, the elderly are heterogenous, but with a lifetime of experience in handling sales techniques, they are generally more conservative than younger persons. Also, in many instances the senior buyer is not acting alone, but is being represented by, or at least receiving counsel from, adult children and peers. Therefore, it is possible to be selling the same product to at least two different persons.

David Wolfe argues that consumers achieve self-worth through seeking desire fulfillment. These desires, in contrast to needs, differ according to age and other factors, such as income, social class, and sex. Wolfe suggests that at least four life experience motivators based on age can be identified.[4]

[4]David Wolfe, "Why Most Seniors Won't Move to a Retirement Community," *National Association for Senior Living Industries News* (November 1986): 5.

Possession experiences affect young people who seek satisfaction by purchase of goods such as automobiles or houses.

Catered experiences are sought by persons as they grow older and include travel, dining out, maid service, and yard service.

Being experiences include the desire to pursue interpersonal relationships, enjoy living, get in touch with one's self

Survival experiences reflect the need to respond to declining health and capability and include a desire for safety, security, and medical support.

Wolfe also points out that the majority of new entrants into today's retirement communities are the ones forced to address the survival experience. National statistics indicate the average age of residents in retirement communities is between 75 and 85 years.

Motivation of the Elderly Prospect. Many seniors don't want to admit that a move to a retirement community may be their final move or that they are losing their independence. The developer and marketing staff must realize that they are asking persons to make this final move. The elderly fear loss of health, either their own or their spouse's, and they fear becoming dependent, which means inability to perform their daily activities.

These fears or needs motivate many of the elderly to relocate, but the level one product (independent living) described earlier, is not fear or need driven. It is difficult to stimulate demand for a product unless it is perceived as needed. The advertising firm, developer, and the sales staff must recognize this problem, in motivating seniors to select level one housing.

Level two (semi-independent) prospective residents are a hybrid of demand- and need-driven consumers. The marketing plan must be modified to meet their needs and expectations as well as to illustrate the benefits of the community to the demand-driven segment. Level three (personal care) and levels four and five (nursing care) clearly attract need-driven users.

The developer who is planning to market an independent living or continuing care retirement community will attract prospective residents who are for the most part, active and independent and thus, difficult to motivate to move into any type of community. This motivation challenge means that the developer who wishes to undertake a senior housing community with services and/or care must be realistic in anticipating the fill-up time. There will also be additional staffing requirements and more extensive promotional materials than needed for marketing conventional apartments.

Profile of Elderly Consumers. The suggestion that the elderly fall into three basic categories is a simplistic view, but it does offer a framework for analysis. The first category is comprised of freedom searchers. They see their freedom to relocate as quite important and do not wish to be restrained or tied down to long-term commitments. Further, they do not want to have estates that must go through long probate. Therefore, they may not own real estate and dislike long-term entrance fee agreements. In general, these individuals do not see themselves as old or needing health care. Typically, this category of elderly will sell the current home and reinvest the proceeds in financial products with greater appreciation rates. Individuals in this group may tend to be compulsive; they avoid limitations or restrictions being placed on their lifestyle. The most attractive product for this segment of the elderly population is a rental environment, with many services available on an a la carte basis.

The second category can be called the anticipators. These individuals thoroughly plan and organize their future needs. They are usually homeowners who are active in conserving their estates and very concerned about catastrophic illnesses. More often than not they have insurance and want to prepare for the worst. Anticipators would prefer to cover the cost of living in a retirement community from interest earned on investments, pensions, and social security. Further, they prefer to retain the equity from the sale of their homes in order to pass that equity on to their estates and adult children. This group of elderly will often look favorably at a continuing care retirement community, because it provides the resident with a long-term assurance of both services and care.

The third group of elderly need nursing support or some level of assistance in their daily living activities; they are categorized as health care users. Individuals in this category may find a level three community (personal care or a nursing facility) will be the only facility that can meet their needs. They, and their families, must be educated about their options.

Because the terminology, programs, and services provided by each level of housing can be confusing, the marketing staff must clearly communicate the differences and how they may meet particular seniors' needs. Creating a resident profile is important in order to align individual needs with the appropriate community. It should reflect project goals and the applicant's physical and emotional condition, personality, and attitudes about mutual support and sharing. What the prospective resident desires versus what the development offers must match. This process will create an atmosphere that responds to the elderly client's desire to be independent. The prospective resident of any community is looking for an environment that will help provide an image of productivity and independence. Anything that diminishes that image will be a deterrent to choosing that community.

Some criteria that will help the marketing staff determine whether the profile of a prospective resident matches the product being offered by the community may include:

Is the prospect medically stable?

Will he or she require constant supervision?

Can the individual make judgments without involving another person?

Would the applicant require more services than available in the community?

Does the community meet the person's needs?

Attitudes Toward Housing.   Elderly individuals often believe that experience is necessary for success. Therefore, they look at the developer's track record. A developer who has no background in retirement housing must attract individuals to the development team with prior experience. It is also important to emphasize the experience of the owner in other development enterprises or businesses related to retirement housing. One place to begin this education process is with the lender. To most elderly, lenders have considerable credibility. If the lender has accepted the concept, the developer is on the road to gaining the needed trust.

The marketing campaign is asking the elderly individual, in certain cases, to give up the pervasive American dream of home ownership. Many in the marketplace feel that leasing indicates transience, something that most elderly have strived to overcome all their lives. One challenge to the marketing staff is to present the idea that it is acceptable not to own a home. (This, of course, assumes that the development is not being sold as condominiums.) The sales staff must convince the prospective residents that moving to the retirement community offers more advantages than remaining in their current homes.

Developers and their marketing staff will be working with prospects who were raised during the Great Depression. To own a home was a lifetime goal for many. It is difficult then, to ask a 78-year-old widow to give up that home. The task is to encourage the acceptance of an alternative lifestyle by overcoming the negative feelings and apprehensions generated by moving out of a home. Life in a retirement community needs to be presented to the potential resident as desirable.

Research conducted by the authors in 1987 suggests certain attitudes toward senior housing are related to geographic region, as presented in Table 6-1. The data are based on a personal survey of over 500 elderly individuals. Table 6-2 shows preferences by age groups for a sample of 372 respondents from the urban Southeast. The data in this table show certain differences in attitudes toward senior housing between persons under 75 years and over 75 years of age. These differences highlight the importance of carefully targeting the potential consumer.

These data indicate that more urban elderly than rural elderly prefer apartments, more urban elderly than rural elderly desire swimming pools, both urban and rural elderly prefer cafeteria-style meal service, and most elderly prefer rental to entrance fee projects.

Most elderly do not prefer central dining, maid service, or an on-

TABLE 6-1. Facility Design Preferences by Region (Percent Preference)

	Rural Southwest	Rural Southeast	Urban Southeast	Urban Northwest
Unit Type				
Efficiency/studio	10	12	6	12
One bedroom	52	42	35	49
Two bedrooms	38	46	58	39
Building Type				
Single family	31	43	25	33
Townhouse	28	30	23	12
Apartment/condominium	41	27	50	55
Services				
Maid service	7	20	42	24
Central dining	24	27	40	36
Nursing home on site	24	38	39	27
Swimming pool	48	32	80	55
Meals in Central Dining				
Cafeteria/buffet	100	84	69	62
Waitress	0	16	30	37
More than one meal/day	17	22	21	32
Fees				
Rental preferred	93	79	39	84
Purchase preferred	7	21	55	16

TABLE 6-2. Facility Design Preferences by Age Groups (Percent Preference)

	Less Than 75 Years	Over 75 Years
Unit Type		
Efficiency/studio	4	10
One bedroom	29	52
Two bedrooms	67	37
Building Type		
Single family	28	14
Townhouse	26	16
Apartment/condominium	46	68
Services		
Maid service	30	65
Central dining	30	54
Nursing home on site	28	58
Swimming pool	83	60
Central Dining		
Cafeteria/buffet	68	69
Waitress	32	31
More than one meal/day	15	30
Fees		
Rental preferred	34	53
Purchase preferred	66	47

site nursing home; however, those over 75 years desire more services, probably because they recognize that they may soon need such assistance.

Similar market research is required in order to assess attitudes of local consumers. Because these attitudes seem to vary considerably by geographic region and age, it is necessary to conduct a thorough market analysis prior to developing a senior housing community.

Summary. Matching the prospective resident with the community is one of marketing's major responsibilities. Most communities' marketing programs are specifically designed around lifestyle, so it is extremely important to identify the appropriate potential occupants. If the lifestyle is aimed more toward the recreational versus the care side, then residents should be independent, not persons who require significant care.

Moreover, it is important to understand the motivation and attitudes of elderly consumers. They are not all alike, so specific research is required to solicit attitudes and opinions. The elderly are motivated by needs and desires, some emotional and some rational. The challenges of marketing senior housing are to understand these motivating factors and to convince the elderly consumer that the housing product is a realistic option.

PRODUCT PLANNING ANALYSIS AND SELECTION

Retirement housing products have not gained uniform, overwhelming market acceptance. The lack of acceptance of troubled retirement projects seems to relate more to the lack of adequate product planning, analysis, and selection than to lack of desire by the elderly for the product.

These are the fundamental reasons for failure of senior housing projects:

1. Failure to test product acceptance
2. Failure to identify the market
3. Poor product definition
4. Unclear product image
5. Inaccurate data collection, analysis, and interpretation
6. Ignoring of market analysis data
7. Pricing that does not match target market
8. High cost of development
9. Poor timing
10. Ineffective marketing support and evaluation

All of us have heard about products such as the Ford Edsel. Selecting the right product for the market is one of the most critical factors in the marketing effort. The choice of product determines who the market will be, how it will be sold, the price, and the method of promotion. A successful project requires several key elements in product planning and selection. These necessary elements in formulating an acceptable marketing strategy are discussed in the following sections.

Defining the Product.   The senior housing product is not a single item or type of project. In fact, since the industry is relatively young, there are a variety of products, ranging from fully independent housing to nursing care. Further, combinations of products can exist in the same organization or on the same campus. This variety can create confusion among the planning and marketing teams. The product, product variety or mix, and relationship among products within a single campus or organization can confound developers and customers alike, unless they are clearly understood and given a priority of importance.

A retirement housing product is much more than the physical or technical characteristics of the building and grounds. Although the technical or functional character of the building may be important to the architect or developer, it may have little to do with the potential consumer's feeling about the product. The consumer is looking for utility or satisfaction of psychological needs that encompass not only the building and grounds, but services, status, security, comfort, safety, and other intangible factors.

The senior housing products that include independent housing, assisted living, supervised living, intermediate nursing care, skilled nursing care, and subacute care are generally classified as consumer goods, which are delivered directly to the user. This is in contrast to industrial goods, which are the raw materials sold for making other goods or services. This distinction is important because it determines the method of planning the product.

Consumer goods can be classified as convenience, shopping, or specialty items.[5] Convenience goods (such as milk, bread, or soap) are those that consumers purchase frequently without spending much time in price comparisons. Shopping goods are those that consumers will generally analyze and compare based on quality, price, style, or suitability. Specialty goods are those that consumers will make a special effort to obtain and are unwilling to replace with substitutes because of perceived unique features or characteristics.

In addition, there are unknown goods and services that the customer does not want or does not perceive needing. These include new products that must be explained, nursing home care that the elderly do not desire, cemetery lots, and encyclopedias.

The retirement housing product has some features that classify it as a shopping good and also as an unknown good. Of course, the developer of a retirement project desires to position it as a specialty good, which will be aggressively sought by elderly consumers because of its unique character or ability to satisfy a need or want.

Further, it is possible for the senior housing product to respond to certain desires of consumers, including status or prestige (snob appeal); sensory appeal (sight, texture, color, design); physical needs (assistance

[5]Philip Kotler, *Marketing Management and Analysis Planning and Control* (Englewood, NJ: Prentice-Hall, 1967), 293.

with physical disability); and psychological well-being (safety and security).

The first step in product planning and selection is to define the business being considered and then to determine if retirement housing is consistent with that business. Retirement housing encompasses elements of the health care, hospitality, and real estate industries. The characteristics of the senior housing product influence the design and conduct of the marketing program. For example, real estate is sold in a different way than services or health care. The senior community is offering a lifestyle, including security and services, whereas an apartment provides primarily shelter, despite the fact that it may be a luxury dwelling.

Product Life Cycle. All products pass through phases much like human life. These phases include birth, growth, maturity and decline. A major decision is to determine where a product is in this life cycle sequence. It is undesirable to introduce a product that is declining in consumer acceptance. For example, with the trend toward outpatient medical care and the decline of hospital inpatient care, very few additional hospitals are needed.

Retirement housing, however, seems to be somewhere between the birth and growth phases. Although this offers significant opportunity, it also produces risk, since market acceptance and consumer behavior are not well defined. With little restriction on new entrants into the senior housing market, the point at which saturation is reached may approach quite rapidly. An example of this rapid saturation is the office and apartment construction activity in certain oil-dependent states during the early 1980s.

Steps in Product Planning. Since the failure rate of senior products is fairly high and competition is increasing, there is little room for products that are poorly defined or planned.

Product planning is more of an organizational task than a particular tool or technique. It involves development of the planning team and the process of analysis and definition. The steps involved in product planning have been discussed in Chapter 2.

At the product planning stage, it is important to seriously consider the product's special features, that differentiate it from other products and to develop ideas that will help position it in the marketplace. The goal of product planning is to systematically analyze and select a product that will appeal to the target market of the elderly. The definition of the product will probably change as more information is gathered on consumer preferences and attitudes and competitor activities.

Market Research and Measurement.   Market research is a process of determining who the customers are, what they want, where they live, and how the competition is performing. A detailed discussion of the market research function has been provided in Chapter 3.

Market Research Benefits.   Market research should provide useful information, not merely be an exercise in data gathering. To be useful, interpretation of the data is required. The developer faces a variety of decisions concerning target markets and product mix; the task of research is to help make better decisions. The functions of market research that support this decision-making effort relate to systematically and objectively collecting, analyzing, and interpreting data in several areas.

Product research—market acceptance of the product or packaging
Population analysis—size, location, and characteristics of the potential client population
Sales research—sales policies and sales effectiveness
Consumer research—attitudes and behavior of customers
Advertising research—the effectiveness of the advertising program in generating leads and sales

In the project planning phases, the primary emphasis is on product, population, and consumer research. Later in the project marketing phase, advertising, sales analysis, and opinion research are also required.

Pricing.   The four P's of marketing are pricing, product, promotion, and place. Obviously, price is related to the target market and type of product. Of primary concern to most developers of retirement housing is the amount to charge in order to fill up the project and make a profit. The answer to this question is a direct function of the type of product, services offered, and amenity package.

In economic terms, price is closely related to value or utility. That is, how much does the product satisfy the consumer's wants or desires? Consumers tend to analyze products and choose the ones that best satisfy their desires. Moreover, the price of a product tends to influence demand, especially for luxury goods or products that have substitutes. For example, if houses are selling for $100,000 but apartments are available for $400 per month, consumers may choose to rent rather than buy. However, for necessity goods such as emergency services, surgery, or goods without clear substitutes, price is not as critical in determining demand.

Retirement housing is a need-driven product only when an elderly person needs support or services in order to live. In most cases, elderly individuals have substitutes available for a congregate care or a seniors housing project. These substitutes include their own home with family assistance, using health care or homemaker services, friends, or spouse, and nursing home care. In these cases, the elderly and their family tend to compare not only the price of those alternatives, but the associated value, utility, or desirability of the choice. Under most circumstances, the elderly prefer to remain in their own home because it is more convenient, familiar, desirable, and/or cheaper.

The price charged for senior housing will, therefore, be determined as a result of a variety of factors including type of product, competition, and cost of production. For the project to be viable, the price must cover costs and return a profit to the developer. Cost-based analysis is a necessary first step in determining the price of the product. The cost of retirement housing must be accurately determined in order for this approach to be used. As pointed out in Chapter 4, it is extremely important to identify all costs.

The following example may be helpful in developing a cost-based pricing model.

Project: 200-unit congregate housing apartment; 190 occupied units (95% occupancy)

Unit mix: 140 one-bedroom units; 60 two-bedroom units

Services: One meal per day; scheduled van transportation; utilities included (except telephone); full-time activities coordinator; nurse on duty (daytime hours)

Total construction cost: $8,120,000

Marketing cost: $600,000

Interest carry during construction: $1,610,000

Total development costs: $15,475,000

Absorption period: 36 months from beginning of construction

Interest on debt: 10.5%

Monthly fixed operation cost (MFC): $52,000

Monthly variable operating cost/unit (MVC): $350

Monthly debt service (MDS): $141,541

$$\text{Break-even price} = \frac{(\text{MFC} + \text{MDS})}{190} + \text{MVC}$$

$$= \$1{,}018 + 350 = \$1{,}368$$

Average monthly rent = $1,368 at 95% occupancy

Following the determination of the break-even price, the next step is to determine the desired return on the investment. If the developer desires a 20 percent annual return on a cash investment of $500,000, the cost must be increased by 20 percent of $500,000, or $100,000 annually. Adding this amount to the annual costs produces:

$$\begin{matrix}\text{Price to earn}\\20\%\ \text{return}\end{matrix} = \frac{[\text{MFC} + \text{MDS} + (\$100{,}000/12)]}{190} + \text{MVC}$$

$$= \frac{(\$52{,}000 + 141{,}541 + 8{,}333)}{190} + 350$$

$$= \$1{,}062 + 350 = \$1{,}412$$

Average monthly rent = $1,412 at 95% occupancy

Finally, it is necessary to compare the price with the price of the competition for a similar product. The confusion surrounding senior housing products and the availability of substitute housing options make price comparison somewhat difficult. As a result, price setting also must incorporate emotional, psychological, and unique elements. This process involves describing the product in terms that create value and uniqueness. This approach attempts to convince the purchaser that a one-bedroom congregate living environment is *not* the same as a typical one-bedroom garden apartment, but rather offers services and a lifestyle that are desirable, valuable, and different from traditional housing arrangements.

The price a developer can charge for retirement housing is, therefore, a function of the type of product, competition, cost, and perceived value. By using the approach to price analysis described on the preceding pages, it is possible to achieve a more realistic pricing structure.

Pricing strategy also encompasses techniques to attract customers and achieve rapid absorption of the project. These techniques are closely related to the promotion strategy and include price discounts, premium pricing for desirable units, unbundled pricing of services, and meeting competitors' prices. Although any of these techniques can be appropriate, the underlying factor is that a project cannot be viable over the long term when the price charged is less than the cost to develop and operate. Therefore, the fundamental feature of pricing is a determination of the break-even price.

Summary. Product planning involves selecting the right senior housing product for the target market. Of primary importance is a detailed description of the product being proposed. Lack of a clear definition can create confusion for the planning team as well as the potential elderly consumer. Retirement housing appears to be a shopping good and an unknown good. Therefore, seniors may not understand it and when they do, will compare it with others in terms of quality, price, and suitability.

Success in product planning requires a thorough analysis of the product and market culminating in a product business plan. These tasks will enable the developer to define a product which is needed by the community, has unique features to distinguish it from the competition, and will be profitable. The following pages address the methods and techniques for promoting the product.

PRODUCT PROMOTION

Promotion includes advertising, special events, personal selling, and public relations. Marketing encompasses promotion plus product planning and analysis. Although it is important and seems to receive the most attention, promotion is merely one element of the entire marketing function. Many decisions and tasks are required prior to reaching the promotion phase.

Promotion has different objectives depending on the stage of the product's life cycle. Promotional activities also follow this cycle. In the early phases of birth and growth, promotion focuses on educating the consumer about the quality, features, and advantages of the product. Also during this phase, credibility and image are developed. In later phases of the life cycle, promotion stresses the uniqueness of the product and how it achieves customers' needs better than competing products. In the final phases, when the market is filled with competitors and little difference exists between products, promotion stresses the psychological factors, appeals to wants and desires, and finally addresses competition head-on with arguments of lower cost, higher quality, or better service.

The promotional budget must be divided among advertising, personal sales, special events, and public relations. The most dollars should be allocated to those activities producing the largest number of leads and closings. The mix of dollars will also change in relation to the product life cycle. In 1988, the promotion budgets for newly constructed retirement housing projects ranged between $3,000 and $7,500 per dwelling unit. Using this rate, the budget for a 200-unit congregate care community would be between $600,000 and $1,500,000 in order to achieve full occupancy. This amount would cover only promotion, not the cost for product planning and market research.

The marketing cost is a function of geographic market area, project image, customer preferences, and objectives. An encouraging note is that once the facility has achieved a stable occupancy, the marketing and promotion budget is minimal, usually between 1 percent and 2 percent of annual gross revenue.

During the early periods of promotion, when developing an image and educating consumers, advertising assumes 60 percent to 80 percent of the cost. In later stages, when potential customers must be contacted, the personal selling effort takes 60 percent to 80 percent of the cost.

Promotional Activities and Materials.   To market retirement housing requires effective promotional activities including direct mail materials, move-in kits for new residents, advertising, press releases, and public relations.

It is important to have the sales office communicate the proper image with clear, understandable closing tools, such as audio-visual displays, simple leases, resident agreements, and artist renderings. Finally, the project concept must be communicated through brochures, signs, advertising, and related presentations. The following tools, techniques, and approaches may be useful.

Advertising.   Advertising consists of nonpersonal (not face-to-face) activities and events that communicate a message through paid media under the project's name.[6] It is different from publicity or public relations, which seeks to create a favorable public image or acceptance, but does not use paid media advertising to achieve that goal. Often, advertising is considered to be a subset of public relations. This subtle distinction suggests that publicity or public relations promotes credibility and awareness and is not paid for by the sponsor. Conceivably one could produce a similar message and pay a magazine or newspaper to print it, and it would be classified as advertising. In practice, pub-

[6]Kotler, *Marketing Management,* 455.

licity and public relations seem a preferred method to promote the image, success, or credibility of a product or sponsor without the negative effect of trying to sell the consumer.

Advertising accomplishes a variety of objectives. These include introducing the project and developer, building and reinforcing images, educating the consumer, describing product features, and motivating consumers to buy.

Too often, because retirement housing developers do not have a clear objective in mind, the advertising program is confusing and counterproductive. It is important that each advertising effort have a clear and measurable objective. For example, an objective of creating 100 inquiries within the next 30 days is much more measurable than simply agreeing to generate sales leads.

Advertising communicates a message. It is most effective in creating interest and awareness among large groups and in heightening demand for the product. Advertising, however, cannot close the sale; one cannot expect advertising to result in a flood of elderly into the sales office with deposit checks in hand.

Alec Benn indicates that most advertising fails.[7] In other words, the advertising does not make any difference in sales. In some cases, the advertising program turns buyers away. According to Benn, some of the most common advertising mistakes consist of:

Putting the wrong person in charge of advertising (the chief executive should ensure that the responsible person benefits from effective advertising or suffers if it is inadequate)

Choosing the wrong advertising agency (pick the agency with expertise in the target market and the chosen media)

Choosing an advertising medium based on low rate rather than on cost per thousand readers, listeners, or viewers

Advertising too infrequently

Making ads too big or too small

Imitating the competition

Trying to be different, unique, or cute

Criticizing or demeaning the customer

Failing to promote the unique features of the product

Not measuring the outcome of advertising[8]

[7]Alec Benn, *The 27 Most Common Mistakes in Advertising* (New York: American Management Association, 1978), 5.

[8]Ibid., 138.

Advertising consists of much more than newspaper copy, radio, or television spots. It can appear in magazines, direct mail, yellow pages, contests, promotions, and special events. The selection of the mix of methods is a function of the client, project type, budget, and community.

Newspaper Advertising. Newspapers are widely read by senior consumers and are one of their primary sources of local news, politics, sports, and activities. In addition, newspapers provide the opportunity for an advertiser to distribute the message to a specific area of a community and to change ads quickly. Another benefit is that newspapers have a short lead time between creation of the ad and its appearance.

This is not to suggest that newspaper advertising is the best advertising medium. It does have certain disadvantages: Newspapers have a great deal of advertising, and individual ads may be overlooked; readers tend to skim material, and so complicated or lengthy advertisements may be ineffective; newspaper reproduction is a poor medium for detailed color photographs and images.

The following guidelines should enhance the presentation of newspaper advertising:

Provide a brief message.

Use a recognizable logo or format for all advertising.

Make it easy to read and follow.

Use large type.

Do not confuse the reader with unnecessary extra words and symbols.

Clearly state the benefits of the product.

Radio. Radio advertising is a useful medium because it is generally directed at specific audiences. In a typical midsize city, there may be 10 or more radio stations serving the tastes of different groups through broadcasts of classical music, news and folk formats, country and western music, light listening, top 40 tunes, blues, and so on. Further, these stations can identify their listeners by audience type and size. This allows the advertiser to select a specific group for the message. It appears that older consumers will listen to news, and to music from their era, such as the 1930s, 1940s, and 1950s, big band sounds, or classical music. Listening preference is also a function of social class and education.

Radio advertising is more expensive than newspaper advertising and also does not last as long. A typical radio spot is 30 or 60 seconds and, unless often repeated, is likely to be missed. Radio messages must be clear, simple, and create images in the mind of the listener. Also, it is helpful if these spots are distinctive, through the repeated use of a theme song, jingle, or personality.

Television. Television is viewed by the average household several hours each day. Elderly viewers watch more daytime television than the younger population. Commercials on television comprise between 10 and 15 minutes of every viewing hour. In some cases, the viewing audience is overwhelmed with advertising messages. Television advertising is competitive, expensive, and not generally targeted to a specific audience.

As a visual medium, television has created expectations among the viewing public of well organized, professionally produced material. Such presentations are not only expensive to produce, air time is costly. The general rule is, if you cannot produce a professional quality spot, do not use television. Corny, down-home folks may be fine for advertising furniture, stereos, water beds and used cars, but they are not effective in establishing credibility and stability for a company that promises safe and secure retirement housing.

Direct Mail. Direct mail sends an advertising message by personal letter directly to the customer. One of its advantages over other forms of advertising is that there is direct communication with the selected customer. There is no competition with other advertisers in the same space, such as in the newspaper. There are quite a few options in terms of size, shape, color, layout, and copy for the material. Finally, response can be measured through coupons, response cards, or a telephone number for the recipient's use.

Direct mail is expensive, with a cost per thousand contacts exceeding $400, not including the costs of artwork and printing. This is in contrast to a newspaper ad that may cost $400 per week, but reaches 10,000 persons, or a magazine ad that costs $850, but reaches a circulation of 25,000 persons. Therefore, one key requirement of direct mail is to select the target group most likely to be qualified for your product. The greatest benefit of direct mail is the ability to make the cost per thousand really count by sending only to customers who qualify by age, location, and income.

In order to be successful in direct mail, it is necessary to follow certain guidelines. In the case of direct marketing to seniors, some of these guidelines take on the appearance of rules.[9]

[9]Herschell G. Lewis, *Direct Mail Copy That Sells* (Englewood, NJ: Prentice-Hall, 1984), 2–14.

Tell the truth.

If you make a claim, be prepared to prove it.

Be personal versus impersonal.

Do not be too clever or cute.

Demonstrate widespread support for the product.

Be clear and specific.

Do not use jargon like CCRC, lifecare, or ACLF.

Do not overstate the product.

H. G. Lewis, in his book on direct mail, suggests that there are four great motivators—fear, guilt, greed, and exclusivity.[10] In direct mail advertising, these elements can be used to influence the elderly market through elements such as security and safety, physical needs, medical problems, and the desire to save or make money or to have a prestigious address.

Direct mail involves sending advertising material to potential residents that will motivate them to respond by calling, sending back a card, or visiting the facility. In order to achieve this response, the direct mail material must meet the fundamental guidelines listed earlier, appeal to the motivators just defined, and present a factual, unconfusing message to *act now*. Expert consultants may be needed to assist the developer in organizing a direct mail program because the appearance and language of the material are extremely important in achieving success.

Direct Mailing Lists. Lists of names and addresses can be obtained through list brokers. Some lists are based on income levels, others on age or motor vehicle registrations. Local social service agencies may also be able to supply names, as well as churches, area agencies on aging, and other organizations. The lists need to be refined and made specific to the particular segment of the senior community a developer wishes to attract. Using a shotgun approach and sending direct mail information to tens of thousands of individuals is foolish and expensive. The ratio that has been experienced by the authors is one lease for every 25 to 30 contacts. Therefore, a developer who plans to build a 200-unit project will need 5000 age- and income-qualified contacts through direct mail to be able to lease 200 units. These figures assume that the contacts' needs and demands are met by the lifestyle promised in the promotional information.

[10]Ibid., 15.

Public Relations and Publicity. Publicity and public relations are planned activities designed to influence the public's opinion and create a favorable image of the product by establishing credibility, stability, and trustworthiness. In addition, public relations will promote the acceptance and prestige of a community. Public relations is similar to advertising except that a developer is not using paid media advertising to achieve a goal.

Public relations is used within several different contexts. First, it means the relationships a developer has with the community or public. Second, it defines the activities undertaken to promote a favorable image. Finally, it implies a value, such as having good or bad public relations. Given these various meanings, public relations requires upper-level management involvement as well as professional expertise.

Publicity is free promotion of a product. Newspapers, radio stations, television channels, or other media present a product because they feel it is newsworthy. A favorable report can create a good image for a facility or organization. Generally, publicity is sporadic, because a developer does not have a newsworthy event every day or week.

Public relations, on the other hand, can be ongoing and comprises all those activities by a developer and the staff that promote a positive image of a product. The primary activities that fall in this category include:

Keeping abreast of the attitudes and opinions of the public

Knowing the attitudes, opinions, and activities of elected officials and government agencies that impact an activity

Dealing with the news media by providing them with information that enhances the image of the organization

Training staff to handle the public in a courteous, helpful, and positive manner and teaching them how to deal with a problem client or request

Organizing publicity and news releases

Organizing special events to generate interest and enthusiasm for a product

Ensuring that all contacts with the public are directed at promoting a positive image

Specific activities within the realm of public relations consist of:[11]

[11]Scott Cutlip and Allen Center, *Effective Public Relations* (Englewood, NJ: Prentice-Hall, 1978), 22–23.

Writing and editing news releases, articles, pamphlets, brochures, and other material seen by the public

Maintaining media relations with individuals at the newspapers, television stations, radio stations, local and national journals and magazines, trade associations, and other media groups

Organizing special events—open houses, press parties, celebrations, and related events

Training staff and management how to interact with the public

Presenting speeches or talking informally with groups, or assisting others in the preparation of such presentations

Reviewing and making recommendations on graphics, artwork, and logos that impact image

Providing guidance on internal and external written and graphic communications such as newsletters, reports, and advertising copy

Coordinating exhibits, shows, and related events in terms of type of material used, message to be presented and expected staff participation

Coordinating opinion and gathering research to assess public attitudes and opinions

Public relations seeks to promote a positive image by a planned and coordinated effort of written, oral, and graphic communication. In accepting this broad responsibility, the developer or sponsor of a retirement community must seek professional guidance to achieve the proper image. In addition, this guidance can be provided to all levels of the organization and can touch all forms of communication, both internal and external.

Personal Sales.   The personal, or face-to-face, sale is the primary method of selling retirement housing to seniors. Although the other elements of promotion create enthusiasm and interest in the seniors community, personal selling is the true indicator of success. The relationship that develops between the marketing representative and the senior consumer is the key to closing the sale.

A variety of marketing books and articles have attempted to describe the process of personal selling. The effective salesperson finds customers, attracts their attention and interest, creates a desire for the product, and influences the customer to buy the product. Perhaps the most vivid, if not the best, example of this function is Professor Harold Hill in Meredith Wilson's *The Music Man.* Almost everyone in River City wanted to participate in Professor Hill's band or believed it was good for the community; Hill created the image and the desire, and closed the sale to the community.

The steps of the sales process are prospecting, qualifying, approaching, presenting, closing, and following up.[12] They are defined by these activities:

Prospecting:	Identifying likely customers
Qualifying:	Screening prospects
Approaching:	Contacting and gaining the attention of the prospect
Presenting:	Demonstrating the desirability of the product
Closing:	Persuading the customer to purchase
Following up:	Making sure the buyer is satisfied

Previously described marketing activities will assist the sales force in prospecting, qualifying, and approaching prospective buyers. The personal selling job becomes much easier if the prospective customer is aware of the product, feels good about the idea, and has a positive image of the developer. Advertised special events and promotions set the stage for approaching the customer, overcoming the negative characteristics of the "cold call."

Selecting Sales Personnel. Although there is no ideal salesperson for retirement housing, certain skills and abilities move the customer from awareness and interest to action. The salesperson should possess the following qualities:

Thorough knowledge of the product being sold

Comprehensive understanding of the competition

Understanding of the important factors that motivate seniors (safety, security, trust)

Friendliness and outgoing personality

Willingness to explore and learn about each customer's personal needs and living environment

Ability to quickly identify the needs or desires of the buyer and present an image of the community that fulfills those needs

Good listening skills

[12]Fred C. Allvine, *Marketing: Principles and Practices* (New York: Harcourt Brace Jovanovich, 1987), 588.

Patience with the senior customers, who may visit five or six times prior to making a decision

Appearance of stability and seriousness

Prior experience in selling services that required creating an image of benefit to the customer

Personal characteristics of sales personnel are perhaps more important in successful selling to seniors than in any other market. These attitudes and characteristics include:

Positive goals and enthusiasm	Satisfaction in helping seniors
Self-confidence	Desire to close the sale
Persuasiveness	Willingness to ask seniors
Maturity	to make a decision
Sincerity	Ability to ask for seniors'
Pride in the product	opinions
Interest in the elderly	

Compensating Sales Personnel.   Compensation plans for sales personnel should be designed to meet three basic objectives: (1) to achieve the sales or leasing objectives of the developer; (2) to allow sales personnel to achieve desired earnings; and (3) to reward high performers. The compensation plan should be adequate to attract qualified, experienced personnel.

Compensation plans come in a variety of packages—salary, straight commission, draw accounts, bonuses, and combinations of these options. Each plan has advantages and disadvantages depending on the desired goals of the developer or sponsor and sales personnel. The most appropriate compensation plan should meet these basic objectives: to pay sales personnel based on their contributions and to recognize high performance; to provide an incentive for sales personnel to increase production and sales; and to promote the goals of the project.

In practical terms, a sales compensation plan will generally include a base salary, commission, and bonus.

The primary goal of the developer or sponsor is to have residents living in the community. Therefore, sales personnel should be rewarded and compensated when they attract permanent residents into the community. That is, sales personnel must be aware of the admission standards of the community, including age and income qualifications. Merely acquiring signed leases may not fulfill the needs of the developer, particularly if these residents do not have adequate income or have medical needs not provided by the community.

Compensation is as varied and broad in sales to the elderly as in any other sales position. It can range from beginning salaries as low as $10,000 to $12,000 per year with large bonus payments, to as high as $35,000 to $50,000 a year with small commissions. Some projects pay only $6.00 per hour but provide a large annual bonus based on the development's overall profitability. The rationale for this plan is that sales cannot usually be attributed to one individual, because the average prospective resident will be seen several times, and many sales members may have assisted in convincing the resident to buy or lease a unit.

Yellow or Silver Pages.   Everyone knows about the Yellow Pages and almost everyone uses them, especially in larger communities. In some areas, Silver Pages aimed at the 65-and-over market are published. In this early stage of the senior housing industry, it is unclear whether potential customers look to the Yellow Pages for a retirement center. Most people do not look for other professional services, such as medical or legal advice, in the Yellow Pages, but rely on recommendations of friends or family, or pick someone close by their home.

A Yellow Pages ad is necessary, however, especially if children or friends are looking for what is available in retirement housing. More importantly, not listing the project implies that it is not stable. Since the ad will be listed with other competitors, it should stand out. To accomplish this, use a logo or distinctive artwork and large, bold letters in the same format or layout utilized for other advertising; keep the copy simple and easy to read; be specific about the services and products offered; and select a display ad rather than a simple listing, as it implies stability and success.

Billboards and Outdoor Advertising.   Billboards are somewhat limited in their ability to deliver more than a simple two- or three-word message. There are various types of outdoor advertising including printed poster billboards, painted signs, animated and lighted displays, portable lighted signs, flags, balloons, and skywriting. In fact, a developer is only limited by imagination, good taste, and the law.

Billboards, which are most useful for giving directions and creating name identification, come in several sizes. The very large boards, approximately 20 feet by 10 feet, are expensive and are often tied up months or years in advance by national or regional advertisers, particularly on major freeways. The smaller (junior) boards are generally available in the area near a facility and can be excellent for giving site directions.

When preparing billboards, make a message short and simple, big and bold. Use a logo, name, or distinctive artwork. Identify the concept of the project in one or two words.

Retirement centers should probably not try to compete with automobile dealerships and fast food restaurants in terms of exceptional outdoor advertising, such as hot air balloon rides, animated gorillas, and searchlights. The elderly want to be sure the developer is stable, trustworthy, and responsible, so the guiding principles of advertising should be simplicity, clarity, and creation of the proper image.

Special Promotions, Gifts, and Special Events. The American Marketing Association has defined sales promotions as marketing activities other than personal selling, advertising, and publicity. They include exhibitions, demonstrations, and nonroutine activities such as contests, coupons, rebates, giveaways, and gifts.[13]

Sales promotions, in order to be effective, must be used with other advertising activities and publicity campaigns. The objective of promotions is to generate interest in a product, introduce potential customers to the lifestyle, reinforce an image, and create a demand. Examples of promotion efforts include:

Drawings for a free vacation or other gifts

Special events, such as a dance, holiday dinners, or a theme party on Halloween, Valentine's Day, or some other special occasion

Contests, such as identifying a famous personality

Competition events, including floral arranging, baking, or a crafts fair

Drawings for a free weekend at the community

Gifts and special promotions might include premiums imprinted with the name of the project. Appropriate items are calendars, pens, pencils, clocks, calculators, note pads, glasses, and cups. Such gifts can be expensive, however, and the benefit is directly related to the value of the gift, as perceived by the client.

On-site promotions can entail special events featuring free weekends

[13]Ralph Alexander et al., *Marketing Definitions: A Glossary of Marketing Terms* (Chicago: American Marketing Association, 1960), 20.

at the community. Sampling the lifestyle is an excellent introduction to the community for persons who are undecided whether to make the move. The program also adds a sense of activity in the community when early fill-up may be running behind schedule and provides an opportunity to train the staff.

Another option might be a weekly luncheon at the project for a specific club, organization, or church group, allowing members to taste the food, sample the services, and generally experience the community. A tour and sales presentation would be conducted with each luncheon.

Once a week or once a month a theme party could be presented, such as Oktoberfest, casino night, or southern hospitality, featuring appropriate foods and activities. There might also be senior arts and crafts shows or fashion shows featuring senior models sponsored by major department stores. All these events will continue to generate leads and promote activity within the community.

Seminars can help create interest in communities, as well as provide a service to seniors. Such seminars can cover the psychological adjustments to aging, tax planning, family relationships, employment opportunities, nutrition, health planning, book reviews, death and dying, theatre reviews, antique shows, garage sales, and picnics.

Grand Opening. The grand opening should create a degree of urgency, with some emphasis on limited numbers of available units. Newspapers should be the primary media, with magazines being secondary support in informing the community about the project's success. Publicity will relate to project completion and the functions that are going to take place during the grand opening. On-site media tours should be conducted, and interviews can be arranged with key spokespersons. Feature stories can describe interior design, with the seniors in mind, or highlight landscape areas such as rose gardens.

The grand opening needs a theme, which can be developed from ideas oriented toward local history, holidays, or other topics. There should be one or two grand opening weekends. The first weekend might be a "special invitation only" arrangement for individuals and families who have expressed an interest in the community. It is important to include family members of the elderly, since they have considerable influence on the decision to move. Valet parking might be provided, as well as buffet services, roses to women in attendance, and other special favors.

The second week of the grand opening would be for the general public and should include entertainment, food, speeches by public officials, and special activities.

Audio-visual Presentations.   Audio-visual aids take the form of either slide presentations, with music and narrative, or videotapes. A presentation normally is between 5 and 12 minutes in length, which is more than adequate to get the concept across to an audience. The audio-visual presentation is a talking brochure, combining many of the same elements and features as the printed material. However, the slide presentation or videotape is usually far more subjective. It can set a tone for the project and explain the development goals. The printed brochure is a more objective marketing tool containing hard facts and figures. Audio-visual presentations are especially useful during the preconstruction phase and in the construction stage. They enable sales representatives to conduct off-site seminars that create an image of the project when nothing yet exists at the site.

Brochures.   The project brochure gives the potential resident a sense of the project and provides an excellent format for explaining the community's advantages. Tables or charts demonstrating the long-run benefits of being a resident in a particular development are essential. One of the best formats for the project brochure is a pocket folder with removable fact sheets. This gives the brochure flexibility, as sheets can be removed, replaced, or added when information changes. For example, if a certain floor plan is sold out, the page can be removed without making the entire brochure obsolete. In addition, the brochure should include photographs or artist renderings of the completed project, information on surrounding areas, benefits, the developer's philosophy, map showing location, and a return postcard.

Resident Contracts and Leases.   Leases and contracts must conform to legal requirements and be readable. The more individuals who become involved with the decision-making process to relocate into a retirement community, the less success that community will have in closing units. Adult children, accountants, attorneys, ministers, and advisors all have a potential negative impact for the retirement product. Usually, no harm is meant, but each advisor creates anxiety. One way to offset this is to make the leases and contracts as simple as possible, reducing the need for advice. This is not to say that the prospective resident should not have assistance with interpreting legal documents. Contracts and leases should be written with the appropriate market in mind, and they should be as readable as possible.

Realtor Incentive Programs.   Because realtors may deal with older people who are selling their homes, an incentive program can be offered to realtors for referrals. Finders' fees can be offered for each referral who actually signs a rental or sales agreement. The sales staff can reciprocate by referring to realtors prospects who are seeking to sell their homes and do not yet have a realtor in mind. The realtors need to be educated about retirement housing and what the project has to offer. Special programs and parties for realtors should be held to encourage their enthusiastic support.

Press Kits. A press kit with fact sheets about the project is required. In addition to photos, the kit should contain information about the developer, the contractors, the development team members, and unique or unusual design characteristics of the project. It is also useful to include general information on assisted living for the elderly. Slides could be developed for use in the broadcast media as well. News releases should be written and distributed when a special event has occurred, such as ground breaking, grand opening, completion of a gazebo, or commission of any special amenities. Feature stories for newspapers and magazines might emphasize the name or theme of a project, the concept of senior retirement communities, the assisted living components in a community, elements of an individual home environment versus a retirement community environment, and advantages of living in the retirement community.

Booklets. A booklet guide to retirement housing is a very useful marketing tool. It can be distributed through direct mail or left at various locations that service the senior community. It should contain sections on planning for retirement, selling a home, housing options for the elderly, senior services in the area, specific facts about assisted living projects, and a checklist of things to look for in retirement communities.

Telemarketing. Telephone approaches vary, particularly for the over-65 group. The following ideas have proved to be successful:

Asking if the respondent is interested in receiving information about the community

Informing the respondent that the sales office and models will be completed soon and encouraging the person to stop by and visit

Indicating that a member of the sales team is going to be in the neighborhood the following week and would like to stop by to discuss the community

Explaining that the developer plans to offer a seminar in 10 days (or some other specific date) that will describe the housing options available to retirees in the community

Telemarketing campaigns are very expensive, so trained staff must be available to properly follow up such a sales effort. If not, the approach will be a complete waste of time.

Newsletters.   An important ingredient in ongoing communications, newsletters are sent to interested persons, the media, churches, and residents in the surrounding community. They keep recipients abreast of what is going on and encourage participation in special events at the project. Newsletters also generate additional sales after the facility is open.

Preview Center and Model Units.   A developer who constructs a preview center with model apartments will enhance and speed up the sales process. Conversely, a developer who tries to save money by not constructing models and preview centers will most certainly spend an equivalent sum for additional advertising to generate leads. It also appears that the fill-up time is much longer, which is costly and gives a negative image. Many prospective residents will not commit themselves unless they can see what they will get for their money. If possible, the preview center with a model should be on site, but if necessary, it can initially be constructed in a trailer or at a shopping center and be moved to the on-site facility once construction is completed.

The atmosphere of the preview center is extremely important in presenting the lifestyle to the prospective resident. Proper temperature, lighting, color, aroma, furnishings, and displays give the desired impression and connote a feeling of harmony. Some physical concerns in the layout of the sales center and model are traffic flow, proper displays and renderings, panels telling the developer's background, models, neighborhood location maps, photographs, and sales literature.

Models, if properly laid out, are an effective selling tool. Most developers construct units that are smaller than the average senior's current home, and that can be a major psychological adjustment. The prospective resident wants to see that his or her furniture will fit into a model unit being considered for lease or purchase. Another reason it is important to construct and furnish the model properly is to see if the architect and designer understand the needs of seniors. This is a good opportunity to test design ideas.

The model unit should be practical and functional so that it meets the needs of the elderly. Are kitchen shelves placed too high and too deep to be useful? Are glass closet doors too heavy to open and close? Are the wall and floor colors distinct enough to show a transition from one living area to another? Is the furniture in the model practical?

Furnish the model simply and realistically; do not include all of the premium or optional features such as extra trim or wallpaper. These will cause dissatisfaction if the prospective resident assumes the features in the model are standard.

Ongoing Sales.   Once the project is established, advertising and marketing goals will change.

Advertising.   At this stage of the advertising program, fine tuning of the image and credibility of the project will take place, depending on the assessment of previous programs and ads.

Resident Rewards.   A system may be devised to reward residents who frequently refer prospects to the development. Such a plan might award points for each successful referral. They could be redeemed for dollars off rent or accumulated for larger prizes such as theatre tickets, dinners, or even trips.

Marketing Costs and Budget Issues.   An effective and aggressive marketing plan requires a great deal of money. The marketing cost per dwelling unit can range between $3000 and $7500, depending on the size of the project and the level of the community. It may require over a year of marketing effort to reach 50 percent occupancy. On the average, a community should lease or sell between four and six units per month. Between 20 percent and 80 percent of the presale clients will not move in and occupy a unit, as a result of illness, death, and other factors.

  These marketing costs may seem extremely high, but it is common for a prospective resident to meet five or more times with the marketing staff before signing a lease, assuming the facility is constructed. If the facility is still in the planning stages, the number of these visits can increase. The sales manager and staff will spend a great deal of time making calls, arranging meetings, and answering questions to relieve prospective residents' anxiety. The following issues and questions must be addressed in preparation of the marketing budget.

Sales Staff and Office.   In preparing the budget for the sales staff and office, the number of sales staff to be hired and the amount of compensation for the sales manager and sales staff must be determined. Will it be straight salary, or salary plus bonuses? Will the sales staff need a receptionist? The developer must also decide whether to build a preview center or to rent office space and simply present sales material.

Media Advertising and Guidelines. The media budget must reflect the advantages and disadvantages of various forms of advertising. Television is expensive to produce and to run on local channels. Generally the results are very limited, resulting in inefficient use of marketing money. If the proper stations are selected, radio is an effective and efficient use of marketing funds. Used in tandem with newspaper ads, radio has proved to be effective as a reinforcement program.

Newspaper advertising is expensive, but necessary. Ads should be combined with other events for more impact. Journals and other periodicals are expensive, with less influence than newspapers.

Other Advertising Sources. Other advertising efforts need to be considered in the budget. The Yellow Pages can be a very reliable source of inquiries. They also promote an image of stability. The Silver Pages are a new type of telephone classified advertising designed specifically for senior use. They offer coupons and list resources for seniors. Directional signs are necessary to help clients find the community. Billboards are expensive and usually require a one-year contract. Such contracts should include at least one repaint at no charge.

Collateral Materials. Although they are necessary, collateral materials are sometimes overemphasized and overbudgeted. Stationery and business cards should be printed in a simple, easy-to-read format with contrasting colors. Newsletters are an excellent form of advertising and public relations. Costs vary depending on quality and quantity. (Reference is to the marketing newspaper, not the in-house newsletter for resident activities.)

Brochures are needed; however, four-color brochures with multiple pages may be expensive. Simple two-color brochures are just as effective. Because brochures need to be updated, do not order more than 5000 (even if a cost break is received). Flyers should also be simple, one-sided supplements to other collateral materials. They are used infrequently to advertise special events.

Direct mail lists can be purchased or rented. They are not expensive, but postage and production can be costly. Reportedly, direct mailers generate an average of five percent response for a mailing. Lists can often be purchased from voter registration offices.

Press kits should be developed with the assistance of the public relations firm. Kits include pictures and background information about the community and are designed for future media reference. Press releases should be written by or with public relations consultants who understand the requirements of news editors.

Sample Budget.   Table 6-3 is a sample marketing budget for a congregate living facility. A detailed breakdown is usually provided for the first 12 months, with summary information provided for the following years. The total budget is $667,718.

Preview Center or Marketing Office.   As previously noted, the preview center or marketing office should be located on site in a highly visible area. The layout is also related to the budget. Some presales and preleasing activities have been successful by building full-scale replicas of the units, a very expensive approach. Others have suppressed presales activities until actual units are available to view, which is the least expensive alternative. In full-scale replicas, models should give the impression of being lived in, with grocery lists on refrigerators, fresh flowers, and quiet music.

In addition to the models, private, cozy, well-lit areas should be provided for closing. Closing should not occur over desks, but at group sitting areas.

Equipment should be available to handle routine administrative functions, including mail outs and correspondence. Unless the volume of correspondence is enormous, mailing machines are not necessary. It is often more cost efficient to contract newsletters and direct mailings. A computer and a word processor or a typewriter are essential to monitor mailing lists and answer inquiries.

Summary.   Product promotion encompasses all of the activities targeted at having consumers purchase a product—advertising, special

TABLE 6-3. Annual Marketing Budget

	Year 1	Year 2	Year 3
Payroll	$ 70,163	$ 53,355	$33,175
Administrative	41,586	16,700	13,350
Advertising	101,134	105,120	35,920
Preview center/model	24,865	4,000	1,800
Brochures, pamphlets	17,590	17,900	3,900
Professional fees	51,213	12,000	0
Miscellaneous, dues, contingency	36,527	18,660	8,760
Total	$343,078	$227,735	$96,905

events, publicity, public relations, and personal selling. Although promotion is only one element of the marketing function, it is extremely important in closing the sales. Personal selling, especially to seniors, is the primary method of achieving success. Therefore, a major concern is to have skilled salespersons.

AN APPROACH TO MARKETING RETIREMENT HOUSING

Background and Perspective. Retirement community marketing has a dual responsibility: to educate the public about housing alternatives for the elderly, and at the same time, to present a product desired by senior adults. Marketing must translate the housing concepts into clear and understandable language in order to influence prospective residents to want to lease, rent, or purchase a unit within a retirement development. Marketing is a yardstick of how successful the development team members have been in providing the correct product to the appropriate segment of the elderly within a service area. All disciplines and professionals who are on the development team support the marketing and sales program, either directly or indirectly.

The marketing approach selected by a developer can enhance or detract from the success of any community. Marketing is a function of location and concept.

Phases in Marketing. There are four steps in marketing retirement housing: the preliminary phase, preoperations, initial operations, and ongoing operations. These steps incorporate product planning, market research, promotion, selling, and pricing. By identifying these four steps, it is possible to describe the application of the marketing elements to a specific project.

In the first step, the preliminary phase, market and feasibility studies are conducted. Results are analyzed, and the product or services are defined. The marketing budget, marketing strategy, and marketing plan are formulated. Collateral materials are designed. Members of the sales staff are hired and trained.

The preoperational phase focuses on the sales activities. The goal is to have a percentage of units rented or purchased prior to opening. This phase may begin when financing is secured.

The third step, initial operations, starts when the community accepts its first residents. As during preoperations, this step concentrates on sales or leasing activities. The marketing budget included in the overall development budget carries marketing through the initial operations phase.

The fourth step, ongoing operations, begins when the project has reached full occupancy. Sales activities continue, but with a new, smaller budget and media campaign schedule. Emphasis is also placed on retaining current residents and evaluating new services or programs.

Preliminary Marketing Phase.   This step achieves a variety of critical objectives and encompasses many of the product planning tasks described previously. These tasks are:

To determine the type of product

To assess the market and evaluate demand for the product

To define the product and service package

To determine pricing

To develop marketing strategy

To prepare a marketing plan

To establish a marketing budget

To establish evaluation criteria

To establish a time schedule

To hire sales staff

To develop policies and procedures

The activities that must be accomplished in this step are market research and feasibility studies, project definition, concept development, pricing, marketing and public relations strategy, and preparation of the marketing plan.

The development of the marketing and public relations strategy begins with a written description of the project, designed to identify the target consumer and the type of services to be provided. This description should present the lifestyle of the community. From the beginning, all marketing staff should understand the community is providing such a lifestyle, not just services and shelter.

The strategy process should begin by answering the following questions: What is the product? Who constitute the market? What is the price? What is the desired image? What are the objectives?

After answering these questions, it is necessary to construct a marketing plan that organizes the elements described in previous pages into an action plan.

Elements of a Marketing Plan.   The first portion of a marketing plan describes the product, its benefits, the market, and essential characteristics of the prospective clients.

Next, a promotional plan and the strategy should be developed. These address the target market and the mixture of promotional options.

Advertising (when, where)	Brochures and pamphlets
Public relations	Promotion options (frequency
Direct mail	of use)
Newsletters	Ways to deal with competition
Signs and billboards	Marketing objectives

The budget for marketing and promotions should provide for salaries and commissions, office operations, advertising, collateral materials, special promotions and events, and professional consultants.

Policies and procedures should be written to cover signing of sales or leases, generating and following up leads, and analyzing the cost per sale.

OUTLINE OF A SAMPLE MARKETING PLAN

Description of Product

Congregate housing community; mid to high income; 200 dwelling units (70 percent one-bedroom)

Services include one meal per day, van transportation, utilities, social activities, housekeeping once per week

Independent lifestyle for active seniors

Description of Market and Prospective Clients

Seniors over age 70 years, primarily female and widow

Location, Any County, Arkansas

Total target population 10,000 persons

Income-qualified market 4,000 persons

Promotion Plan and Strategy

Strategy to reach target market
    Meet with local seniors organizations
    Provide public press releases

Place articles in newspaper and senior magazines

Use advertising to enhance awareness

Use direct mail and newsletters for targeting income-qualified elderly

Select logo and theme

Promotion mix

Schedule presentation to 10 key seniors groups

Prepare newsletter and send monthly to age- and income-qualified neighborhoods

Prepare advertisements for *Evening News* to run each Sunday for three months, then daily for two months, then weekly for seven months

Furnish and open preview center and sales office on November 1, to be staffed six and one-half days per week, eight hours per day

Purchase three billboards for one year, located at major intersections within five miles of site

Prepare two-color brochures of moderate price including site and floor plans, amenities description, fact sheets, map to site, and pictures

Prepare additional collateral materials consisting of letterhead stationery and envelopes, thank you cards, and business cards

Purchase Yellow Pages display advertisement

Identify and purchase direct mail list

Evaluate promotional mix weekly and monthly for effectiveness and provide flexibility to alter mix

Ways to deal with competition

Describe unique features of the product, including amenities, location, and services

Emphasize experience in senior housing

Seek endorsements of respected community and organization leaders

Confirm comparable prices in terms of services provided

Marketing and promotion objectives

Lease a minimum of five units per month

Achieve an overall project occupancy of 50 percent by July 19___; 75 percent by December 19___; and 95 percent by June 19___

Budget for marketing

Establish sales staff salaries, benefits, and commissions

Determine costs of office and model setup and office supplies and furnishings

Establish costs for advertising and promotion expenses and special promotions and events

Provide for purchase of collateral materials

Set aside funds for professional consultants

Methods of evaluation

Determine whether lease or sales goals are met

Determine whether project occupancy goals are met

Determine whether promotion cost per lead generated is within target range

Marketing time schedule

Identify each task

Establish target date for beginning activity

Assign dates for beginning and completing each task

Sales staff and operation of sales office

Hire and train sales staff, approximately one salesperson per 50 to 75 units

Hire one clerical worker for each four salespeople

Provide staff orientation and ongoing training with emphasis on selling to seniors

Marketing and sales policies and procedures

Define mission of sales staff

Establish office hours and telephone answering service

Develop procedures for handling inquiries and sales, records and reports, and inquiry follow-up

Determine methods of handling concessions, allowances, deposits, and refunds

Develop thorough understanding of contracts and agreements

PREOPERATIONS MARKETING PHASE

The second step in the marketing of retirement housing is the preoperational phase, which focuses primarily on sales activities and strategies. The goal is to presell or prelease as many units as possible.

Sales staff, previously hired and trained, have started to generate traffic and secure leases. During this phase, sales meetings are conducted at least weekly to discuss goals and methods of overcoming potential resident objections, and to provide support or leadership to sales staff. Personnel should be available in the sales office seven days a week, including holidays. Activities should include in-house tours and presentations, as well as sales appearances at clubs and organizations in the community.

Preopening Sales Program.   The preopening sales program must place a strong emphasis on selling combined with community relations and education of the elderly and their families. The primary goal is to make the public aware of the product and to interest them enough to seek additional information.

The first action in creating awareness is to contact people who advise the elderly, such as clergy, physicians, and bankers. These advisors will be helpful in supplying information about the elderly needs for an area. It is an excellent opportunity for the marketing director to explain, as clearly and simply as possible, the lifestyle, shelter, services, and care, if any, that the community has planned. Such advisors may also provide immediate feedback concerning the positive and negative features of the project. In promoting public awareness, the marketing staff should work closely with the media. Real estate and business editors in particular should be targeted in the beginning of the campaign. If the community has a religious affiliation, then the religion editor should also be contacted.

It is also important not to overlook the neighbors to the development. Keeping neighbors in the community informed about the project eliminates rumors that can result in negative public relations. The developer or owner should meet the neighbors, inform them of the plans using illustrations, and receive their input. This groundwork helps a developer to generate a positive image that will promote interest in the community.

An effective technique for generating interest during the preopening phase is direct mail followed by focus groups, seminars, and small gatherings or parties. The elderly in particular enjoy receiving mail and like to be in the know concerning events in their neighborhood. A postal telegram and reply card is an effective method of determining interest in the project and helps create a mailing list of potential clients.

Reports and records are also developed during this phase to analyze the sales effort. Examples of information that should be gathered include:

Who is making the inquiry—consumer, family member, or other?
How did the person hear about the community?

What type of service is being sought?

Other information, including name, address, and telephone number

Policies and procedures are developed to provide appropriate follow-up. If inquirers are qualified, their names are added to the inquiry list for personal sales follow-up.

Public relations continues during the preoperational phase and will include coverage for human interest stories concerning developers, residents, or features of the community. Other public relations activities may include:

A speakers bureau

A newsletter that includes activities of area agencies serving seniors

Articles about aging for local newspapers or journals

Sponsorship of senior athletic events, such as tennis or golf tournaments

Sponsorship of food drives and voter registration campaigns

The sales manager or other personnel should be active in community organizations such as Rotary, the Chamber of Commerce, and other appropriate community service groups. Lifestyle seminars and education sessions can also be sponsored. It is not necessary to wait until the community has facilities to begin sponsoring programs if local auditoriums are used to host sessions.

The end of the preoperational phase can be marked by a grand opening celebration, which must be budgeted and planned in advance. The celebration should cover at least two weekends, with events planned every day, such as presentations by well-known speakers or celebrities, entertainment, family events (including children and grandchildren), and get-togethers that allow potential residents to meet other residents. Invitations should be sent to local politicians and to other community leaders, and the local press should be contacted for coverage.

Initial Operations Marketing Phase.   The third step, initial operations, begins with the opening of the project and occupancy by the first residents. Sales activities take an approach that is different from the preoperations phase. The marketing objective continues to emphasize selling, but there are new goals, relating to monthly absorption numbers and retention of sign-ups, and new selling strategies. Sales staff now have a community with actual programs representing the lifestyles. The initial operations step is in effect until the community becomes fully occupied. Sales staff activities include selling, generating leads through a new ad campaign, working with previous inquiries, and following up until new residents move in.

Operational staff should support sales staff and be prepared to satisfy promises made by sales (within reason), handle move-ins, and resolve new resident concerns. Operational staff also become salespeople through their attitude and services. When initial operation begins, all services and features sold to the residents must be available. Operational staff will be expected to handle parties and special events, beyond routine schedules.

A sales goal during this phase is to generate traffic. Events and parties create a sense of activity. Touring potential residents through an empty community is not ideal for selling a lifestyle. Sales staff continue follow-up contacts after deposits are made, through the move-in and adjustment period. Satisfied residents are the best sales tool.

Public relations activities are an ongoing process designed to enhance public awareness. Following are a few examples of public relations during the initial operations phase.

Contact voter registration offices and offer the common area as a polling place during elections

Sponsor craft fairs at the center

Sponsor art exhibits

Sponsor makeup classes at a local department store

Sponsor investment and retirement planning

Develop a catering and banquet business both for revenue and public image

Ongoing Operations Marketing Phase.   The final step of senior community marketing, ongoing operations, begins when full occupancy is reached. The marketing plan and budget provided during development will not address plans and expenditures after fill-up. Consequently, a new plan and budget must be developed. The goal of marketing a full community is to keep current residents. A new budget is included as a line item in the operations budget. When the community is full, management generally reduces the marketing budget to an amount that can be funded from operating income. Strategies must be redefined, including reassignment or termination of marketing staff. In smaller facilities, management may assume the marketing tasks. In larger communities, full-time or part-time staff may still be needed.

Advertising will be reduced, but not stopped entirely. Obviously, some advertising must be continued to maintain occupancy levels. Collateral materials will still include brochures, stationery, and business cards.

CHAPTER SUMMARY

Marketing of retirement housing consists of four steps—preliminary operations, preoperations, initial operations and ongoing operations. The preliminary phase defines the market, develops the strategy plan and budget, creates the image and gets ready to sell. Preoperations is the time to create interest and leads. Initial operations focuses on filling the project as rapidly as possible. Finally, ongoing marketing helps keep residents in the community and fills vacancies quickly. These steps include many activities; all are important to achieve a successful marketing program.

The elderly are a heterogenous consumer group with a variety of experiences and values shaping their attitudes. Generally, they are conservative consumers who have experienced a lifetime of marketing gimmicks.

In reality, there are two markets for retirement housing, the adult child and the elderly consumer. Many senior community markets are need-driven. Residents generally move to such communities because they require support and assistance. Often, the adult children, especially daughters and daughters-in-law, make the initial inquiry. Therefore, marketing will also need to be directed to the children or grandchildren.

Like other consumers, the elderly seek reinforcement that they are making the correct choice. Often, they visit a community with other family members several times before making a commitment to move into a unit.

Generally, elderly consumers respond negatively to pressure and hard-sell techniques. Salespeople must be perceived as sincere and must develop a trusting relationship with prospective residents.

BIBLIOGRAPHY

Allvine, F. C. *Marketing: Principles and Practices.* New York: Harcourt Brace Jovanovich, 1987.

American Hospital Association. *Basic Guide to Hospital Public Relations.* Chicago, 1984.

Benn, A. *The 27 Most Common Mistakes in Advertising.* New York: American Management Association, 1978.

Cutlip, S. and Center, A. *Effective Public Relations.* Englewood, NJ: Prentice-Hall, 1978.

Evans, J. and Berman, B. *Essentials of Marketing.* New York: Macmillan, 1984.

Holtz, H. *The Secrets of Practical Marketing for Small Business.* New York: Prentice-Hall, 1982.

Kotler, P. *Marketing Management and Analysis Planning and Control.* Englewood, New Jersey: Prentice-Hall, 1967.

Lewis, H. G. *Direct Mail Copy That Sells.* Englewood, NJ: Prentice-Hall, 1984.

McMillan, H. N. *Marketing Your Hospital.* Chicago: American Hospital Publishing, 1981.

Peter, J. P. and Donnelly, J. *A Preface to Marketing Management.* Plano, TX: Business Publications, 1985.

Ruckman, W. G. *Compensating Your Sales Force.* Chicago: Probus Publishers, 1986.

CHAPTER 7

OPERATIONS AND FINANCIAL MANAGEMENT

CHARLES A. CARTER, JAMES L. LAUGHLIN,
and DIANNE B. LOVE

INTRODUCTION

This chapter acquaints the reader with the unique aspects of managing different types of retirement housing. Because responsibilities and activities may vary depending on the amenities and services offered, the information is designed to aid the developer or sponsor in learning what to expect in the management of a retirement housing community.

The quality of any organization is measured by the effectiveness of its management. The senior housing industry is no different. Inexperienced or inappropriate management can destroy even the best designed and marketed senior housing community. To ensure success experienced management, seasoned in the administration of the types of services provided, must be present. Being successful in the management of related fields including health care, real estate, or hotel and motel operations is not necessarily a guarantee of success in the retirement housing industry.

Likewise, experience in managing a small senior apartment community may not adequately prepare an individual or corporation for the challenges of a large senior adult community, which provides complex health care and related support services.

In addition to possessing the conceptual, technical, and human re-

lations skills general to management, retirement housing management must also have a knowledge of aging populations, an understanding of health care systems, and the attitudes of the hospitality industry.

FACTORS THAT CAN AFFECT MANAGEMENT

The following factors can impact the ease or difficulty of being able to
manage a community:

Experience or inexperience with nonhousing services
Size of community
Levels of support systems to be provided
Segment of the elderly participating in the community
Location of the project

A successful manager's approach to retirement communities needs
to be responsive, flexible, and pliable. The management plan needs to
meet the day-to-day operational needs of each resident through a useful
and effective system of procedures. Management is generally measured
by the results.

These results could take the form of such items as absorption rates
reached in a timely manner, reduction in turnover, or higher profit
than anticipated.

It has been estimated by the American Institute of Architects that
if the lifetime of a community is 40 to 50 years, hard costs (cost of
construction, development, and land cost) account for approximately 3
percent of the cost of the development, and approximately 97 percent
can be attributed to the community's operation and management. However, all too often the development team, under the developer's direction, concentrate only 3 percent of their time on plans for a community's
management, and 97 percent for all other disciplines and functions
associated with the development process.

Management goals are several, including providing effective and
efficient housing, many times coupled with quality services and care,
so as to meet residents' expectations. Management should attain these
goals within projected budget costs. Management must also permit the
residents to maintain their independence as long as possible, while
aging in place. Individuals should have the opportunity to control their
lives and schedules. Unfortunately, not every management dealing
with senior communities considers these expectations.

As an example, few retirement managers would disagree that residents should maintain their independence as long as possible; yet many managers assign seating in the central dining rooms denying a choice for the elderly resident. Assigned seating makes the food handlers' job easier while eliminating the important socialization element of choosing one's dinner companions.

MANAGEMENT'S ACCOUNTABILITY

The management of senior housing is accountable to three specific groups: the residents; the staff; and the owner. The order or priority of this accountability will shift according to the circumstances. The authority and responsibility of performing tasks can be delegated; the accountability cannot. Failing to recognize this obligation will create problems.

Management is accountable to the residents for a safe, secure environment that enhances their quality of life. Management is bound by not only the terms of the lease agreement, but also by a moral obligation that will become more critical as competing projects enter the market.

Often quality assessment is a matter of perception. Residents must perceive that management is sincerely interested in their welfare and should believe that services are fairly priced. Visibility and accessibility enhance the residents' positive perception of management. Regardless of the burdens of the daily operational regimen, management, including department supervisors, must allow time to interact with residents. Because food service can be the source of considerable criticism, the food service supervisor should interact with the residents during mealtimes and encourage comments on the quality of the meals. Such interactions demonstrate the staff's sincere interest in the services being offered.

Management must also satisfy the staff members' basic needs for guidance, recognition, support, and discipline. Failure to do so will often result in poor services because the staff must feel that their needs are being addressed before they will address the needs of the residents. Other consequences of poor labor relations may be excessive turnover or the presence of organized labor, which can compromise management's ability to perform efficiently.

Equally important is management's obligation to the owners. Management should operate a property as though it owned the property. This philosophy should apply to protecting both the owners' equity and reputation. Management must exercise professional business practices to increase profits, protect equity, and provide an appropriate return on the owners' investment. Since the owners' reputation often parallels the quality of the property, management is always accountable to the owners to protect or enhance their reputation.

Management of senior housing can be difficult. There is a fine balance between providing a catered lifestyle and creating a dependent relationship with the residents. How does management offer support without taking all the challenges out of daily life? There is no simple answer. Retirement housing management is a function of art and experience.

Another concern is the amount of amenities and services that will be provided. Too many services may price the development out of the market. Too few amenities, and it cannot be distinguished from other communities. Offering many amenities may also reduce the need for the residents to leave the complex for services. Considerable professional input from different sources is necessary to establish balance so that the development will be part of the surrounding community, and not an isolated shelter for the elderly. If not properly planned and managed, senior communities may become ghettos for the aged, a fear that has been voiced by some sociologists.

Managers of retirement housing deal with unique problems, which become more apparent in supportive or assisted living and nursing homes. The more services provided, the more involved staff become in the residents' lives. Staff members, because of daily contact, may function as a surrogate family. They must be constantly reminded of the need for confidentiality.

Aging in place has been listed as one of the bigger problems faced by management. When is a resident no longer living in the appropriate setting? This major dilemma confronts families of the elderly every day. In retirement communities, the answer lies somewhere between policy and judgment. An example of such policy is restricting individuals with walkers and wheelchairs from independent and supportive living arrangements. Judgment is the empathy and reasoning used in enforcing policy. In senior communities without alternative levels of service, the problem of moving a resident is even more difficult.

Management lists the time consumed in handling individual resident problems as unique to this industry. Again, there is no easy solution. Operating a retirement community requires considerable patience and empathy, yet the strength to say no. The resident services department should address most individual problems, allowing administration to resolve issues affecting the whole community. However, even effective resident services cannot satisfy all individual resident needs. Management must accept these demands as part of the job.

In licensed nursing homes, staff and licensure issues cause the majority of the challenges. Working with ill senior adults requires a certain type of personality. Retaining good, qualified staff is a continuous battle.

Nursing homes are one of the most regulated industries in the nation. Complying with the varying interpretations of the standards by inspectors has always been an effort. In the past, noncompliance meant submitting a plan of correction and initiating the correction as cited in the plan. New governmental mandates have added additional burdens. Administrators not in compliance may be held financially or criminally liable, depending on the seriousness of the violation. Management of a nursing home is not an entry level position.

Prudent management of finances is especially important. Many existing projects that have not had adequate management have suffered financial failures in recent years. Even in those cases where projects do not fail, their profitability may be low because of poor financial administration.

HOW TO SELECT A MANAGER OR ADMINISTRATOR

Experience.   Experience is a very elusive term in this market. Does the development team look for a manager who has experience in real estate, health care, or the hospitality industry?

Is it important to have someone who has only worked with and administered a continuing care retirement community (CCRC) or who has dealt with conventional rental housing? Is it easier to train someone in the food service side of the industry and hope they bring real estate management experience to the community; or is it better to find someone else who has hospitality skills, including food service and housekeeping, and provide training in the real estate shelter side of the business?

If it is a new development, has the manager had prior start-up experience or worked only with ongoing communities? Additional traits that need to be analyzed include attitude concerning the elderly, understanding of the aging process, knowledge of the characteristics of this population segment compared to the general population, overall business skills, and marketing ability.

Reliability. It is quite difficult to determine reliability. In checking references, the developer should not question current clients of the manager or management firm but instead should contact previous employers to learn their assessment of the candidate's performance.

If possible, visit sites that the management prospect is currently working with, talk to the residents, and get some sense of how well their obligations are being met.

Management Systems. Sometimes, managers state that they are not accountants or property managers or environmental managers. Determine up front what kind of flexibility they have built into their operating systems. Are financial statements prepared in a timely fashion? Do they utilize both a cash and an accrual method of accounting? The cash method alone does not show an accurate financial picture of where a community stands at any given time.

How do follow-ups take place? Has the board of the current community taken on functions that should be the responsibility of the manager or the management firm? What types of financial or management information systems have been developed?

Look carefully at the budgets and the documentation to substantiate the budgets. How well are reserves established in the budgets? How many different forms or types of budgets are established, and have they been regularly funded?

Study the staffing closely to determine whether there is overstaffing or understaffing. Can more than one individual handle problems involving a certain community?

It is important to look at the basis for the cost per meal. Raw food cost and labor cost per meal both will indicate how well a management firm is administering the food responsibilities.

MANAGEMENT CONTRACT AND EMPLOYMENT AGREEMENTS

Termination Clause. The termination clause needs to be a two-way street. It should be no more difficult for the manager to terminate the contract than for the community to do so. For the ongoing contract, there should be no more than a 30- to 90-day period of time for termination, with or without cause. It will generally take a community 60 to 90 days to select a replacement management firm, so do not make that time period too short.

The term of the contract can be anywhere from three to five years. The exception to this rule would be a management firm or an individual brought on to do the start-up. In the case of a start-up manager, in addition to all the standard terms, there should be a clause that describes the payment of fees.

Normally, a firm handling start-up will work twice as hard in the first year as in the fifth year of a contract. To have the fees paid evenly would be unfair if the contract could be terminated with only a 90-day notice. The termination notice may be on an annual basis for start-up management, and it is not unusual for the management company to be paid 150 percent of a straight one-year fee to offset the additional effort put forth in establishing the initial management plan.

For example, if the contract over five years for a firm is $500,000 and the community agreed to pay the manager 150 percent of a straight year contract for the first year, the firm would receive $150,000 in year one and $125,000 in year two, assuming it was 125 percent of the base year. Year three would normally be a straight year fee, equal to $100,000; year four would be $75,000; and year five would be $50,000. This distribution would more equitably represent the amount of effort expended by the management company in the early years.

Insurance Requirements. Insurance protects the developer or board of directors as well as the manager. Managers should not be permitted to unilaterally terminate, modify, or change any terms of insurance policies that would affect the community. The management firm should not be allowed to change its own insurance policies without giving the community a reasonable notice of between 10 and 30 days.

A fidelity bond should be required by the contract in an amount adequate to cover the monies handled by the manager, as well as the total monies handled by the management firm for all of the communities it administers.

Fees. The most utilized payment method is to compensate the management company based on a percentage of gross revenue. The percentage on a yearly amount would be between 5 and 12 percent, with the norm between 5 and 7 percent. The higher percentage would be for a smaller project in most instances. In some cases, a specific yearly amount is adequate, particularly for the start-up phase. The third approach is to take a percentage of net profits, generally between 5 percent and 20 percent.

If the manager is responsible for managing an ownership facility, such as a condominium or cooperative, the fees may be based on a per unit amount.

If commercial or office space is part of the project, the fees may be based on a square footage basis; it is impossible to measure the number of users who may initially occupy the commercial, retail, or office space.

Communities that have properties both for sale and for rent utilize a mixed or varied fee structure. Condominium units would be on a per unit basis or fixed amount per month basis; rental units would generally be on a percentage of gross revenue. Condominiums cannot be based on a net profit approach because no profit is generated on a monthly or yearly basis. Money in excess of expenses is generally credited towards accelerating reserve amounts in many of the ownership communities.

Educational Requirements. There is no one source for competent, qualified management personnel or firms in this country today.

Nursing homes must have a licensed nursing home administrator, but administrators of any other part of a retirement community do not have to have a formal license. Licensing standards for nursing homes vary from state to state, and often are not difficult. Some states do not require a college education. Many states that do stipulate a college degree do not require that it be in a health-related industry or profession. Most states require a six-month internship and education ranging from a high school diploma to a four-year college degree, as well as a passing grade on a written test administered by the state. This examination includes questions on both state and federal minimum standards.

The Institute of Real Estate Management offers a Certified Property Management (CPM) designation, but it has not yet been oriented toward the retirement industry. The Community Association Institute offers a Professional Community Association Management (PCAM) designation oriented toward residential age-integrated condominium communities without any emphasis or special training for retirement communities.

Many universities offer degrees or certificates in gerontology, but may not address, except in the most cursory ways, the issues of housing and shelter for the elderly.

A developer needs to look for management talent in the hospitality industry, social service agencies, conventional housing management companies, and the health care industry. It is difficult to find individuals with experience and expertise in all phases of senior housing management.

UNIQUE ASPECTS OF SENIOR HOUSING

There are unique aspects that distinguish management of retirement housing from other forms of property management. The two most striking differences are the special needs associated with the elderly, and the variety of services and amenities commonly offered in senior housing.

One special need of seniors is to age in place. Almost invariably, developers build for the current needs of the market. As seniors age, there is a gradual increase in their need for additional services and programs. Some senior housing communities are not designed to accommodate residents who need more assistance or service.

The aging in place issue causes the language in lease or resident agreements to differ from standard leases for other properties. Transfer policies must be developed with clauses in the agreements that allow management to terminate leases when a resident can no longer satisfy the criteria or functioning level for that project.

Staff will need to be trained to recognize deteriorating health conditions. Awareness of subtle changes in residents' behavior or cognitive abilities may help in getting proper medical attention and may prevent minor problems from becoming life threatening.

A major problem resulting from aging in place is the negative impact on marketing. As the retirement community population ages, residents become more frail and less active. Ultimately, the community may develop an identity as an "old people's home." Marketing then confronts the challenge of changing this image. If occupancy falls, the problem may be exacerbated by accepting more frail elderly to increase the number of residents.

One method to address the problems of aging in place is designing the property with several levels of service. Providing different service levels will reduce relocation trauma and allow residents to be matched to appropriate programs. In addition, offering several levels of service broadens the community's market appeal.

Resident Selection. Residents who are semi-independent dislike living with moderately dependent residents who require staff assistance. And, moderately dependent residents prefer not to live with fully dependent residents. Proper resident selection for senior housing projects is important not only to maintain satisfaction among the other residents, but also to ensure the availability of appropriate services according to resident needs.

Prior to marketing, well-defined, written criteria for the functional level of residents in the community should be developed and thoroughly explained to sales personnel. Procedures must allow management to refuse admission anytime during the processing of an application.

Some retirement housing projects have sophisticated admission procedures with detailed health and cognitive skills inventories. Others require various degrees of financial disclosure. Since no two individuals are alike, no tool exists that can accurately predict whether an individual will fit comfortably into a community. Consequently, the ultimate approval rests in management's subjective appraisal of an applicant.

Services and Amenities. In order to justify the need for additional services and amenities in senior housing, functional levels must be assessed. Only during the past few years have Americans become acutely aware that this society is beginning to age and that everyone over 65 years of age is not alike. In addition, the definition of old or aging is changing. Rather than using age to describe special needs and services, this text utilizes functional levels. Because some individuals who are 60 behave as if they are 80, and others who are 80 act like 60-year-olds, levels of function are more appropriate criteria.

Four categories are used to define levels of resident independence: fully independent, semi-independent, moderately dependent, and fully dependent. It is important to understand these levels as they relate to the amenities of senior housing projects. The array of provided services is one factor that separates the management of senior housing from other types of property.

The services most commonly provided in senior housing are food, resident services, transportation, safety and security, housekeeping and laundry, maintenance, and licensed health care. Each service will be discussed in greater detail in the following pages.

FOOD SERVICE

In fully independent communities, food service is not necessary. In nursing homes, licensure requirements stipulate the type of food service. However, in semi-independent and moderately dependent living arrangements, the type of food service is open for debate. Generally, communities for the semi-independent resident include one or two meals per day, in the monthly fee. The decision to provide cafeteria-style or waiter-served meals depends on the ambience of the community. Food that is prepared for nursing home residents should not be served to other residents, because they tend to view it as institutional food. Whether food service is provided by in-house management or contracted out, the importance of preparation and presentation should never be discounted. Food service staff with institutional backgrounds may not be as successful in providing the proper atmosphere as staff trained in a restaurant operation. It is important to match backgrounds with the food service. Because of the captive audience, it becomes a challenge to create menus and presentations that prevent all the food from looking and tasting the same.

Evaluating a Food Service Program.   Almost an infinite number of questions can be asked in evaluating food service. Some of the more important ones are discussed here.

Will the food preparation be provided in-house or will it be provided by a catered contractor? Small projects often make arrangements with outside food vendors to provide one or more meals to the community. Often there are too few residents to justify bringing aboard a dietician, cooks, and food handlers. It makes sense in many instances to contract food services until achieving a certain percentage of occupancy such as 30 to 50 percent of the units.

Kitchen facilities will still be necessary for the caterer's use while serving the residents.

Are special menus and diets going to be a part of the food service program? Is the staff able to provide salt-free diets, liquid diets, and vegetarian diets, to name but a few, or is the food service program going to be limited in offering such special menus? Will two or more entrees be offered at lunch or dinner, or will there only be one entree? Such decisions will affect the department budget.

Food service programs are menu-driven. It has been stated that an army travels on its stomach, but even more than an army, a retirement community travels on its stomach. If the food services are effective and presented well, generally the majority of the remaining problems are small. However, if the food service program is poor, it does not matter how well the lawns are manicured, or what social activities a community may offer, life will not be pleasant for the manager, the staff, or the developer.

Hamburgers and potato salad will equate to one set of food costs;

steaks, poached salmon, and wine with dinner will create a significant increase in the services plan. The developer and manager need to build a food service program around the menu.

Will guest meals be offered? Are meals going to be completely optional, or will one or two be optional? Should one, two, or three mandatory meals be paid from the monthly service fee by each resident, whether they utilize these meals or not? May residents have as many entrees as they desire, or are they limited to one per resident per meal? Making all meals optional makes it extremely difficult to be able to budget closely, because there is no way of planning for the number of residents who will eat at any given time. Will 25 percent of the residents want breakfast and 100 percent want lunch, or will no one want breakfast and 75 percent want dinner?

A community food service program needs to evaluate providing room service or tray service. When will a resident be permitted to have room service, if at all? Must a doctor determine if a resident is too ill to walk to the central dining facility? Should the room service be charged as an extra, or can a certain number of those meals be included in the monthly fee?

What ambience should be planned for the dining area? At one extreme is the austere dining room, with Formica tabletops, no host or hostess, and plastic dishes. At the opposite extreme is a country club atmosphere with a plush decor, host or hostess, tablecloths, wineglasses, china, silverware, and candles or centerpieces for the tables. Along the same line, will alcohol, beer, or wine be a part of the food service program?

Another consideration is the policy on tipping. The authors' feeling is that no tipping should be permitted to any staff members within a retirement community, for the simple reason that the retirement community is each resident's home, and people do not tip when they are at home. It is strongly recommended that a no tipping policy be established within all departments of a retirement community, and particularly in the food service area.

It must be decided whether or not to open the dining room to the public. One advantage of this is the involvement of the public, particularly the elderly. By having an opportunity to sample the food and service, they receive a sense of the retirement community. It also permits the developer to offset a part of the food costs. One idea is to provide a Sunday brunch that is open to nonresidents.

The developer who plans to open up the dining facility to the public needs to remember that one does not ever stop selling. The quality of food and the manner in which it is presented are of utmost importance when inviting the public to participate in the food service program. One poorly presented platter can mean the difference between favorably impressing or alienating a potential resident.

Number of Meals Served. In a nursing facility, although 100 percent of the patients take three meals per day, generally, they will only complain about 5 percent of the time. The residents in a CCRC consume an average of 1.5 meals per day, and will contribute 95 percent of the complaints. Generally, one or two meals a day are the most desired by members of a level one or two community. Level three residents usually want three meals per day, and levels four and five always offer the residents or patients three meals per day.

In moderately dependent environments, three meals per day are typical. The provider is allowed more flexibility in the presentation than is possible in nursing homes. It is recommended that the method selected provide a variety of options for the residents.

Food Service Options. In determining the type of food service, certain options and considerations are related to project variables, such as the residents' level of functioning, the type of image the senior community wants to present, and the costs. A list of common food service practices follows.

Food Service Options

Consideration: What are the residents' functional levels?

Independent: No meal service or optional meal service; buffet or waiter served

Semi-independent: One or two meals, noon or evening; buffet or waiter served

Moderately dependent: Two or three meals, morning, noon, or evening; staff served

Dependent: Three meals, morning, noon, and evening; staff served; snacks available

Consideration: What ambience does the community want to project?

Cafeteria atmosphere: Buffet style, several entree options

Country club atmosphere: Waiter served, limited entrees

Institutional atmosphere: Staff served, no entree options

Consideration: What are the costs of the program?

Buffet style: Limited control of food cost, portions, and waste; lower labor cost; menu choices for residents

Waiter served: Moderate control of food cost; moderate labor cost; limited menu choices and a restaurant atmosphere for residents

Tray service: Controlled food costs; low labor cost; other staff members sometimes involved; regimented atmosphere

RESIDENT SERVICES

Resident services may be a new term or concept for many developers and sponsors. Often, resident services personnel are perceived as being responsible only for social and recreational programming. In reality, resident services should also supervise resident orientation, manage resident transportation services, develop referral sources, and serve as a resident advocate.

The resident services department is influenced by several conditions and will vary by retirement community. In retirement housing designed for more active, independent, and affluent residents, the responsibilities of resident services more closely parallel that of a social director. Such residents generally have the energy, skills, and funds to pursue their own leisure activities. Consequently, resident services assume a less active role.

In communities catering to occupants who are less affluent and more dependent, resident services should play a greater role in daily activities by developing and expanding recreational and social programs. The more frail the resident population, the greater the need to use resources within the retirement community. Consequently, resident services must develop a network of community resources and referral services to aid the residents.

The less independent the living arrangement, the greater the need for social and recreational programming. Most independent communities will not need extensive social and recreational programming. Semi-independent residents may need a part-time resident services director to schedule programs and serve as a resource person. Residents in assisted living (moderately dependent) will need a full-time resident services director. Due to decreased energy and mobility, social and recreational options have narrowed for these clients. They require appropriate programming and more staff involvement.

People have varied interests. A balanced resident services program should include a variety of activities from the following areas: health and wellness, education and self-actualization, diversionary crafts or hobbies, volunteerism and vocations, religion, and recreational and social events.

All retirement communities will need to furnish some recreational equipment, depending on the type of residents and the availability of funds. Generally, the quality of the resident services program is more a function of the leadership in the department rather than the type and amount of equipment provided. Following is a list of basic items commonly used in retirement communities:

Game tables (30-inch height, on pedestal)

Pool table

Videocassette player

Television (25-inch or larger screen)

Portable cassette player/radio

Folding tables (6-foot) and armless, stackable chairs

Shelves for greenware and other craft projects

Art display stand

Exercise mats, stationary exercise bikes, hand weights

Bingo game (portable game with cards)

Small kitchen area with refrigerator and stove

Assorted supplies, including playing cards, craft supplies, table games

Portable dance floor

Loudspeaker equipment

Resident services program expenses are often overlooked in the operations budget. The amount budgeted to cover parties, dances, program supplies, and other activities will vary according to the available funds. Industry standards do not exist; however, an amount ranging from two to five dollars per resident per month should be sufficient. The budgeted amount does not include capital equipment purchases or staff salaries and benefits.

In summary, the resident services department is an important factor in enhancing resident satisfaction. In communities of less than 100 units, many of the responsibilities of resident services will be a function of the administration. However, in larger communities, regardless of the level of resident dependence, the administration can be freed from some time-consuming individual resident problems by hiring a resident services director.

TRANSPORTATION SERVICE

In fully independent communities, scheduled transportation is generally not an issue. Most residents will continue to drive since that capability is regarded by the elderly as the ultimate sign of independence. In semi-independent and moderately dependent settings, fewer residents will be capable of driving. Transportation can become a real problem if the senior community's location requires transportation for shopping and medical treatment.

Management must establish and maintain policies regarding transportation services. Many residents will depend on the community to provide transportation. The opportunity for travel continues to be appealing to the residents in most senior adult communities. In moderately dependent and fully dependent environments, the issue of transportation decreases. However, even the least mobile individual should have opportunities to leave the confines of the community.

Historically, retirement communities have used vans and cars for resident transportation. Some retirement communities even use limousines as a marketing ploy to project an image of class or distinction. Since transportation is such an important feature in retirement communities, many facilities are selecting minibuses over vans. Although vans are less expensive to lease, purchase, and operate, minibuses are better designed to accommodate the retirement community resident. The minibus is easier to board and more comfortable.

It is difficult to predict the transportation needs of every retirement community, but certain ratios of vehicles to residents are commonly used. In communities for semi-independent and moderately dependent residents, with less than 100 units, one minibus or van is often sufficient to handle routine transportation needs. In communities exceeding 100 units, approximately one van or minibus per 75 units appears appropriate.

Generally, one designated driver is sufficient in most communities, with other staff members also driving on major outings. For large outings, contracted bus service is often the most efficient method of transportation.

All retirement communities should establish policies governing the transportation schedule prior to any marketing efforts. Since transportation is often a marketing feature, marketing staff must avoid making promises that the operations staff cannot satisfy. If the retirement community wants to offer transportation for health care services, residents' medical appointments must be coordinated through the staff to prevent schedule conflicts. In addition, limiting the distance for appointments is important.

SAFETY AND SECURITY SERVICES

Safety and security issues are important to all service levels. Often, developers interpret security as being free from the dangers of bodily harm. The elderly, however, may interpret security as not having to move to a different location to receive needed services. Seniors may select communities that provide multilevels of service in order to be secure from relocation. This does not discount the need for the provision of physical security.

Developers must recognize the potential impact of the aging process on sensory abilities and mobility. However, they must also be sensitive to not creating an environment that is perceived to be for the handicapped. Carpet design, surface composition, time lags for elevator doors, and contrasts in sign lettering are just a few areas that can contribute to a safe and secure environment.

Independent and supportive living communities in most metropolitan areas need security personnel. Whether they must be present 24 hours per day will depend on the availability of other staff and the design of security programs. Generally, security personnel are necessary for evening and night shifts in most communities. Management may contract security or develop an in-house security staff.

Contracting for security services is generally more expensive and prevents management from assigning other tasks to security personnel. Being trained in weapon use is not as important as understanding what to do in emergencies dealing with the elderly.

HOUSEKEEPING AND LAUNDRY SERVICES

The need or demand for housekeeping and laundry services will vary by retirement community. In semi-independent living arrangements, housekeeping is often provided once a week or every other week. Communities for semi-independent residents may not include housekeeping in their monthly fee to keep prices competitive; instead they offer the service à la carte. Some seniors in semi-independent settings do their own housekeeping to avoid the added expense. Other than linen, personal laundry service is generally not included in the monthly fee, but is offered a la carte. Some view these functions as signs of independence.

In moderately dependent living arrangements, both housekeeping and personal laundry services are generally included in monthly fees. Many states that license facilities for the moderately dependent resident dictate provision of housekeeping and personal laundry service. However, the environment should not be free of all challenges or activities of daily living.

Licensed health care facilities for the fully dependent resident are required to provide both personal laundry and housekeeping services according to licensing standards.

MAINTENANCE SERVICE

A competent maintenance staff is essential in retirement housing for several reasons. As with conventional housing, a well-maintained property protects the owners' equity. Preventive maintenance programs reduce major repair costs and extend the useful life of the equipment. Properly maintained properties enhance market appeal. The senior resident is very sensitive to the appearance of the community. Poorly maintained properties are often considered a reflection of the quality of management.

Residents of retirement communities tend to be higher risk candidates for falls and accidents than residents of conventional properties. Consequently, emphasis must be placed on safety issues. All equipment, including emergency alert systems, elevators, and fire protection equipment, must receive priority attention.

Since the responsibilities of the maintenance department in retirement housing extend beyond those of conventional housing properties, a larger staff is normally required and should be accessible on a 24-hour basis. Untimely response to maintenance problems can damage management's credibility and affect the community's reputation.

During initial operations, management often underestimates the need for maintenance. Although under warranty, new equipment often malfunctions and requires adjustment by maintenance personnel. Sufficient staff should be available to correct equipment problems, aid resident move-ins, and begin development of a preventive maintenance program.

LICENSED HEALTH CARE SERVICES

Most developers are reluctant to become involved in licensed health care. It is a highly specialized system requiring management experience in long-term care operations. Licensed health care is not a service that senior adults openly discuss. However, in semi-independent and moderately dependent environments, residents are concerned about its availability. They want the security of knowing the service is there if they need it.

SENIOR HOUSING AMENITIES

Senior housing communities differ significantly from other housing properties in the number of common amenities provided. These design features or services are generally part of the base rate and are not included in calculating the service component. For example, libraries, spas, and on-site postal facilities are service amenities. Design amenities would include emergency call systems and assistance devices installed near commodes and bathing facilities. The number and kinds of amenities to include are debatable. Generally, the decision is predicated on the level of independence and the financial status of the resident population. Obviously, the more amenities, the more it costs to build and maintain a community. Most developers have a tendency to provide more services than the residents will use. The following common amenities may be provided in retirement housing projects.

Libraries. A feature common in most retirement communities is the library. Although not utilized by everyone, libraries offer a sanctuary and an opportunity to keep the mind active. Semi-independent and moderately independent residents tend to use libraries more than dependent residents. Libraries do not need to be large but should be readily accessible.

Swimming or Lap Pools. Except in fully dependent and moderately dependent living arrangements, swimming pools are common and are often used as a marketing tool. In addition to being aesthetic, pools may be promoted as providing excellent exercise. Although some pools are underutilized, communities with enclosed pools cite a higher rate of use. Regardless of use, some managers recommend including a pool if the community can afford the cost to build and maintain it.

Putting Greens.   In the current market, putting greens do not appear to be an essential feature of retirement housing. Some retirement communities install greens with artificial surfaces. Although less expensive to build and maintain than natural grass greens, their artificial appearance may detract from the landscape. The cost for the construction and maintenance of natural grass greens is hard to justify. Because of limited utilization, most newer communities do not include putting greens.

Game Rooms.   Whether designated as a game room or a recreational area, space should be provided for small group activities. Playing cards or parlor games may satisfy a social need in many retirement communities. Although unproven, there appears to be a relationship between the location of game areas and their utilization. Areas adjacent to high traffic areas seem to be used more than secluded areas. Apparently, people want to be near activity.

Pool Tables.   Like libraries, pool tables are one of the more common amenities in retirement communities. Unlike libraries, resident utilization varies considerably from community to community. Of all amenities, pool tables are generally low on the list of essential features.

Whirlpool Spas.   Whirlpool spas are used in most communities if they are designed for safety and privacy. They are used for therapeutic reasons, regardless of the type of community. In moderately dependent and fully dependent environments, staff must be in attendance for safety reasons.

Chapels.   Chapels experience limited use in retirement communities without any religious affiliation. If a developer feels strongly about incorporating a chapel in a retirement community, a room that can accommodate multiple uses is recommended.

Lounges for Alcoholic Beverages.   An amenity being offered in several new retirement communities is a lounge that serves alcoholic beverages. Some communities only offer setups, while others operate full-service lounges. Since operating a lounge increases operations expenses and liability risks, management and developers must thoroughly evaluate the pros and cons.

Banking Facilities.   Some retirement communities offer banking facilities on site. These services are provided through automated teller machines or through contracts with local banking institutions. Developers may need to survey state banking regulations concerning branch banking restrictions.

Post Office.   Some communities provide an area for weighing and preparing packages for mailing. Usually adjacent to mail drops and mailboxes, it is an inexpensive feature to develop and manage.

Exercise Areas.   Exercise areas are becoming standard amenities in most retirement communities. Recognizing the contribution of exercise to overall health, residents often participate in group sessions featuring aerobics or stretching exercises. Rather than being furnished with expensive fixed or free weight equipment, these exercise areas are normally open floor space that can accommodate rows of chairs or exercise mats. Exercise equipment is usually limited to fixed bicycles, treadmills, and mats.

Greenhouse and Garden Areas.   Greenhouses and garden areas are not as popular with retirement housing residents as generally believed. Although some residents have an interest in gardening, the elderly do not automatically become gardeners as they age. In living arrangements for moderately dependent and dependent residents with limited mobility, greenhouses provide diversionary activity. Some retirement communities have built raised garden plots for residents' convenience.

Walking Paths and Landscaping.   Many residents in retirement communities enjoy a well-landscaped walking path in a secure area. Walking is a popular exercise for many of the elderly. Of all the features designed into a retirement community, a safe, lighted area with paths is an essential amenity.

Crafts and Hobby Areas.   Rooms or areas for residents to pursue hobbies or crafts should be available. However, whether these areas should be designed and designated solely for crafts or hobbies is debatable. Often single purpose areas are not utilized sufficiently to justify the cost of building and maintaining them. The best alternative is to develop a multipurpose area for different group functions, including crafts and hobbies.

Elevators.   Any retirement housing property with multilevels must have elevators. In addition to conveying residents, elevators are used by housekeeping and maintenance, and in moving furniture. Consequently, installing service elevators in addition to passenger elevators is ideal.

Emergency Alert Systems.   Because retirement communities cater to a high-risk population, an emergency alert or monitoring system is a common amenity. In nursing homes call systems are required, and their presence is obvious. In housing for the more active senior, alert systems are less obvious.

Two different types of alert systems are used. The active system, which requires a resident to activate it by pulling a cord or pressing a button, is generally installed in bedroom or bathroom areas. Critics question its usefulness since the resident who needs assistance may not be able to reach or operate the system.

The passive system, often installed on commodes or apartment entrances, is designed to alert staff if no activity occurs in the apartment. This system may be a sophisticated electronic system or a simple apparatus attached to a door hinge that indicates whether the door has been opened recently.

Handrails or Other Assistive Devices.   A question often asked by developers is whether handrails and grab bars should be installed. In nursing homes, licensure standards specifically require handrails. In communities for the semi-independent and moderately dependent, the answer is yes—with discretion. Although residents do not like an environment that appears to have been designed for the handicapped, they welcome features that accommodate their decreased agility. For example, railings can be designed into the decorating scheme in hallways, and bathrooms can be designed for safety and comfort without installing obvious grab bars.

Barber Shops and Beauty Salons.   A barber shop or beauty salon in communities for independent and semi-independent residents may discourage their participation in the surrounding community. Beauty and barber shops are essential for moderately dependent and fully dependent residents.

Because only licensed barbers or cosmetologists can operate the shop, developers should discuss design and equipment needs with an experienced operator.

SELECTING PROFESSIONAL MANAGEMENT

After market analysis, design, location, and marketing activities, the continued success of a retirement community relies on professional management. Lenders are becoming more aware of the unique management expertise necessary and are requiring developers to hire management with proven experience in retirement communities.

Managers must understand the subtleties of administering services and programs for the elderly. Their special needs should not be interpreted as dependence. Regardless of their functioning level, residents should be offered alternatives and choices. The basic need of all seniors is to remain as independent as possible. Developers should select a management firm that demonstrates a knowledge of the difference between a care-oriented environment and an environment that encourages independence.

As mentioned earlier, the developer should tour communities currently under management by the prospective company, evaluating the property conditions or appearance, the quality of the staff, and the overall atmosphere.

A well-maintained site will reassure the developer that the management company understands its responsibility in protecting the property's value and reputation. It also demonstrates the implementation of proper maintenance systems.

In observing staff, evaluate their appearance, demeanor, and work habits. An ill-groomed staff is an indication that management may not have adequate recruitment and screening policies. The staff's reluctance to visit or smile may signal poor employee and management relations. Faulty work habits reflect limited training, inadequate supervision, and questionable employee policies.

The overall atmosphere will be readily apparent during the tour. Warmth, friendliness, and activity mean that management personnel are knowledgeable and confident about their responsibilities. This atmosphere is apparent in the interaction of the staff and residents and the relationship between management and their employees.

The developer should also ask to see written policies, procedures, and established business systems. These provide evidence that management can handle the business operations efficiently as well as provide a pleasant environment.

Regardless of the services provided in a retirement community, professional management must demonstrate the necessary abilities and skills to fulfill the following responsibilities:

Develop a management plan

Develop, implement, and update policies and procedures

Develop and monitor an accounting system

Hire, train, and supervise all staff

Monitor policy adherence

Analyze monthly income and expenses

Develop and supervise budget control including utility, food, and payroll

Develop, organize, implement, and monitor preventive and operational maintenance programs for grounds and equipment

Negotiate, execute, and monitor service contracts

Manage all tax accounts including payroll

Monitor quality of services (food, housekeeping, maintenance, health care, and resident services)

Monitor resident satisfaction through opinion polls, suggestion boxes, and resident meetings, both collectively and individually

Monitor local, state, and federal legislative and industry activities that influence project operation or viability

Monitor community market needs and implement appropriate programs

Attend local, state, and national meetings and conventions concerning the industry

Remain abreast of current developments in the industry through trade journals

Conduct periodic staff meetings, monitor employee relations, and discourage the need or desire for union intervention

Collect rent and other fees and pay bills in a timely manner

Prepare annual operating, personnel, and capital budgets

Monitor security procedures

Provide statistical data of residents (age, sex, income, medical needs, vacancy rates, hospital and nursing home utilization) for market analysis and policy development

File and maintain records and reports according to state and federal
requirements

Participate in local events

Interact with the resident population daily

Although the responsibility for some of the activities can be passed
on to subordinates, management is still accountable. Whether management is hired or organized internally, a management plan is necessary. This is discussed more fully in a subsequent section on management's role in the planning process.

On-Site Versus Contract Management.   There are advantages and
disadvantages to any approach or option taken by a developer in implementing project management.

Advantages of On-Site Management

The developer or board of directors generally has closer control over
an on-site manager than over an off-site manager.

An on-site manager can often prevent escalation of minor problems
by responding quickly and appropriately.

The on-site manager may be more attentive to the community's
needs.

The on-site manager can develop custom services.

The cost for the on-site manager can be less because no overhead or
profit is included in a monthly fee.

Disadvantages of On-Site Management

One individual is seldom well-qualified and knowledgeable in all
the skills and tasks that are required—accounting, landscaping,
insurance, building maintenance, supervising a food service department, communications, public relations, and marketing.

There may be a void when the manager becomes ill or goes on
vacation.

Termination of employment may cause problems if there is no backup
person.

If a personality conflict develops between the board or a developer
and the manager, replacing the individual can be difficult, whereas
a management firm can simply reassign personnel.

In summary, the advantages for an on-site manager are control and cost, and the disadvantages are lack of support and knowledge.

Advantages of Contract Management

Backup and continuity of management are provided.

Day-to-day management problems can be assumed by the manager both on and off site, allowing the board members and developer to concentrate on policy decisions.

Contract management firms usually have had experience with more problems than an individual on-site manager.

Management companies can also serve as an intermediary when there are disputes or personality conflicts between the residents or board members and the on-site manager.

Disadvantages of Contract Management

Most of the files, records, and staff are not on site; the on-site manager may be someone with little experience who is backed up by the management firm from another location.

Communications can break down because the management firm is not physically present.

The cost of this type of management approach is usually higher due to increased overhead and profit.

Board members may feel a lack of involvement in running their own community.

In summary, the advantages of the contract management firm are backup for the on-site manager and experience. The disadvantages are the increased cost and lack of control.

Combination On-Site and Contract Management. This perhaps is the most frequent choice utilized by the typical level two or level three project. It permits the contract management contractor to have the kind of close relationship that is mandatory in the retirement community, and the community benefits from the experience and resources of the management firm. This combination, however, is the most expensive, because the board or developer is paying for not only an on-site manager, but also the staff and overhead of the contract management company.

Transitional Management.   Transitional management takes place in start-up communities where the developer has little or no experience with managing a retirement community. An experienced firm or individual will help guide the developer or sponsor through the start-up phase to a determined point in the life of a project. After the senior community has been in operation for that period of time, the management firm's responsibilities will be complete. A manager hired by the developer will take over, or the transitional manager will have trained a local firm to assume the ongoing responsibilities. The management of a retirement project is complicated by such start-up tasks as the staff phase-in, initial purchasing agreement, and the various resident mixes. Very few of these problems are understood by management firms without prior start-up experience with a retirement community. The more varied the levels of residents that make up the community census, the more difficult and costly the start-up mistakes can be.

New developers or sponsors often hire too many staff and fully staff the day before a project opens instead of phasing in staff and services as more residents enter the community. Introducing the staff, services, and contractors in a timely manner and purchasing the supplies necessary to meet the promises made to residents while still meeting the budgets can be a complicated balancing act. The fewer nonshelter services provided, the easier and quicker the transitional period can take place. Conversely, the more services or care that have been promised, the longer the transitional management firm needs to be involved. It is much easier for a manager to take over an operating facility that has already had its problems ironed out.

In summary, the determination of what type of management alternatives is not unlike any prudent business decision. The pros and cons must be evaluated based upon the needs and methods of doing business. There are no standard solutions, only alternatives.

THE DEVELOPMENT PROCESS

Often developers overlook management's role in the development process. Management experience can help prevent problems caused by selection of inappropriate services, inaccurate operational expense projections, purchase of inappropriate equipment and furnishings, and poor interior and exterior design.

Selection of Services and Amenities.   The selection of services and amenities is based on information gathered during the marketing analysis. However, this process is inexact and cannot unconditionally guarantee that the suggested services and amenities are essential. Experienced management can lend insight into which services or amenities are most commonly utilized and can assist in developing priorities with accompanying data on the cost of operation. Developers can use management's knowledge to weigh the benefit of an amenity or service against its cost.

Operational Expense Data.   To determine the financial feasibility of a proposed property, developers need realistic data on operations costs. This knowledge is essential in the development of budgets and other pro forma documents.

Furnishings and Equipment.   Management can also assist in selecting the most appropriate equipment and furnishings for the services being provided. Inappropriate equipment will add unnecessary costs to the development budget and increase future operations expenses. Improper or insufficient equipment can ultimately influence the overall quality of the services.

Interior and Exterior Design.   Knowledgeable management can be a resource for the architect by explaining, in practical terms, how certain systems work. Security, landscape lighting and design, and parking are just a few exterior design issues needing management's opinion. The placement of janitorial closets, the design of employee areas, and business offices are examples of interior design concerns. Management should review design documents and render opinions for the consideration of the development team.

MANAGEMENT PLAN

During the development process, a management plan must be created that includes strategies for operational management and defines management's philosophy governing services provided to the residents and conduct toward the staff. The plan should also provide an organization structure and policies and procedures for the community. The plan should be completed several months prior to opening the facility.

Policy statements should cover the following concerns.

Resident Relations

Criteria for acceptance
Health care
Orientation information
Suggestions and grievances
Fees, rent policies, and other financial considerations
Safety and maintenance
Guidelines concerning visitors, pets, mail, keys, messages, and use
   of common amenities

Food Service

Budget and menu planning
Vendor contracts and food purchasing
Food preparation and presentation
Dining room setup, hours of service, and meal schedules
Storage and inventory control
Staffing, schedules, and job descriptions

Maintenance Services

Maintenance of units and common areas
Preventive maintenance
Vehicle maintenance
Emergency equipment maintenance
Service agreements and outside service representation
Staffing, schedules, and job descriptions

Resident Services

Type and schedule of social and recreational events
Transportation
Health and wellness programs
Programs and services available in the surrounding community
Resident orientation
Resident organizations
Staffing, schedules, and job descriptions

Housekeeping and Laundry Services

Standards and routines for residential units
Standards and routines for common areas
Laundry procedures
Chemical and supply purchasing
Inventory control
Staffing, schedules, and job descriptions

Human Resources

Organization chart
Statement on nondiscriminatory practices
Statement on organized labor
Employee policies
    Terms of status
    Health examinations
    Orientation and training
    Hours of work
    Reasons for termination
    Grievances
    Promotions or change of status
    Starting salary and pay increase structure
    Payroll periods and deductions
Employee benefits
    Vacation pay and schedule
    Holiday pay
    Leaves of absence (medical, personal, bereavement, military,
        jury duty)
    Health insurance

Accounting System

Payroll
Accounts payable
Accounts receivable
Chart of accounts
Security deposits

Purchasing

Records and reports

Complications of Management Plans. A major difficulty for a manager initiating a management plan is to ascertain and establish guidelines for the assessment of the prospective residents' independent living skills. When a resident can no longer perform certain skills, the retirement facility may not be able to still provide a functioning environment.

As an example, in a level one community, residents would have to be able to perform their own housekeeping chores, except perhaps for occasional aid with heavy cleaning. If that same community has planned to serve both level one and level two residents, then housekeeping chores such as vacuuming, washing floors, and cleaning bathrooms would be performed on a regular basis for the level two residents. A resident who regularly needs extensive help with housekeeping functions or who refuses to maintain an acceptable level of cleanliness in his or her unit might require level three (or higher) services. If the management plan has not provided for such an intense level in the housekeeping function, it would be necessary to find an alternative community for that particular resident.

There can be as many as 25 critical or contributory factors that require evaluation and incorporation in any management plan, ranging from being able to prepare one's own meals to being able to use drugs or alcohol. Bathing, dressing, toiletry, and mobility all need to be evaluated in determining what level of supportive services should be provided, as opposed to what the residents expect to have provided. The manager must understand the general physical, emotional, and social requirements of the residents, as well as individual levels of care and needs.

The policies of communities that provide extensive services and health care are generally dictated to a great extent by certification and licensing requirements.

Management Services. The management plan is broken down first into basic services and then into special services that meet the needs of the senior housing environment. Basic management services include preparation of budgets, accounting and cost control, collection of assessments or rents, routine cleaning and maintenance of common areas, purchasing of supplies, staff supervision, insurance program implementation, and day-to-day general operations.

Services related to the special needs of the elderly and the level of care to be provided are also incorporated into the management plan. They can encompass a variety of items from installing grab bars in bathrooms or ordering left-handed refrigerator doors to establishing a referral system when it is necessary to transfer a resident. Probably the most difficult task for a manager is informing a resident that relocation is necessary because the provided services are no longer sufficient to permit the person to age in place.

Management should treat all residents equally and not plan to cater to those in wheelchairs. Most residents do not want special treatment because they have a handicap or are frail. The management plan also must be pragamatic and sensible. No plan can be all things to all residents.

For example, retirement communities often provide assistance with heavy cleaning of individual units, such as shampooing rugs, moving furniture, waxing floors, washing windows, and cleaning appliances. The management plan must have a clear statement about its manner of involvement in such services. The policy can be simply to supply each resident with two or three names of reputable contractors, or management can arrange access to the unit for estimates, negotiate the price, supervise the work, and determine whether the job was done satisfactorily before the resident pays the contractor.

Obviously, management's involvement could take as little as a few minutes or many hours. If there are 200 units in a project and it takes four hours per unit, to go through the various steps for heavy cleaning, it could easily take six months to complete the task. Myriad other services may be just as time consuming, if not more so. It must be clearly stated in the policy, and explained to each resident exactly what to expect from management.

Another point that needs to be made is that a manager can do too much for any one or all of the residents. What, at first glance, appears to be concern, may actually deprive the residents of self-reliance. Managers also have to be alert to residents who have bogus maintenance problems, such as a leaky sink that never drips when checked. Sometimes depression or loneliness is the real reason for the call, and the resident needs to communicate with someone.

MANAGEMENT'S ROLE DURING PREOPERATIONS

The preoperational phase, which generally parallels the construction phase, commences with groundbreaking and ends when the first resident moves in. Management may or may not be directly responsible for the marketing. If another company is hired to market the community, management should be involved and should participate in marketing policy and development. It is necessary to be aware of and in agreement with promises made to prospective residents by marketing. Prospective residents may become familiar with management staff through marketing, prior to moving into the community. This can help with resident adjustment.

In some instances, management, whether on-site or contract, also markets the community. When management assumes this dual role, it may prove better at management than marketing, but the promises made in the sales processes are generally fulfilled when the resident moves in.

During the preoperations, management will continue to fine-tune the operations budget. Assumptions may change according to sales activity or changes in the economic conditions that influence costs. Several errors of assumption are commonly made in the development of operations budgets. One such mistake is an overly optimistic absorption rate that assumes everyone who reserves a unit will move in. National averages for absorption of units is approximately four to six move-ins per month. Obviously, this will vary by market areas. Underestimating costs can be another problem. Utility companies or other senior communities can only provide estimates based on past experience. Insurance costs, food costs during initial operations and staffing expense during hiring and training are also frequently underestimated.

Overestimating revenues or underestimating costs may create problems if limited operating capital is available. For this reason, it is recommended that a contingency expense item be included in the initial budget.

For new management companies or even existing companies, considerable time during the preoperational phase will be spent in the development of policies and procedures.

Management must also solicit, compare, and execute vendor and service agreements, such as:

Agreements with food vendors

Elevator service contracts

Pest control

Trash pickup

Landscape maintenance (may hire staff)

Fire and emergency equipment inspection and service

Pool maintenance (may use own staff)

Security (may hire and train staff)

The last major responsibility of management during the preoperational phase is recruiting, hiring and training staff. Approximately one month prior to operations, department supervisors should be hired. After orientation, department supervisors should begin developing procedures and setting up their areas of responsibility. Approximately two weeks before initial operation, support staff should be hired and trained. When the first resident moves in, all services and features cited in the residence contract must be operational.

Management should recruit staff who have warm, outgoing personalities and positive attitudes toward senior adults. Management cannot change staff personalities, and sometimes it is difficult to change attitudes. Success in building a quality staff depends on management's approach and the availability of personnel. It is important to develop a policy that emphasizes only certain attitudes are acceptable in dealing with residents. Training should incorporate a familiarity with the many social, psychological, and physiological aspects of aging.

A visitor to Disney World, impressed by the enthusiasm and friendly nature of the staff, asked how they trained the staff to be so outgoing and helpful. The Disney World manager responded, "We don't train them. We recruit and hire the personality, then we train the staff in their job task."

The ratio of staff to residents is always of concern. The following numbers are rules of thumb; they are not intended for application to a specific project because each community must be looked at on its own. For an ACLF, the average number of staff members is between 35 and 55 (excluding nursing care). They are responsible for social activities, administration (including manager or director), transportation, food services, housekeeping, laundry, maintenance, and security. The size of the community and complexity of the resident programs will impact the number of staff.

Staffing requirements for a CCRC with nursing facilities, personal care, and all other support systems could easily reach 98 to 115 employees if the community has 250 independent apartments, a 50-bed nursing center, and 25 personal care units. There would likely be six personal care staff members. Food services would require 30 employees, and the nursing center would also need 28 to 30 workers. Another 35 to 45 employees would be necessary for all other tasks. The gross salary for a CCRC would range between $1 million and $1.4 million and for an ACLF, between $550,000 and $800,000.

MANAGEMENT'S ROLE DURING INITIAL OPERATIONS

During the first six months to one year after opening the community, management will focus on three specific areas.

First, management will become an active member of the marketing group. Marketing should be scheduling parties and special events to generate traffic. Management must ensure that the staff fully understand their role. Not only are they expected to perform their assigned tasks and serve residents, they must also cooperate with marketing efforts. Sometimes conflicts develop between overzealous marketing and operations staff. Management must see that daily routines are not disrupted, while resolving problems between staff with two different orientations.

Management's second responsibility will be to iron out the wrinkles of operations during the first six months. Ideally, all the equipment and furnishings will be in place when operations begin. Realistically, management will need to be prepared to test new equipment or to wait for other equipment. The first six months is also filled with shakedown activities, such as repairing inoperable elevators, replacing air conditioning units that do not work, and testing housing and food service routines. Although equipment may be under warranty, unexpected problems may occur.

A third area of attention should be resident orientation and adjustment. Residents, regardless of the level of service, are moving into a new community. They need to be coached in the routines and introduced to staff. Some communities use other residents to orient newcomers, others utilize staff. The ideal situation is to conduct resident orientation before the move. Moving and unpacking can be very upsetting for anyone. It is essential to instruct residents on emergency procedures before or immediately upon move-in. Other community routines can wait until after the resident has had time to unpack and settle down.

Semi-independent and moderately dependent living environments require round-the-clock staffing, although partial staffing may be possible at night. Nursing homes require full staff constantly.

Business Operations. Management must establish policies and procedures to pay bills in a timely manner, collect receivables, and prepare accurate and timely financial statements. Most properties do not have an inexhaustible supply of operating capital; consequently, responsible management must be aware of their financial position.

Staff Training and Development. Training and development should be an ongoing process with regular training sessions after orientation and initial training. Nursing homes are required by law to provide training; other senior housing should have such programs as a matter of policy.

Resident Services. Although the resident services department does not necessarily assume responsibility for resolution of a resident's problem, it directs the individual toward the sources that can help solve the difficulty. This department can reduce the administration's involvement in such problems.

Food Service and Menu Development. Food service is a challenge in all senior adult communities except independent living. In essence, residents will be eating in the same restaurant daily. It is necessary to achieve variety in presentation and menus while maintaining quality. Some management firms contract food service out to groups experienced in restaurant operation.

Housekeeping Service. Although housekeeping's role may vary from community to community, the quality should not. In fully dependent and semi-independent living, housekeeping is required either daily or weekly. Supportive living may or may not include housekeeping in the service package. Some residents view maintaining their home as a sign of independence. Consequently, housekeeping in semi-independent living environments may need to be offered a la carte.

Transportation. Transportation may become a problem in any community, including nursing homes, when policy does not provide specific guidelines or when communities attempt to cover all the residents' transportation needs. Personnel and vehicles may be committed for hours if providing transportation for all medical and dental appointments. Management must be cautious in promising transportation. "Scheduled transportation" is a more appropriate term to prevent misunderstandings and disappointments.

Maintenance. A preventive maintenance system and work order system must be developed to effectively utilize maintenance staff. Except in emergencies, resident needs are number one priority. During initial operations, management should anticipate greater demands as residents move in and new equipment malfunctions. Management should plan for part-time workers to assist residents in hanging pictures and performing other menial tasks during move-in periods.

Physical Management. Too often, in the physical management of a community the administrator, director, or manager does not have the necessary technical knowledge of the various components (equipment, buildings, grounds). The facility maintenance program is the most often overlooked task. Some managers have the attitude, "If it's not broken, don't fix it." A manager must develop a sound preventive maintenance and repair program for each component that will need repair or replacement within the retirement community. Not providing proper preventive maintenance can multiply difficulties for the manager and the residents.

What impacts and compounds facility maintenance in the senior adult community is that failures or deficiencies not only affect cash flow but also can cause much discomfort for the residents and, in some instances, a possibly life-threatening deterioration in health. For example, an 80-year-old woman sitting in the lobby at her community may suffer from hypothermia if the air temperature inside the room drops below 65 degrees. Loss of central heat for any length of time because of a power outage or a boiler malfunction might be devastating to some residents. The manager's role is to anticipate worst-case scenarios and establish procedures so that the staff can implement them should there be an equipment failure. Each portion of the maintenance program needs an organized and coordinated approach.

The developer, with assistance from the manager, must set guidelines that will clearly mark any components that require facility maintenance. The information developed for such a program will affect the cost of operating the community. Complete operating manuals and documentation are essential to implement preventive maintenance whether a component or element requires one-time service or ongoing maintenance (such as the pool, elevators, painting, and housekeeping).

Repairs cannot be made on an as-needed basis. Each piece of equipment must be listed, its components must be periodically inspected, and the appropriate manuals and data should be conveniently filed to make maintenance an easier task. Each equipment manual should include scheduling for maintenance, procedure for repair, and evaluation of the item's effective operation. If a piece of equipment needs routine repairs, oiling, or replacement of parts, it should be clearly listed, and a trained staff member should periodically inspect the item. If the equipment is complex, requiring additional experience or training, it may be necessary for the manager to contract with an outside service company.

Health Care Services. In facilities without licensed health care on site, it is advisable to budget for a licensed nurse. Although seldom needed for emergency situations, the presence of a nurse provides a sense of security. In semi-independent living arrangements, nurses should establish wellness programs and interface with the medical community for support services, including educational activities for residents and staff. In facilities with licensed health care on site, knowing medical assistance is next door gives security to the residents. Management should not require licensed staff to leave the floor of the nursing home to visit other sections in the community. This is a violation of licensing standards.

There continues to be debate about licensed health care adjacent to semi-independent or fully independent complexes. Some argue that more active residents do not like living next to a nursing home. The problem is not its presence, but how management and marketing handle its presence. Many developers feel on-site health care is essential to handle the aging in place problem as communities mature.

SUMMARY

A critical issue in the success of any senior community is experienced and appropriate management. Experience in other businesses or in general property management does not guarantee success in communities for the elderly.

The unique feature of housing for the elderly is the various types of services and amenities available. It is sometimes difficult to determine what services and amenities to provide and how to charge for them. Obviously, such decisions impact on the cost and management expertise necessary to achieve a quality product at a reasonable price.

Experience in management techniques and considerable knowledge about senior adults are essential. Depending on the developer or owner's business plan, the management organization may be developed internally or contracted out to another organization. If it is contracted out, the developer or sponsors must be certain that both organizations have similar management philosophies, business goals, and attitudes toward seniors.

Management should become involved early in the development phase of a community through participation in specific tasks—selection of services and amenities, pro forma budget development, equipment and furnishings selection, exterior and interior design, and development of a management plan.

During the preoperations phase, management should fine-tune the management plan by writing specific policies and procedures, continuing to work on operational budgets, and securing vendor and services agreements. Approximately six weeks prior to initial operations, management should begin hiring and training staff, and testing equipment.

In the initial operations phase, all services and features must be provided whether the community has 1 occupant or 50. Management has an obligation to protect the owners' equity, provide quality and consistent services to the residents, and provide leadership and support to the staff. Failure by management to address these responsibilities may lessen the chances of a community's success. Failure of a retirement facility tarnishes both the general community and the senior living industry as a whole.

FINANCIAL MANAGEMENT

One of the most vital aspects of managing any property, prudent financial management is especially important in retirement housing. The lack of adequate financial management in many existing projects is evident from the number of financial failures in recent years. In other cases profitability has been low because of unsound financial planning and management.

The financial management of a facility involves budgeting as well as operations. Budgeting includes the preparation of the operations budget, the cash flow budget, and the capital budget. Financial management provides the information, and interpretation of that information, to assist planning and controlling the operations of the retirement center. The financial management system includes periodic financial statements such as the income statement or balance sheet, budgets and performance reports, financial operations, and an annual audit.

To be useful, information must be timely and in sufficient detail to incorporate in the decision-making process. Proper financial reporting, however, does not cause the user to suffer from information overload.

This section focuses on the elements of financial management unique to retirement housing. The major emphasis is on additional revenues and expenses, such as food service and housekeeping. Facilities with health care centers will have additional regulations in the form of licensure requirements, as well as Medicare and Medicaid regulations.

In order to perform the functions of financial management, the following components are required: organization structure, chart of accounts, information system, budgets and performance reports, financial operations, and annual audit.

Organization Structure.   The first step in constructing a sound financial management program is the development of an organization plan that identifies the jobs and responsibilities of each employee. It is necessary to define responsibility centers in which to accumulate costs and to identify the person with the authority, as well as responsibility, to control those costs.

In order to hold department heads accountable for their performance, they must have clearly established areas of responsibility. Responsibility centers are generally departments such as maintenance, dietary, and housekeeping. Costs are accumulated by department as well as for the whole facility. The performance of each department can then be evaluated.

Responsibility Centers.   For performance reporting, responsibility centers (departments) can generally be divided into two types: standard cost centers and discretionary cost centers.

Standard cost centers are departments or activities in which the relationship between inputs (personnel or supplies) and outputs (activities) is direct. An example of a standard cost center is housekeeping, in which there is a direct relationship between inputs (personnel or supplies) and outputs (activities) is direct. An example of a standard cost center is housekeeping, in which there is a direct relationship between the square footage to be cleaned and the amount of time and supplies necessary to clean it. The dietary department is also a standard cost center in which there is a direct relationship between the number of meals served and the labor hours, raw food, and other supplies used.

Standard cost centers are easier to budget for and to control because the amount of inputs (costs) required is a direct function of the units of outputs produced. Table 7-1 provides an example of a dietary department budget.

Discretionary cost centers are more difficult to manage because there is no direct relationship between the inputs and the outputs. In many cases it is difficult to measure the outputs. Examples of discretionary cost centers are general and administrative services and social services. In both cases, it is relatively easy to measure the inputs of hours worked, or supplies used. It is very difficult to measure the outputs. For example, how do you define the output of the administrator or recreational director? However, the difficulty in measuring output should not be used as an excuse not to control cost. Measures of performance, such as profitability or activities conducted, should be used.

Chart of Accounts. In order to accumulate costs by department or responsibility center, it is necessary to develop a chart of accounts, which is the basic structure of an accounting system. It is a listing of account titles with numerical symbols, designed to compile financial data concerning the assets, liabilities, equity, revenues, and expenses of the project.

The number assigned to each account is used in the general ledger to identify the account (responsibility center) to which to assign each item of cost as the invoices are paid. The department head assigns an

TABLE 7-1. Dietary Department—Annual Budget (Occupancy, 90%)

Fixed cost		
Cook	$ 24,053	
Dining room manager	29,207	
Total fixed cost		$ 53,260
Variable cost		
Consultant or dietician	5,000	
Purchased service	0	
Utilities	14,000	
Raw food	240,775	
Personnel	84,148	
China and glassware	7,705	
Disposables	4,815	
Other	4,815	
Total variable cost		361,258
Total food service cost		$414,518

account number to each invoice when approving it for payment. When paying the invoice, the accounts payable department assigns the cost to the account number appearing on the invoice.

As an example, the chart of accounts would include housekeeping department expense accounts for salaries, disposable equipment, supplies, and purchased services. If the project includes a health care center, the chart of accounts would show revenue and expenses for the health care center, including revenue accounts for skilled nursing care, intermediate care, and personal care. Expense accounts for skilled, intermediate, and personal care would also need to be added, as well as expense accounts for physical therapy, medical records, and other departments unique to a health care environment.

Information System.   The accounting information system comprises the journals, ledgers, and other records in which the transactions of the organization are compiled. It also consists of the persons responsible for maintaining these records.

The information system should accumulate not only financial data for the assets, liabilities, capital, revenue, and expenses of the project, but also statistical data. The number of meals served, the square feet of the project, the FTEs (full-time equivalent), and other similar data are necessary to determine the productivity of each responsibility center.

The cost-benefit relationship of the information should always be considered. It is possible to accumulate almost any information and to record it in great detail. However, the designer of the information system should always ask whether this additional information will result in improved decision making by the users of the information and if the improvement exceeds the cost of accumulating and processing the additional information (cost vs. benefit).

The accounting system maintains those accounting records and reports necessary to properly safeguard the project's assets, provide management with financial information necessary for managerial decisions, apprise the owner and creditors of the financial status of the facility, and meet regulatory requirements. More specific discussion regarding the information system is provided in the financial operations section presented later in this chapter.

Budgets.   From a strategic planning and control point of view, budgeting is the most important element of the financial management process. A budget is a detailed plan for the future that is used for planning and control purposes. There are three basic types: the operations budget, the cash budget, and the capital budget.

The operations budget presents the projected revenues and expenses of the organization for a specified period of time, usually a year. It is used to plan the personnel and other expense requirements for each department for the following year as well as to provide a standard against which to compare the actual results. The cash budget is a projection of the cash receipts and disbursements for a specified period of time and indicates future cash requirements. The capital budget is a plan for acquisition of major assets, such as buildings and equipment, over a period of time, generally three to five years. It is a long-range planning tool.

Operations Budget. In the operations budget, revenue is generally broken down by source, such as rents, gifts, government payments, or insurance. The expenses are listed according to responsibility center.

In preparing revenue projections, a retirement center differs from a standard multifamily facility in that, in addition to rental income, there is also income from services provided to residents and possibly revenue from a health care center. Some additional sources of revenue include income from additional meals, rental of special purpose rooms, parking, extra housekeeping services, extra laundry services, beauty and barber shop, gift shop, special clients, tray service, and room service.

For a life care center, consideration must also be given to deposits, entrance fees, and earnings on those fees, as well as the expected turnover time for apartments, which generally ranges from 12 to 14 years.

In addition, lenders require that revenue for a retirement housing facility be separated into base rent and service revenue.

Revenue Projections. For an existing facility, the starting point for projecting revenue is the project's past performance. Revenue data should be collected for the past three to five years as a basis for projecting revenue for the next year. In trending the past revenue data forward, such factors as inflation, competition, and the general economic outlook for the specific geographic area should be considered.

For a new project, the starting point is an analysis of the competition and industry standards as well as the cost of the facility. However, care must be taken in adapting industry standards or operations of another facility to a specific project.

Among the most important determinants of cost in a retirement facility are the provided services and how they are offered. Therefore, the starting point in projecting the revenue is defining the service package. What services will be available? Will they be bundled or unbundled?

The food services revenue will certainly be different for a facility that offers three meals per day as opposed to a facility that only offers one meal. The type of meal and the way it is served (cafeteria style or table service) will also influence the cost. Before a budget can be prepared, such questions must be answered. Merely taking the budget for an existing facility and modifying it to reflect size difference in another facility will result in serious problems.

The information needed to project the rental revenue from a retirement center includes the average rent per apartment (taking into consideration the number and mix of apartments), the number of rentable apartments, the type of services provided, and the number of residents per unit. Here also it is necessary to consider whether the services are to be offered as a package or à la carte. A life care center, must project the turnover of residents.

The revenue for a retirement housing facility is provided from base rent, service revenue, other revenue, and revenue from the health care center.

The base rent for a retirement housing facility is similar to the rent from any multihousing facility and consists of the average rent per apartment times the expected number of occupied apartments. The potential base rent is then adjusted to reflect the estimated vacancy periods and the estimated turnover. The apartment turnover rate for retirement housing facilities, especially newer ones, is generally lower than for a standard multihousing facility. However, a retirement housing project takes substantially longer to fill up than does a typical multifamily housing facility. The lease-up rate for a retirement housing community ranges from four to six apartments per month. Data for projecting the base rent of a new facility are found in the market feasibility study and the budgeted operating cost of the facility. This information must reflect inflation, competition, and general economic conditions expected in the future.

The monthly rent includes the base rent and the service revenue (the payment for the services provided). For a life care project, there is an entrance fee and a monthly fee. Entrance fees range from a low of about $20,000 to a high of as much as $350,000. Interest income on the entrance fees must also be estimated.

Projection of service revenue depends the package of services to be offered—meals, housekeeping, laundry, social services, and health care—

and whether these services will be bundled or unbundled. If the services are unbundled, then the demand for each service must be determined as well as its price. Most retirement housing facilities offer bundled services to reduce the difficulty in forecasting the demand for the services.

Once the service package and the method of offering have been determined, a competitor price analysis should be conducted. The cost of providing the services can then be determined. Inflation and general economic conditions are factored in to arrive at a final price.

The calculation of the total amount of service revenue is computed by multiplying the price of the service package by the number of occupied apartments. This amount must then be weighted for the expected number of residents per apartment, which ranges from 1.5 for new facilities to 1.25 for mature facilities. For example, if the service revenue per person is $400 for a project with 200 occupied apartments and the average number of residents per apartment is 1.5, the service revenue per month would be $120,000. An alternative is to state the rental fee as an amount per apartment, such as $1,500 with a $300 double occupancy charge for 100 units. In this case monthly revenue would equal $330,000.

Monthly revenue = (Rental fee) (number of occupied apartments)
+ (double occupancy fee)
× (number of double occupied units)

The final revenue projection is the projected collection loss. For existing facilities, historical data is the best indicator, but it should be adjusted to reflect any changes in the economic or operating environment. New facilities must rely on industry standards or rates experienced by similar facilities. New facilities projections should also reflect economic conditions and collection policies of the facility.

In projecting the amount of revenue from a facility, adjustments must be made for vacancies or turnovers, any rent concessions, and delinquencies. The sum of the revenue from all sources, less these allowances represents the total amount of revenue expected to be generated by the property. Table 7-2 provides a sample revenue projection schedule.

Cost Projections. Cost projections should be made for each responsibility center, such as dietary, maintenance, and general and administrative. There are two general approaches to cost projections. The

TABLE 7-2. Revenue Projection

Unit type	1B/1B Patio	1B/1B Balcony	2B/2B Patio	2B/1B Balcony	2B/2B Patio	2B/2B Balcony	2B/2B Patio	2B/2B Balcony	Averages	Totals
Base rent	$ 775	$ 775	$ 1,150	$ 1,150	$1,100	$ 1,100	$1,300	$ 1,300		
Service income	650	650	750	750	812	844	800	800		
Revenue per unit	$ 1,425	$ 1,425	$ 1,900	$ 1,900	$1,912	$ 1,944	$2,100	$ 2,100	$1,712	
Double occupancy adjustment									400	202
Number of units	46	92	12	24	4	12	4	8		
Square feet/unit	649	672	908	926	991	1,029	1,034	1,034	760	
Total square feet	29,854	61,824	10,896	22,224	3,964	12,348	4,136	8,272		153,518
Base rent sf/month	$1.19	$1.15	$1.27	$1.24	$1.11	$1.07	$1.26	$1.26	$1.19	
Service income sf/month	1.00	0.97	0.83	0.81	0.82	0.82	0.77	0.77	0.85	
Total rent sf/month	$2.19	$2.12	$2.10	$2.05	$1.93	$1.89	$2.03	$2.04	$2.04	
Base rent revenues per month	$35,650	$ 71,300	$13,800	$27,600	$4,400	$13,200	$5,200	$10,400		$181,550
Service income per month	29,900	59,800	9,000	18,000	3,248	10,128	3,200	6,400		139,676
Double occupancy per month	-0-	3,680	1,200	2,400	800	2,400	800	1,600		12,880
Monthly revenue	$65,550	$134,780	$24,000	$48,000	$8,448	$25,728	$9,200	$18,400		$334,106

incremental approach uses historical trends, projecting past cost experience into the future. Caution must be exercised to adjust costs for changes in inflation, technology, services offered, and general economic conditions. The primary limitation of this approach is that any inefficiencies in the system are continued into the future.

The second, and preferable, method for cost projections is the input/output approach, which defines the outputs in terms of productivity measures such as meals served, square feet cleaned, or pounds of laundry processed. Once the expected volume of output is estimated, cost standards for each activity are used to determine what the total cost should be. For example, if the raw food cost per meal is $3.00 and the project expects to serve 200 meals per day 30 days per month, the total raw food cost for the month is $18,000. All of the other costs for the dietary department would be calculated in a similar manner.

The input/output approach is the only alternative when budgeting for a new facility. Standards can be established by utilizing industry averages, time and motion studies, or data from similar facilities.

For the input/output approach, all costs are classified as either fixed or variable. Generally, total fixed costs remain the same regardless of the volume of services. An example of a fixed cost is the administrator's salary. Variable costs change directly with the volume of activity. Examples of variable costs are raw food costs, which vary according to the number of meals served. Since management has the greatest degree of control over variable cost, the use of the input/output approach to budgeting is preferable.

In preparing a departmental budget using the input/output approach, all departmental costs are identified as either fixed or variable based on their response to changes in the volume of activity (outputs). The amount of each cost is then determined through either an analysis of past performance, industry standards, or time and motion studies. The volume of services has been determined in the revenue projections. The fixed costs of the department are listed by major category of cost. The sum of the fixed costs is the total fixed cost for the department. The variable cost by major category of cost is then determined by multiplying the variable cost per unit of service by the projected volume of services. The sum of the variable cost represents the total variable cost for the department. The sum of the total fixed cost and the total variable cost represents the total cost of the department. (See Table 7-1.)

An additional advantage of the input/output approach is the ability to project costs for different levels of occupancy. This is especially important for new facilities in the lease-up stage. The budgeting of operations costs at changing levels of occupancy provides information necessary to properly project cash requirements.

Operations budgets should include allowances for contingencies and cycles. Departmental budgets should be prepared monthly and aggregated to provide an overall budget. All projects have some seasonality to their costs, such as utility costs, which are much higher in the southeast and southwest during the summer months than in the winter months. Taking an annual budget and dividing by 12 to determine the monthly budget would obscure this trend and could lead to insufficient funds during the summer months.

It is preferable to budget payroll on a departmental basis rather than on a separate payroll budget. Because they constitute a significant portion of the cost of operation, careful attention should be given to controlling payroll costs. The best method of control is to include the cost in the budget of the person responsible for training and supervising those employees, that is, the head of each department.

A retirement housing facility and a multifamily facility will have similar budgeted costs for operations and administration. However, a retirement community will have additional costs for food service, housekeeping, social services, additional insurance, professional services, and if a health care center is on site, for the operations of that center.

Usually one to three meals per day are provided to residents. The cost is determined by the number of meals served daily, the type of meal served, and the kind of service (cafeteria style or table service).

The staffing for the dietary department includes a dietician, dining room manager, cooks, assistant cooks, helpers, dishwashers, and porters. Staffing requirements for the dietary department of a 100- to 200-unit facility offering one meal per day buffet style should be cooks, 6 hours per day; assistant cooks, 8 hours per day; buspersons and dishwashers, 6 hours per day; dining room staff, 20 hours per day; and dining room manager, 4 hours per day. For a waiter-served meal, the dining room staff should be increased to 32 hours per day. The staffing represents staffing seven days per week.

In addition to personnel costs, the budget for the dietary department would include raw food costs, china, glassware, silverware, linens, table decorations, disposables, utilities, and miscellaneous food service costs. An example of a budget for the dietary department is provided in Table 7-1.

Retirement housing facilities generally provide housekeeping and laundry services to residents. As with the food service costs, the housekeeping department budget depends on the type and frequency of the services. Housekeeping may be provided on a weekly or biweekly basis with or without flat laundry services. The most common package provides housekeeping and flat laundry service once a week.

Staffing for the housekeeping department would include a housekeeping supervisor and housekeepers. For a retirement center, staffing generally consists of one housekeeper per 15,000 to 17,500 square feet. For a nursing care facility, one housekeeper can effectively clean 20 rooms if each has a bathroom. One housekeeper can effectively clean 30 rooms with connecting bathrooms. Additional staffing will be required for public areas. Also included in the department budget would be cleaning supplies, small tools such as vacuum cleaners and carpet shampooers, as well as any services purchased externally, such as drapery cleaning. The cost of cleaning the common areas and the offices is also included in the budget. An example of the housekeeping department budget is provided in Table 7-3.

Another service unique to retirement housing communities is social services—organized activities, transportation, educational programs, exercise and wellness programs, and arts and crafts programs and retail activities. Again, the budget for the social services department reflects the range and frequency of services.

A typical budget would include salaries for the director, a nurse, drivers, a resident coordinator, an assistant activity director, and a consulting physician. The budget would also cover costs for office supplies, vehicle operation and maintenance, supplies and equipment for activities and any miscellaneous costs of providing social services to residents. An example of the social services department budget is provided in Table 7-4.

TABLE 7-3. Housekeeping—Annual Budget (Occupancy, 95%)

Number of apartments	192	
Fixed costs		
Personnel		$ 17,181
Variable cost		
Personnel	$90,577	
Supplies	4,798	
Small tools	1,535	
Miscellaneous expenses	1,727	
Total variable cost		98,637
Total cost		$115,818

TABLE 7-4. Social Services—Annual Budget (Occupancy, 95%)

Number of apartments	192	
Fixed cost		
Personnel	$82,222	
Physician contract	2,500	
Total fixed cost		$ 84,722
Variable cost		
Personnel	17,436	
Utilities	15,800	
Office supplies	2,879	
Vehicle maintenance	5,757	
Supplies	4,798	
Miscellaneous expenses	4,798	
Total variable cost		51,468
Total cost		$136,190

Additional areas of cost difference between a standard multifamily facility and a retirement housing facility are insurance and professional services. Because retirement complexes provide a broad range of services, such as restaurant services, hotel services and health care services, the insurance program must cover these activities as well as the additional limitations of the typical resident.

If the facility has a health care center on site, the question of malpractice for health care professionals must be addressed. Typically the nursing care facility encourages individual nurses to provide their own malpractice insurance. In addition, the liability insurance for a community with a nursing home on site is significantly higher than for a standard multifamily housing facility due to the residents' physical limitations.

Retirement housing is subject to licensures and regulations not usually encountered in standard multifamily housing facilities; among them are nursing home regulations, personal care regulations, CCRC regulations, and Medicare and Medicaid certification. Compliance with these regulations adds to the cost of operations.

Professional services also cause increased costs for retirement housing facilities. In addition to the professional services required by a standard multifamily facility for management, accounting, and legal needs, a retirement community may require the services of outside professionals such as physicians, nurses, a dietician, and other health professionals. The types and extent of need for outside professional services are functions of the health status of the residents, the availability of an on-site health care facility, and the range of health care services.

Significant cost savings can be obtained by sharing departmental supervision and other operations. For example, the maintenance supervisor can also supervise the housekeeping department. Complexes with an on-site nursing home have additional opportunities for sharing costs by combining supervision of the food service, housekeeping, maintenance, and social services departments. The two centers can also share kitchen facilities.

Cash Flow Budget.   The cash flow budget is the most important for the project. The absence of a cash flow budget can result in insufficient funds to pay creditors and can mean lost investment income on excess cash. In order to time cash receipts and cash disbursements, the cash flow budget should be prepared monthly; the monthly budgets are then aggregated to form an annual budget.

The cash flow budget has three sections. The first section is the cash receipts from operations. In order to satisfy lender requirements the cash from operations must be broken down by base rent and service fees. The second section is the cash disbursements for operations. The final section is the cash reserve requirements. The cash reserves generally consist of reserves for debt service, replacement, and captial expansion. For a life care facility, reserves will be needed for nursing care.

An example of a cash flow budget is provided in Table 7-5.

Capital Budget.   A unique feature of capital budgeting for a retirement housing facility is the issue of Medicare and Medicaid reimbursement. Under Medicare and Medicaid, capital expenditures are subject to additional restrictions with regard to reimbursement. In addition, some states require capital expenditures above a certain level to be approved through the certificate of need (CON) process prior to the expenditure. Capital expenditures without the required approval are not reimbursed by either Medicare or Medicaid. Certificate of need and Medicaid regulations vary from state to state; therefore, the developer or sponsor should obtain expert assistance if the facility has an on-site nursing home.

The capital budgeting process involves two types of decisions: the replacement of the property and the expansion of the facility or addition of services. Replacement may be required due to either the wearing out or functional obsolescence of the property. Functional obsolescence means that the item is still operational but is outdated and needs to

TABLE 7-5. Retirement Center Cash Flow Budget

Beginning cash balance
Cash receipts from operations
  Base rent
  Service revenue
  Other service revenue
  Other revenue
Total cash from operations
Cash disbursements for operations
  Payroll
  Payments on accounts payable
  Other disbursements
Total cash disbursements
Cash from operations
Deduct
  Debt service
  Replacement reserve requirement
  Capital expenditure reserve requirement
Add
  Replacement reserve fund cash
  Capital expenditure reserve fund cash
Net cash flow

be replaced because of exorbitant maintenance costs or for aesthetic reasons.

The second type of capital budgeting decision involves whether to expand or add services, such as a health care center. These decisions require the same kind of analysis utilized in the original feasibility study of the project (see Chapter 4).

The question of when to replace existing facilities is best addressed through the inventory process. The administrator should conduct an annual property inventory consisting of a listing of the on-site property items, the quantities of each item, the acquisition date of each item, its current condition, and the replacement cost. Usually the on-site personnel are not competent to determine current condition or replacement costs of property items; outside consultants may be required.

The completed property inventory will serve as the basis for developing a schedule of the items that will need replacement during the next three to five years. The actual replacement of the property, plant, and equipment will depend on the availability of funds to meet the capital demands. Replacement funds may be provided through either additional investments of the owners or from funds retained from operations for this purpose. Realistically, the wearing out of the property, plant, and equipment begins when those assets are placed in operation. Therefore, earnings from operations should be retained to provide for the eventual obsolescence of the facility.

In addition to serving as a basis for the capital budgeting process, the current property inventory should be compared with the property records of the facility to ensure that all property, plant, and equipment are properly safeguarded.

Performance Reporting. Performance reporting is the link between the budgets and the actual revenues, expenses, and volume of operations. This comparison of the actual results with the budgets serves to evaluate each department as well as the project as a whole, and it also provides feedback to improve the budgeting process.

A comparison of actual results to the budgets produces an analysis of variance. The variance can be favorable, which means that actual revenue exceeds budgeted revenue, or that actual costs were less than budgeted costs. If the actual revenue is less than the budgeted revenue, or the actual costs exceed the budgeted costs, the variance is unfavorable. However, just knowing whether there is a variance and whether that variance is favorable or unfavorable is insufficient for effective management. The reasons must also be determined.

Revenue Variances. Revenue variances can be divided into volume variance and price variance. When the volume of services, meals served, or apartments rented differs from the budget, a volume variance occurs. When the price charged for the service or the rent is different, a price variance occurs.

The volume variance is calculated by multiplying the difference between the budgeted volume of service and the actual volume of services by the budgeted price. If the actual volume of services exceeds the budgeted volume, the variance is favorable. If the actual volume of services is less than the budgeted amount, the variance is unfavorable. Possible causes of a volume variance could be increased competition, weak marketing efforts, or insufficient demand.

The price variance is calculated by multiplying the difference between the budgeted price of the services and the actual price of the services by the actual volume of services. If the actual price of the services exceeds the budgeted price, the variance is favorable. If the actual price of services is less than the budgeted price, the variance is unfavorable. Possible causes of a price variance are increased competition, which forces the price down in order to attract additional tenants, or an increase or decrease in the use of unbundled services.

For example, if the budget is based on renting 200 apartments at a budgeted rent of $1,200 per apartment, the budgeted revenue would be $240,000 per month. If during the month 195 apartments were actually rented at an average rent of $1,250 per month, the actual revenue would be $243,750. The difference between the actual revenue ($243,750) and the budgeted revenue ($240,000) would be a favorable variance of $3,750. The volume variance would be the difference between the budgeted volume (200 units) and the actual volume (195 units) times the budgeted rent ($1,200), or a $6,000 unfavorable variance. The price variance would be the difference between the budgeted rent of $1,200 per unit and the actual rent of $1,250 ($50) multiplied by the actual number of apartments rented (195). The price variance of $9,750 would be favorable. The volume variance ($6,000 unfavorable) subtracted from the price variance ($9,750 favorable) would equal the total variance of $3,750, which is favorable.

In many instances, the volume variance and the price variance may offset each other. For example, lowering the price of a service generally results in an increase in demand. If the increased demand exceeds the revenue lost by decreasing the price, lowering the price was the correct action. However, if the increased demand does not exceed the lost revenue, lowering the price was a mistake.

Cost Variances. Cost variances result when the actual costs for a responsibility center are different from the budgeted costs. The cost variance can be favorable when the actual costs are less than the budgeted costs, or unfavorable when the actual costs exceed the budgeted costs. The total cost of a department is the sum of the total fixed cost and the total variable cost for that department. The actual cost of a department may vary from the budgeted cost because of a variance in fixed costs or in variable costs for the department. Therefore, the cost variances can be defined as either fixed cost variances or variable cost variances.

Fixed costs are generally easier to budget and control than variable costs. For example, the administrator's salary is a fixed cost which is usually determined prior to the beginning of the fiscal year; thus, a significant variance from the budget is unlikely. The fixed cost variance is generally defined as the difference between the actual cost and the budgeted cost and is identified by line items such as salary, and depreciation.

Variable costs are more difficult to budget than fixed costs, but they provide management with more opportunities for control. More attention is given to identifying the causes for variance. The total variable cost of a department is determined by multiplying the cost or price of each component of variable cost (such as wage rate per hour) by the number of units (such as hours worked) used. The difference between the actual variable cost and the budgeted variable cost can thus be broken down into a quantity or volume variance and a price or cost variance.

Quantity refers to the number of hours worked or the number of units of an input, such as housekeeping supplies per unit cleaned. The quantity variance is calculated by multiplying the difference between the budgeted quantity of the input (housekeeping hours) and the actual quantity by the budgeted variable cost per unit of input. If the actual quantity of the input exceeds the budgeted quantity, the variance is unfavorable. If the actual quantity of input is less than the budgeted quantity, the variance is favorable. Possible causes of an unfavorable variance are poorly supervised or inadequately trained employees who misuse or waste time or supplies.

The price or cost variance is calculated by multiplying the difference between the budgeted variable cost and the actual variable cost per unit of input by the actual quantity of input. If the actual cost exceeds the budgeted cost per unit of the input, the price variance is unfavorable. If the actual cost is less than the budgeted cost, the price or cost variance is favorable. Possible causes of an unfavorable price variance are increased cost of personnel or using a higher paid person than the task requires.

In some cases, the price or cost variance and the volume or quantity variance may offset each other. For example, using a higher paid worker may result in greater productivity, or operating more expensive equipment may result in less hours to perform a specific task. In calculating cost variances, the actual cost of providing the services should be compared to the actual volume of services provided, not the budgeted volume.

If the budgeted preparation time for one meal is 12 minutes at a budgeted wage rate of $4.50 per hour, the budgeted labor cost to prepare 6,000 meals should be $5,400. This is calculated as 1,200 hours to prepare 6000 meals multiplied by the average rate of $4.50 per hour. If the actual number of hours worked was 1,250 hours at an average rate of $4.40, the total labor cost for the 6,000 meals was $5,500. The unfavorable quantity variance of $225 is the result of using 50 hours more than the budgeted hours at the budgeted rate of $4.50 per hour. The price or cost variance is $125 favorable, as a result of paying ten cents less an hour for the hours worked. The total unfavorable variance of $100 is the remainder of the $225 unfavorable quantity variance and the $125 favorable cost variance.

Statistical Reports.   In addition to performance reports, which describe costs and revenues, statistical reports should also be prepared on a monthly basis. They should contain such information as occupancy by type of unit, number of meals served, FTEs by department, and FTEs per unit of service. Such statistics are needed to plan staffing levels and determine the type or types of units most in demand. Table 7-6 is an example of a statistical report.

Monthly Financial Reports.   Monthly financial reports should be prepared for the management and owners of the project. The financial statements that should be provided monthly are the income statement, which lists the revenues and expenses of the project; and the balance sheet, which lists the assets, liabilities, and owner's equity for the project. These reports should be compiled on both a monthly and year-to-date basis. In addition, a cash flow statement for the project should be provided, and the monthly reports should include an analysis of the financial statements.

TABLE 7-6. Statistical Report for Operations—November 1, 1987, to November 30, 1987

	Number	Square Feet	Occupied Single	Occupied Double	Percent Occupied
Units by size					
A	63	529	50		80
B	153	613	110	20	85
C	45	775	25	15	90
D	45	729	15	25	90
Total	306		200	60	85
Total residents	320		200	120	
Other square footage					
Common area		91,626			
Community building		20,200			
Dining area		4,000			
Building total		310,622			
Meals served	10,560				
Employees (FTE)					
Food service	20				
Maintenance	7	44,375			
Housekeeping	16	19,414			
General and administrative	10				
Social service	4				
Total	57				

There are two basic types of financial analysis: horizontal analysis and vertical analysis. Horizontal analysis involves comparing actual revenues and expenses for both the month and the year-to-date with the corresponding budgets and with reports for the same period for the prior year. Vertical analysis involves stating every component of the financial statement as either a percentage or stating it on a unit of service basis. For the income statement, each individual item is stated as a percentage of net revenue. For the balance sheet, each item is stated as a percentage of the total assets. In the unit of service approach, the items may be stated on a per apartment or per resident basis. Both types of analysis provide information useful to management for decision making.

Horizontal Analysis.   A comparison of the actual monthly revenues and expenses with the budget for the month should be performed on a departmental basis as well as for the project as a whole. This comparison allows management to see how well each department has succeeded in achieving the goals set in the budget. By further separating the differences between the actual results and the budget into price and quantity variances, the reasons for the variances can be determined and corrective action can be taken when necessary.

A comparison of the actual results for the current year with the actual results of the previous year indicates how well the departments are performing relative to their prior performance. The major limitation of a year-to-year comparison is that one may be comparing inefficiency with inefficiency. However, when such an analysis is also compared with a budget using the input/output approach, management may find valuable information.

Examples of horizontal analysis are provided in Tables 7-7 and 7-8.

Vertical Analysis.   Vertical analysis is useful when comparing a project with other projects, or with an industry-specific database. For the income statement, all the components are stated as percentages of net revenue. For the balance sheet, all components are stated as percentages of total assets. Presenting the components of the statements as percentages removes any size bias, and thus comparisons with different size projects can be made. A comparison with another project will assist management in determining the efficiency of its operation.

Another form of vertical analysis is to state each cost component on a unit of service basis. For example, food service cost may be expressed on a cost per meal basis. This type of analysis is especially useful on

TABLE 7-7. Horizontal Analysis

| | Actual | | Standard | | Year |
	Total	Unit Cost	Unit Cost	Variance + or −	To-Date Total
Food Service (per meal, unless otherwise shown)					
Food cost	15,229	1.44	1.40		
Personnel	18,497	1.75	1.84		
Utilities (departmental)	967	.24/SF	.24/SF		
China and glassware	521	.05	.05		
Other	4,474	.43	.43		
Total cost	39,688	3.76	3.80		
Social Services (per unit, unless otherwise shown)					
Personnel	6,256	20.44	27.00		
Vehicle maintenance	650	2.12	2.38		
Miscellaneous	1,409	4.61	5.15		
Utilities (common areas)	9,318	.08/SF	.10/SF		
Total cost	17,633	57.62	55.45		
General/Administrative (per unit, unless otherwise shown)					
Personnel	13,317	43.52	54.00		
Insurance	4,580	14.97	23.00		
Taxes	26,402	.085/SF	.09		
Security	4,166	13.61	21.00		
Utilities (apts.)	17,695	.09/SF	.09		
Total cost (excluding mgmt. contract)	66,160	234.61	264.00		
Housekeeping (per square foot)					
Personnel	9,138	.029	.035		
Other	542				
Total cost	9,680	.033	.040		
Maintenance (per square foot, unless otherwise shown)					
Personnel	3,714	.012	.016		
Purchased services	3,167	.010			
Other	1,517				
Total cost	8,398	.027	.037		
Total operating expense	141,559	.495/SF	.625/SF		
Per apartment		502.01	619.00		

TABLE 7-8. Personnel Productivity Horizontal Analysis

| | Actual | | Standard | Variance | Year |
	Total	Unit Cost	Unit Cost	+ or −	To-Date Total
Total Personnel					
Full-time employees	36	.11	.12		
Part-time employees	14	.044	.06		
Full-time equivalent	50	.156	.18		
Food service	20	.063	.07		
Social services	4	.013	.015		
General and administrative	10	.031	.036		
Housekeeping	12	.038	.040		
Maintenance	4	.013	.017		
Square foot/maintenance employee		77,656	50,000		
Square foot/housekeeper		25,885	19,000		

the departmental level. When cost components have been stated on a unit of service basis, comparisons can be made to other facilities and to industry-specific databases. Without the restatement of components of cost in percentages or units of service, comparison with other projects is distorted. The only valid comparison would be between identically sized facilities with the same occupancy levels. In addition, most databases either group facilities together, or group them within a certain range. Thus a comparison in absolute terms with a database may result in a comparison of apples and oranges. Table 7-9 provides an example of vertical analysis.

Ratio Analysis. In addition to horizontal and vertical analysis, financial ratio analysis should also be performed. Ratio analysis is a form of trend analysis, useful in identifying the direction in which the project is headed. The two types of ratios discussed are the ones of primary usefulness to project managers—liquidity ratios, which measure the ability of the project to meet its current obligations as they become due; and capital structure ratios, which measure the extent to which the project will be able to meet its long-term obligations or secure additional financing.

Liquidity Ratios. Liquidity ratios measure the ability of a project to meet its short-term obligations as they come due. The *current ratio* is one of the most widely used measures of financial strength of an or-

TABLE 7-9. Vertical Analysis of Balance Sheet as a Percentage of Total Assets

	1986	1985	1984	1983	1982
Cash and marketable securities	2.74	11.09	8.58	2.22	7.71
Gross accounts receivable	9.19	9.94	3.65	9.77	8.32
Allowance for uncollectibles	−0.38	−0.19	−0.13	−0.10	−0.54
Contributions receivable	0.67	1.32	2.20	5.24	5.49
Inventory	1.86	1.87	1.84	2.42	1.14
Prepaid expenses	0.70	0.42	0.35	0.44	0.55
Other current assets	0	0	0	0	0.34
Total current assets	14.78	24.45	16.50	19.99	23.01
Other assets	2.54	1.97	25.91	28.85	10.03
Property, plant, and equipment	82.68	73.57	57.59	51.16	66.96
Total assets	100	100	100	100	100
Accrued payable	0.20	0.49	0.42	0.34	0
Accounts payable	3.47	5.14	6.29	3.46	3.81
Salaries, wages, and fees payable	5.87	6.29	5.65	8.48	15.65
Payroll taxes payable	4.41	4.54	3.71	6.05	0
Current portion, long-term liabilities	0.58	0.41	0.46	0.21	0.24
Interest payable	0.06	0.01	0.01	0.02	0
Other current liabilities	0.33	0.54	0.74	0.64	0.79
Total current liabilities	14.92	17.42	17.28	19.19	20.49
Long-term debt	12.04	1.90	3.10	2.10	2.95
Total liabilities	26.96	19.32	20.38	21.29	23.44
Total equity	73.04	80.68	79.62	78.71	76.56
Total liabilities and equity	100	100	100	100	100

ganization. The current ratio is equal to current assets divided by the current liabilities. Current assets include cash, marketable securities, accounts receivable, prepaid expenses, and inventories. Current liabilities include accounts payable, notes payable, and any other liabilities expected to be paid from current assets. The current ratio indicates the number of times the current assets would "pay off" the current liabilities. A decreasing current ratio from period to period indicates a weakening of a project's ability to meet its current obligations as they come due.

The *quick ratio* is a more stringent measure of financial strength. The quick ratio does not include the project's inventory and prepaid expenses in the numerator of the ratio; it is equal to cash, temporary investments, and accounts receivable of the project divided by the current liabilities. As with the current ratio, a declining trend in the quick ratio indicates a weakening ability of the project to pay its current obligations as they come due.

The *number of days' revenue in net receivables* is an indicator of a project's collections management. This ratio is calculated by dividing the net accounts receivable by average daily revenue. Average daily revenue is equal to total revenue for the year divided by 365. An increasing trend in the number of days revenue in net receivables indicates that the quality of receivables management has detoriated.

The *average payment period for current liabilities* indicates how long it takes for the project to pay current liabilities. The average payment period for current liabilities is equal to current liabilities divided by daily cash operating expenses. Daily cash operating expense is annual cash operating expenses divided by 365. A high or increasing ratio from year to year indicates a failure to pay bills promptly, which could be caused by either a problem in the accounts payable department or a cash shortage.

The *days' cash on hand ratio* is equal to the cash and marketable securities divided by the average daily cash expenses. This ratio indicates the ability of the project to meet short-term obligations. A decreasing ratio from year-to-year indicates a cash flow problem.

Capital Structure Ratios.   The *equity financing ratio* indicates the portion of the assets that are financed by the owners as opposed to debt sources. The ratio is calculated by dividing the stockholder's equity by the total assets. A decreasing equity financing ratio indicates that more and more of the assets are being financed by debt. Such a situation could make it difficult to obtain additional financing or favorable loan terms on future debt.

The *cash flow to total debt ratio* is a measure of the project's ability to pay its current and long-term debts. It is calculated by dividing cash from operations by total liabilities. A decreasing ratio is a predictor of future difficulty in paying liabilities as they come due.

The *long-term debt to equity ratio* is a measure of the relationship of long-term debt to equity. It is calculated by dividing total long-term debt by stockholders' equity. An increasing debt to equity ratio is an indicator of decreasing soundness of the project's financial structure.

The *times interest earned ratio* is an indicator of the ability of the project to meet annual interest charges on debt. The ratio is calculated by dividing net income plus interest expense by interest expense. A decreasing ratio reflects a weakening ability to pay interest as it becomes due, which might indicate serious financial difficulties.

The *debt service coverage ratio* is a measure of the ability of the project to pay the annual interest and principal on its debt. The ratio is calculated by dividing net income plus depreciation and interest expense by the annual principal and interest payment (annual debt service). A decreasing debt service coverage ratio from year to year is an indicator of a decreasing ability of the project to pay the annual debt service. An inability to meet this obligation could lead to bankruptcy.

The *internal rate of return* of a project is the rate that discounts all cash flows, including the original cash outlay, to zero. It is equivalent to the yield to maturity on a bond. The internal rate of return is used to compare different investments of similar risk in the investment decision-making process.

Feedback.   Feedback is the communication of the variances to management so that corrective action can be taken. It is the link between the budgets (planning) and performance reports (control). The information provided by the performance reports should be used to make adjustments in current activity and to modify future budgets. The variance analysis identifies why there is a difference between the budget and performance—what management expected to happen and what actually occurred. For example, an unfavorable quantity variance for dietary personnel may indicate improperly trained or inadequately supervised employees in the dietary department. Training programs may be necessary for the workers, or additional supervision may be required.

The variance analysis and performance reports identify the areas of the project that require additional attention and corrective action. Thus, management knows where to concentrate effort to achieve the maximum results.

Financial Operations.   The financial operations of a retirement housing facility are very similar to the financial operations of any real estate project. The primary differences are in the areas of rent collection options, types and levels of insurance coverage, and the operation of an on-site nursing home. Because of the complexities of state and federal regulations, a specialist in the area of nursing home reimbursement should be utilized in developing the accounting system and preparing the cost reports.

The day-to-day financial operations include, but are not limited to accounts receivable, cash management, accounts payable, insurance coverage, payroll, administration, internal control, and preparation of financial statements needed for the annual audit.

Accounts Receivable.   The accounts receivable include the collection of the rents and fees, the processing of delinquency, and the processing of miscellaneous income. If the project has a health care center, insurance reimbursement and possibly Medicare or Medicaid collections will be required. Medicare and Medicaid reimbursement is a very specialized and complex subject; Medicaid reimbursement procedures differ from state to state and therefore, Medicare and Medicaid reimbursement is not discussed here. For projects with health care centers, experts in Medicare and Medicaid reimbursement should be consulted. Some public accounting firms offer such services.

Collection of Rents.   The objective of rent collection is, of course, to collect as much rent as possible as soon as possible. However, in a senior housing project this goal is somewhat different than in a general apartment setting. The elderly generally will pay their rent in a timely manner unless they have a serious problem. The administrator should consider eviction of a resident for nonpayment of rent to be a solution of last resort.

The first question in accounts receivable is whether or not to invoice residents for rent. Whichever approach is selected, it is the administrator's responsibility to be certain that the residents are apprised of their responsibilities.

If the tenants are expected to pay on the first day of each month, it is the responsibility of the administrator to be certain that the residents are aware of the method of payment required; the address to which payment is submitted; the manner of processing payments; and the person to contact in case of questions.

If management prefers to collect rents on a lock box basis, some form of billing or invoicing system is required so that the payments are applied to the correct units.

Collection Options.   The preferable options for collecting rents are either an on-site office, where payments are accepted and processed, or a central collection service, in which rent payments are transmitted either from an on-site office or directly by the residents. On-site offices provide regular contact with most of the residents and are convenient for residents, and for the families who administer the funds.

Delinquency.   Probably one of the most delicate elements of the rent collection process is dealing with delinquencies. In a retirement facility, delinquency is generally the result of severe financial circumstances. In addition, the responses of the elderly resident must be carefully considered as well as those of his or her family. It is important that management maintain regular contact with residents and their families. If financial difficulties are being experienced, management can help the resident or family find alternative means of payment or more appropriate housing. Assistance in locating alternate housing options for a resident in financial difficulty can be obtained from the area Council on Aging, American Association of Retired Persons, area churches, area social services organizations, local housing authority, discharge planner of the local hospital, and United Way.

Miscellaneous Income.   Even in projects where services are offered on a bundled basis only, the administrator will be faced with more miscellaneous income than in an apartment complex. The most common types of miscellaneous income are:

Income from additional meals	Extra housekeeping services
Room service	Extra laundry services
Rental of meeting rooms	Beauty and barber shop
Parking	Gift shop
	Special clients

Control is important in dealing with miscellaneous income. The administrator should have reports that list the number of meals served, room rentals and setups, and so forth to compare with the income generated. Written procedures should be developed for handling miscellaneous income, and employees should be trained in the use of such records.

Cash Management.   Cash management is the proper accounting for and safeguarding of cash. In addition, cash management includes proper investment of cash. Since cash is the most easily misappropriated asset, it is important to maintain proper safeguards. In addition, any excess funds should be invested in order to increase the investors' return on the project.

For rental properties, there are two components of the cash management program that need to be stressed: collection of the rental fees as soon as possible and investment of all excess cash in income-generating temporary investments.

The collection of rental fees has been discussed in the previous section. The second goal of cash management should be to maintain a zero balance in cash accounts that do not produce investment income. Financial institutions offer a number of options, such as money market funds that provide returns on invested cash. The manager of a retirement housing facility should determine what financial services, such as checking accounts, lines of credit, investment vehicles, and other financial services are required for the facility, and then ask financial institutions to bid on the package of services. Cash should be deposited in the facility's account on a daily basis, and all available funds should be in income-generating accounts. The lock box approach can be used to ensure that cash is credited to the facility's account on a daily basis.

Accounts Payable. The accounts payable function assures the proper payment of bills. The administrator should monitor all accounts payable transactions so that obligations are met in a timely manner and cash flow is maximized. Obligations should be paid in a manner that takes advantage of all available discounts from suppliers and maintains good credit ratings.

The administrator should periodically review accounts payable to ensure they are being paid in accordance with contractual obligations and sound business practice. This will require a well-structured purchase order system that links into the accounts payable function. Figure 7-1 provides an example of a purchase order.

The best approach involves a purchase order system with the administrator or someone else in authority approving purchases above a certain minimum amount, such as $500. A copy of each purchase order is sent to the accounts payable clerk and to the person requesting the purchase, and a copy is kept by the person responsible for issuing the purchase order.

The receipt of the merchandise should be acknowledged by a receiving report which is sent to the accounts payable department. The receiving report and the invoice are then matched with the purchase order to determine the accuracy of the price, quantity, and extensions. The accounts payable department then issues a check for the amount of the invoice. Figure 7-2 provides an example of a receiving report.

Insurance Coverage. The insurance requirements for a retirement housing facility are higher than for other types of real estate developments. Additional liability insurance is necessary because of the additional limitations of the residents. A facility with an on-site nursing home will need to consider malpractice insurance for the health care professionals. Generally, the health care professionals are required to provide their own malpractice insurance.

Sufficient insurance coverage is extremely important to the continued financial viability of a retirement facility. In addition to the prob-

Figure 7-1. Purchase Order Form

RETIREMENT COMPANY, INC.
PURCHASE ORDER   No. 11

Acct. no. _____   Deliver to _____

                                Extension no. _____

Acct. title _____

    Vendor _____

    Address _____

    City, State, Zip _____

    Attn: _____

    Phone No. _____

Item No.	Specifications	Quantity	Price	Unit Extension

Requested by _____ Ext. _____ Approved by _____

For Use by Purchasing

Confirmed with _____ Date _____

Delivery Date _____

lems generally encountered with insurance, a senior housing facility often has difficulty in putting together an insurance package that covers the range of services provided—restaurant services, hotel services, apartment services, and health care services. The insurance industry, however, has recently begun to package insurance programs for businesses such as nursing homes.

The administrator of a seniors housing facility may simply provide the information necessary to identify the property and service to be insured, or may be entirely responsible for securing the necessary insurance.

Figure 7-2. Receiving Report Form

RETIREMENT COMPANY, INC.
RECEIVING REPORT

Vendor _____

Address _____

City, State, Zip _____

Delivery date _____

Item No.	Specifications	Quantity	Condition

The minimum insurance coverage a facility should have is property and casualty insurance, liability insurance, health insurance for employees, and worker's compensation. If the facility has a nursing home on site, the question of malpractice insurance must also be addressed.

Payroll. The payroll function can be conducted either by the facility or by a service bureau. For a single facility, a service bureau may provide a more efficient system. The payroll function for a retirement facility is generally similar to the payroll system for any other type of facility. The primary differences will occur in the areas of shift differentials, on-call time, and holiday pay. Specific policies need to be established to properly compensate employees for atypical work schedules. The policies should be clearly explained to newly hired personnel, and any changes to existing policies must be communicated to all employees.

Internal Control. In order to properly account for all transactions and to safeguard the assets of the project, the accounting system needs to include a system of internal control. This is a series of checks and balances that increase the reliability of the accounting data and protect against fraud.

The first step in an internal control system is to make sure that no one person has the responsibility of a transaction from beginning to end. Under such a system, the work of one employee is verified by that of another, thus reducing errors. Another component of an effective internal control system is the separation of the custody of the asset from the accounting for that asset. The person who has physical control of the asset should not be the person who maintains the records for it; thus the misappropriation of an asset would require the cooperation of two or more employees.

Another important component of an internal control system is an internal audit. Internal audits are performed with the objective of verifying that the accounting procedures and policies of the project are being properly followed and that all project assets are accounted for properly. For a single facility, the administrator is responsible for seeing that formal procedures exist, employees are properly trained in those procedures, and those procedures are being followed. Internal audits will also increase the level of confidence the outside auditors have with the accounting information of the project and thus lower the cost associated with the annual audit.

Other components of an effective internal control system are financial forecasts, serially numbered documents, and competent personnel. Comparisons of actual results with financial forecasts strengthen control because variations from planned results are investigated in a timely fashion. All documents such as checks and purchase orders should be serially numbered to call attention to any missing item. Formal accounting procedures should be developed, personnel should be properly trained in these procedures, and adherence to these procedures should be monitored.

No matter how well the internal control system is designed, it will not work unless personnel are properly trained and are competent to perform their assigned tasks. Great care should be given to the proper selection and training of all employees.

Financial Audits. The final step in the financial management process is the annual financial audit. An audit is a thorough investigation by an outside certified public accounting (CPA) firm. The firm should review accounting records and other evidence regarding the items of the financial statements. The audit enables the CPA firm to express a professional opinion as to the fairness and reliability of the financial statements.

INDEX